The Ground of Being

Neglected Essays of Paul Tillich

Edited by

Robert M. Price

Front cover photo of Paul Tillich's gravestone in the Paul Tillich Park, New
Harmony, Indiana, USA; Sculptor Ralph Beyer. "And he shall be like a tree
planted by the river of water, that bringeth forth his fruit for his season; his leaf
also shall not wither, and whatsoever he doeth shall prosper."

Photo by Michael Gaeble. All rights released. Wikimedia Commons. Cover
design by Qarol Price.

This book is gratefully dedicated to my
pastor and mentor, Donald Morris,
who suggested the project so many years ago.

Acknowledgements

"What Is Wrong with the 'Dialectic' Theology?" originally
appeared in the *Journal of Religion XV* (April 1935).

"Introduction" to *The Kingdom of God and History* originally
appeared in *The Kingdom of God and History* (London:
George Allen & Unwin LTD, 1938.

"The Gospel and the State" originally appeared in the *Crozier
Quarterly* XV (October 1938).

"Freedom in the Period of Transformation" originally
appeared in *Freedom: Its Meaning* (ed. Ruth Nanda
Anshen, Harcourt, Brace & World, 1940).

"Existential Thinking in American Theology" originally
appeared in *Religion in Life* (Summer 1941).

"'Faith' in the Jewish-Christian Tradition" originally
appeared in *Christendom* (Autumn 1942).

"Kierkegaard in English" originally appeared in *American-
Scandinavian Review* XXX (September 1942).

"Vertical and Horizontal Thinking" originally appeared in
American Scholar XV (January 1946).

"Redemption in Cosmic and Social Thinking" originally
appeared in the *Journal of Religious Thought* III (Autumn-
Winter, 1946).

"Existentialism and Religious Socialism" originally appeared
in *Christianity and Society* XV (1949).

"The Present Theological Situation in the Light of the
Continental European Development" originally
appeared in *Theology Today* IV (October 1949).

"A Reinterpretation of the Doctrine of Incarnation"
originally appeared in *Church Quarterly Review* CXLVII
(January 1949).

"The Recovery of the Prophetic Tradition in the

Reformation" originally appeared as a Christianity &
Modern Man Publication after its delivery at the
Washington Cathedral Library, November –December
1950).

"The European Discussion of the Problem of the
Demythologization of the New Testament" was
delivered as the Auburn Lecture for Union Theological
Seminary (November 10, 1952).

"Victory in Defeat: The Meaning of History in the Light of
Christian Prophetism" originally appeared in
Interpretation VI (January 1952).

"Jewish Influences on Contemporary Christian Theology"
originally appeared in *Cross Currents* II/3 (1952).

"Religious Symbols and our Knowledge of God" originally
appeared in *The Christian Scholar* (1955).

"The Idea of God as Affected by Modern Knowledge"
originally appeared in *The Crane Review* I/3 (Spring
1959).

All appear here with the kind permission of the original
publishers where these still exist. Permission to use all the
essays was generously granted by Mutie Tillich Farris, Paul
Tillich's daughter.

PREFACE

Now that we have entered a truly new world whereby we are losing our established categories, none has become so discordant as has theology itself, which has been torn asunder by violent forces both visible and invisible. Of course, theology is a discipline or way now wholly elusive in its actual form, and in its commonest expressions in Church theologies it is wholly isolated and without deep or genuine impact. One name above all others stands for its transcendence of this impotence, and that is Paul Tillich, whose spirit was never more needed than it is today. Price is committed to the spirit of Tillich, and to employing Tillich to illuminate our contemporary theological condition, and hopefully to do so in such a way as to open a path to a resolution of our theological dilemma.

A major problem here is the work of Tillich itself, not only a very uneven and inconsistent body of work, but one not often decisively expressed. This is a positive condition insofar as Tillich can be employed in so many manners and ways, and this has certainly occurred, but nonetheless it is not possible to speak of a Tillichian school or way. Tillich himself was decisively shaped by his commitment to and work upon Schelling, but this dissipated as time went on and Tillich was soon without a clear philosophical ground, even if he remained a philosophical theologian. That alone deeply distinguished him in the Protestant world, but more than any other major Protestant theologian Tillich was not only open to Catholicism but committed to conjoining the Protestant principle with Catholic substance. While there are few signs of this in Protestantism, there have been enormous transformations of Catholic theology which are reflective of such a goal, and there have been Catholic Tillichian theologians.

Tillich was not only open to Catholicism, but ever increasingly committed to a truly ecumenical theology that would include Hinduism, Buddhism, and Chinese traditions, just as he has had a major impact in Asia. Indeed, Tillich promised or called for the first genuinely ecumenical theology and that may well become his greatest importance. While virtually all Christian theology is too conservative for this, there are deep potentialities for it in Catholicism, and even in a new lay or secular theology that could move in a Tillichian direction without naming Tillich. So let us hail the possibility of a new and even universal Tillichian movement, one that Robert Price is calling for, and that has the potentiality of genuinely transforming theology.

Yet this could only be a radical movement, one distancing itself from all established theology, and seeking all too solitary paths that have never been explored theologically. Tillich himself is exemplary of such a path, and it is notable how distant he is from all theological bodies or schools. Nor can we forget what a powerful preacher Tillich was. This can be demonstrated in his published sermons, but as one who was under the spell of Tillich's voice, I can certainly give witness to it, and despite his heavy accent, he could hypnotize even secular or irreligious hearers, for he could transfix everyone who could hear him.

It is remarkable how little attention serious scholars have given to preaching or homiletics, yet it is certainly one of the deep grounds of our most powerful religions, and it is simply not possible to divorce theology and homiletics. This can clearly be observed in all major Christian theologians, and is even a source of theological offense, and if Tillich evokes less offense than most theologians, that offense is present in his strongest theological writing, and all too significantly is weakest in his lesser theological writing.

One way to remember Tillich is to recall the famous Tillich-Eliade seminar on Theology and the History of Religions at the University of Chicago: after this seminar when I attended it the three of us would retreat to the Eliades' apartment and continue it, and this proved to be the most exciting theological conversation in which I participated. Few are aware of how deeply theological Eliade was, just as few realize how profoundly Tillich was committed to non-Christian traditions; it is not accidental that a tradition has arisen about the absolute polarity between Barth and Tillich, and Eliade even created a potent myth about their theological reconciliation. Those were days in which theology was still alive, and Tillich was never more passionate than in theological discussion. His wife, Hannah, would often attempt to restrain him in theological debate because of a fear for his health, and his final stroke did occur in an intense theological discussion with younger theologians, leading *Life* magazine in their obituary for Tillich to attribute his death to me.

If I were to write an obituary I would want to write it on theology itself, but theology is alive as can be observed in Tillich's continual impact, and this is a healthy impact if only because of the breadth of Tillich's theology, one broader or more universal than any other, and one loyal to great masters such as Augustine, Luther, and Schelling. Again and again I have been told by teachers of religion that they discovered Tillich's sermons to be their most effective pedagogical instrument, and this makes perfect sense, for these sermons are for the most part religiously real and actually understandable, and that is an extraordinarily rare combination. Tillich had the reputation of being our most radical theologian, and that is not unjustified, just as he can also be thought of as our first death of God theologian. And it was just as such that he was a genuine theologian, for subtract the radical in Tillich, and the theologian disappears, which is just as it should be. ❖

Thomas J. J. Altizer

CONTENTS

ACKNOWLEDGMENTS   iv

PREFACE - Thomas J. J. Altizer   vi

INTRODUCTION – Beneath the Ground of   11
    Being – Robert M. Price

What is Wrong with the "Dialectic"   22
    Theology?

THE KINGDOM OF GOD AND HISTORY   42

THE GOSPEL AND THE STATE   77

FREEDOM IN THE PERIOD OF   92
    TRANSFORMATION

EXISTENTIAL THINKING IN AMERICAN   117
    THEOLOGY

"FAITH" IN THE JEWISH-CHRISTIAN   123
    TRADITION

KIERKEGAARD IN ENGLISH   134

VERTICAL AND HORIZONTAL THINKING   141

REDEMPTION IN COSMIC AND SOCIAL   148
    HISTORY

EXISTENTIALISM AND RELIGIOUS   162
    SOCIALISM

THE PRESENT THEOLOGICAL SITUATION
IN THE LIGHT OF THE CONTINENTAL 169
EUROPEAN DEVELOPMENT

A REINTERPRETATION OF THE DOCTRINE 184
OF THE INCARNATION

THE RECOVERY OF THE PROPHETIC 201
TRADITION IN THE REFORMATION

THE EUROPEAN DISCUSSION OF THE
PROBLEM OF THE DEMYTHOLOGI- 254
ZATION OF THE NEW TESTAMENT

VICTORY IN DEFEAT: THE MEANING OF
HISTORY IN THE LIGHT OF 270
CHRISTIAN PROPHETISM

JEWISH INFLUENCES ON CONTEMP- 284
ORARY CHRISTIAN THEOLOGY

RELIGIOUS SYMBOLS AND OUR 298
KNOWLEDGE OF GOD

RELATION OF METAPHYSICS AND 312
THEOLOGY

THE IDEA OF GOD AS AFFECTED BY 321
MODERN KNOWLEDGE

BENEATH THE GROUND OF BEING

The Eternal Tillich

Just the opposite of Hegel, who deemed his own system the eschatological culmination of human thought, Paul Tillich feared that, already in his lifetime, his thought and speculation had become obsolete. He confided to his friend Reinhold Niebuhr, "Am I so soon cast on the ash heap of history?" Rather like the later Process theologians, Tillich thought the most terrible prospect of damnation lay in "being forgotten in eternity." And one suspects he feared this fate had encroached upon him already. But such fears were groundless. While Tillich's thought has quite naturally lost some of the luster it once possessed, displayed in the "new merchandise" cases of theological bookstores, this is because it has been so thoroughly worked over and assimilated. Some may cast it aside as the latest curiosity, already exhausted by the jaded. But one suspects they had never seen the deep richness of Tillich's work to begin with, much less discerned its deep roots in the historic Christian tradition. Much of what the superficial dismissed as semantic mischief and glib modernism was really a set of neglected treasures from the common tradition. Reading Tillich and his critics, then and now, one feels Tillich has forgotten more historical theology than his critics ever learned.

But interest in Tillich has never died out. His works continue to be reprinted, assigned, and read with new wonder by new generations of seminary students. Thanks to Dr. Michael Kogan at Montclair State College, I discovered Tillich through *Dynamics of Faith* when I was a college junior.

Later, at the same school, I plunged headlong into Tillich's works under the guidance of the late Robert F. Streetman. Pieter de Jonge's Tillich Seminar at Drew University in 1979 was a great feast for Robert Corrington and me, with most of the others hanging on for the ride. So *my* interest in Tillich has never flagged. I have been delighted over the years to see and buy new collections of his essays. Even they were not sufficient, so I got hold of a good bibliography and began hunting down all the still-stray essays by the Master. My pastor, Don Morris, suggested to me back in 1981 that I assemble a number of these into a book. You're looking at it.

But theology has moved on, as Tillich's lament to Niebuhr implies, and one would be a fool to ignore new developments in theology and philosophy out of what amounts to brand loyalty. Tillich had shown me that one dare not suppress suspected aspects of the truth without becoming an idolater. So I was willing both to recognize lacunae in Tillich and to seek the efforts of others to close those gaps. Eventually I found myself attracted, indeed mesmerized, by Jacque Derrida and Deconstruction. This was by way of reading a score or so of books by Don Cupitt, inspired in turn by an enlightening article on the latter by Everet Tarbox. I felt that in Cupitt and Derrida I had found new inspirations rivaling Paul Tillich in importance. But naturally, as part of the process of trying out a new paradigm, I had to see how much of the old I could assimilate into the new. After all, Einstein assumes most of Newton instead of replacing him outright. How much, I asked myself, could I as a Derridean retain of Tillich? Or did I have to choose between two incompatible ways? I think it is worth going into this question a bit at least by way of explanation or justification for a new collection of Tillich in a time when some would see Tillich as occupying merely a stratum of the ash heap of history, and not even one close to the top.

The Onto-Theological Argument

Tillich's theological approach seems to me the entire vindication of Derrida's charge that Heidegger's philosophy ought to be called "onto-theology." That is, by discussing Being as a super-existence underlying all existing things and from which they proceed, Heidegger has made Being into God. Bultmann and Tillich saw this, though Heidegger denied he was talking about God when he discussed Being. Derrida, in effect, shares the judgment of Tillich and Bultmann. Furthermore, the assumption that human beings find Being open and apparent to them in the mirror of their consciousness is, for Derrida, deceptive "Presence Metaphysics," the error that seduced Descartes and his followers to believe that what they knew "clearly and distinctly" must be true. Derrida rejects self-evidence metaphysics partly because of his Sausserian view of language as being differential rather than referential in character. Words refer not to things but to more words, the words of signification that explain the significance of the words. There is no crossing the "Barrier" between Signifier and Signified, hence no reason to posit any Transcendental Signified at all, that is, beyond words. Even within the game of their own usage, words have unstable meanings. They promise to deliver some final or exhaustive meaning but always disappoint, always leaving some portion of the desired explanation hanging in limbo, yet unknown or unspoken. It is the ever-lingering Delay of the Parousia of the Word.

Also, language is inherently unstable and ambiguous to the extent that every single use of language lets loose reverberations of signification unintended by the speaker/writer and unrecognized by him as his own returning prodigal, his own black sheep, once he sees it or hears it again. One may make one's message pretty clear and yet simultaneously unleash a counter-argument that subverts it and *must* do so because of the Dionysian play of language despite the dour Apollonian uses we may assign it. So nothing, no seeming truth, is self-evident. If one looks hard enough, one will always find the seams of construction. Early twentieth-century science fiction writers toyed with the notion that someone might discover that gold is not a simple element but rather a combination of elements. If one had this secret, one could make gold for oneself. Wonderful stories by Robert W. Chambers and John Taine made use of this premise. It was a good symbol of the "deconstructive" procedure that Heidegger and Derrida called for, so as to show the constructed, non-natural, not self-evident, manufactured character of this or that supposedly tacit, self-derived concept, picture, or experience. As Dilthey showed, even the present moment, which seems to glow with the Zen halo of the "be here now!", the Eternal Now, is a subtle construction, a melding of the remembered past, the anticipated future, and the experienced (but always just-*subsequently* experienced) present. Nothing pops into being from nothing: there is always a *hidden process of relation*.

For Derrida, these pre-conditions for speaking of ontology (something Heidegger and Bultmann, like Tillich, wanted to do) in fact made it impossible ever to speak constructively of ontology. Every utterance one might venture as to the truth ostensibly underlying all things ("Being," for example) is already vitiated by a signification virus. We have broken the rules by stepping up to the plate. There can be no Transcendental Signified, no one God to whom all points converge, at which all symbols point.

Lighter Than Air
Already, if we accept any of this, Tillichianism appears to be in deep trouble, to stink of that historical ash heap. Or does it? First, Tillich's doctrine of religious symbols, which seems dependent on the notion of the *participation* of the symbolic thing in the symbolized reality, ultimately Being-itself, would seem to be useless. And yet much of the attraction of

Tillich's thought for some of us has been the way in which he seems to lace together the most ill-matching strings, demonstrating that opposites do converge (as in his *Biblical Religion and the Search for Ultimate Reality*). We might seek refuge in the Buddhist Nagarjuna, who made possible a Mahayana Buddhist aesthetic. Nagarjuna warned his pious brethren not to be affronted by the illusory character of nature or of painting. Why scoff, deride, and devalue a copy or an image simply because it has no underlying *dharmas*? No solid reality beyond experience? No, this only seems a shortcoming as long as one expects some confusing thing, the existence of a "realer" reality behind the perceived one. (One senses Bishop Berkeley's ghost, too!) The spring flower, the autumn leaf, the soap bubble, the wild strawberry: all are beautiful in the ephemeral moment in which we see them, the only moment they have in the sun. Somehow it is the very groundlessness which frees all objects from the burden of "real" ontological weight. Maybe it is this airy grace that religious symbols require, that makes them sacred, their *lack* of connection with "reality." It would be a result quite close to that of Camus: true art, in all its transformative power, is really artistic at all only insofar as it is gratuitous, sprinkled gaily into the void of freedom for its own sake.

Tillich tells us right out that the character of Being itself is that of its own self-affirmation over against the inertia of non-Being: "The light shines out in darkness, and the darkness has not yet snuffed it out." Furthermore, "Whatever does not kill me makes me stronger," as Nietzsche said, because Being is made proportionately stronger the more non-being it can assimilate successfully, like the willow that grows stronger the more flexible it becomes from the winds. All this is daring and grand. All this supplies the ontological basis, if there is one, for why Tillichian counselors might urge the despondent not to commit suicide. (While I was taking that 1979 Tillich Seminar, I used to hear a pop song on the radio that said, "In every moment there's a reason to carry on.") But it does more than that: this declaration of Being as constituted by its own overcoming of its opposite is as frank an admission as one might wish of Derrida's contention that supposed "Being" is in fact vitiated from the first moment by the inherent instability of the very speech which seeks to articulate it. *At its very heart, in the originary moment, Being is based upon something else, namely: non-Being.* By thus building his onto-theological castle upon the void, Tillich has unwittingly ruled out as impossible the erection of any enduring systematic philosophical edifice such as he attempts in the *Systematic Theology.* He has also anticipated the whole of Derridean Deconstruction.

This move cuts to the heart of the architectonic principle which has always governed theoretical system building and reveals the endeavor as the product of a theologian's (and everyone else's) low tolerance for ambiguity. Derrida reveals Tillich's thought as fatally "Logocentric" from start to finish, a vain effort at distilling essences and elevating them over actual existences. Of course it was precisely in its Logocentric character that Tillichian theology found its greatest continuity with traditional Christianity, the religion of the incarnate Logos. Deconstruction upends or dissolves the duality and hierarchy of flesh versus spirit. And in so doing Deconstruction invites us to consider whether Tillich's onto-theology may after all be helpfully translated into a different language game altogether. Is there some way in which Tillich's "New Being" may be understood as a "New Becoming" (with all the vitiating non-Being that this implies)? Is there some way in which Tillich's "Spiritual Presence" may be understood as a kind of "Material Presence"? Can his "Eternal Now" become a "Resultant Now," to be better lived and more fulfillingly explored by deconstructing it? Perhaps so. Again, we might find help in Buddhist thinking on some of the same problems.

Though it sounds for all the world like Mahayana

Buddhism is talking about metaphysics and even mythology, with all its levels of existence and processes of perfection, its Buddha-fields of salvation and Dhyani-Buddhas, Buddhist thinkers often perplex Westerners by denying that the whole business has a thing to do with Being at all! All is Sunyata, Void. There are no ontological *dharmas* underlying anything. All is *maya*. All is Samsara, all is a soap bubble. So what of the dream-geography of the *Bardo Thödöl*? What of the Peaceful and the Wrathful Deities? The glorious Buddhas and Bodhisattvas? They are as "real" as they need to be for one to become enlightened. But "in themselves" (a merely verbal "state" in which nothing actually exists), they are zero. Buddhism is describing or, better, mediating *experience*. Perhaps that is what Tillich's talk of New Being does, too. Once Tillich, effusive in his praise of his friend Carl Jung, remarked that Jung was not merely mapping out the working of the mind but had actually disclosed the very ontological structures of Being as manifest to the mind. But had he? Cupitt argues for a non-Realist understanding of Jung which sees him precisely as mapping out the programming of the mind, nothing "more." But however we understand Jung's intention, we might suggest a reverse conversion of Tillichianism into Jungianism in Buddhist terms. That is, why not admit that Jung was "merely" mapping out the channels of consciousness, whatever it is, and that Tillich's own categories, with all their jargon, are descriptions of the way the human interior life works? His dialectic between freedom and destiny, for example, surely rings truer as describing an experienced choice than as a theoretical doctrine of predestination, whether in a traditional sense or some more abstract version.

Sons of Dasein
It is worth noting that Tillich and Derrida share some important analytical tools, no doubt because both were heavily influenced by Heidegger. For instance, Tillich

already knows the doctrine of the Trace, whereby, thanks to the shaping of each term by its adjacency to related and contrasting terms, each term is somehow the reflected Other of both its synonyms and its antonyms! "Apple" denotes "not an orange" as much as "not a crab apple." Each piece of signification bears, then, a necessary relation, though often a paradoxical one, to its own opposites (which in turn is why all paired opposites and hierarchies must be upended, their relationships plotted anew). Tillich understands all this well when he explains how "faith" is not the enemy of doubt but that the relationship of both is altogether different, at once both complementary (you can't have one without the other) and constitutive (without the element of doubt, faith would pass over into knowledge, with a different opposite: error). The faith-doubt dialectic in Tillich is a prime example of the Derridean Trace.

Again, the Derridean "nonconcept" of the *parergon*, the defining character of the marginal, occurs in Tillich's discussion of the Circle of Faith, and the perception that it somehow includes those gathered at the rim of the circle whether they find themselves inside or outside it. How can the Christian faith be conditioned to the point of being defined by other viewpoints which its rejects? Anyone with a basic knowledge of Christian theological syncretism knows this lesson well. And who would deny that every emergent stage of Christological orthodoxy contained the heresy it rejected, enshrining within its very formulation a rejection of the doctrine it opposed yet thereby immortalized along with it, like Pontius Pilate having become an article of the Apostles Creed! One might believe in the divine sonship of the Logos without reference to temporality, but once Arius had posited a post-temporal begetting of the Logos, and Athanasius posited the opposite, an element of temporality was forever included in the sonship concept.

Deconstruction itself, as Derrida readily admits, is a direct borrowing from Heidegger's doctrine of *Destruktion*, or destructuring for the purpose of analysis. Heidegger famously deconstructed the Greek *aletheia*, showing that the word commonly rendered "truth" started out meaning a *divulging, uncovering, revelation*. The philosophical implications are great, and Heidegger showed how they have remained implicit in the usage of "truth" even when the first meaning has been long forgotten. Tillich's discussion of "faith" as originally meaning "concern" rather than factual affirmation, while it strikes many as a convenient redefinition, is actually a Heideggerian deconstruction of a too-familiar word, the cracking open of a fossilized shell to allow the hidden implications to become evident.

Penultimate Concern

If there is no Transcendental Signified to which all signifiers point, pointing instead only to one another, what becomes of Tillich's talk of an Ultimate Concern? Is not such a preoccupation monomaniacal? Walter Kaufman thought so. Rejecting Tillich's notion, Kaufman argued that the sane and balanced individual has a smorgasbord of proper and penultimate concerns. Any one of them (say, patriotism, religious loyalty, or family loyalty) might eventually come to the fore in a pinch, in extremis. But ordinarily we switch back and forth between concerns. It is hard to believe Tillich did not in practice agree, since he warned that only an idolatrous concern resulted in narrow psychological fixation. Rather, he seemed to envision a psychological integration where one avoided compartmentalization. Every concern must be viewed as compatible or incompatible with one's most serious concerns. These latter might be different faces of the same concern anyway (hence not contradictory), as when one calls the Ultimate "Truth" while wearing one's philosopher's cap, "God" while talking theology, and "Beauty" while listening to Bach.

One might compare Tillich's practice of the Ultimate

Concern as something like an ever-shifting kaleidoscope, since the ever-new shifting of perspective results in new flowerings-forth of the same elements in recombination, nothing discarded, rejected, destroyed. Nothing inconsistent is introduced. Otherwise we should never have had the Tillichian theology of culture, where one understands the deepest values and beliefs of a culture by reading the explicit in terms of the implicit. Nor should we have witnessed the publication of the variegated essays making up this book. Here Tillich addresses other thinkers, including Kierkegaard, Martin Buber, Rudolf Bultmann, critiquing and affirming, borrowing and objecting. Here we also see him relating politics to faith, Judaism to Christianity, religious symbols to facts of experience. What made it possible for Tillich to juggle all these seemingly disparate entities was his great skill at "correlation," not only between the questions of culture and the answers of the gospel, but even between each and all areas of human endeavor. He had no trouble seeing the interrelation of all things in an almost Buddhist manner. He would have said it was possible to relate A to B to Z because all alike rested upon and proceeded from a common Ground of Being, which is God. After Derrida, we might instead say that the universal linkage Tillich discerned is simply the existential side of the fact that all signifiers are interrelated as they bounce into and among one another like Democritan atoms, ricocheting against the Barrier.

The disparity and almost randomness of many of the topics treated in this book typify, finally, another feature of the postmodern intellectual landscape, the inevitable resort of the scholar to *bricolage*, the handyman's reliance upon a kit full of theoretical tools that have proven their utility time and again, no matter whether they still belong to the same set one bought them in. No matter even whether one still uses them for the intended purpose! Even as one rejects the totalistic claims of Structuralism, for instance, one may still find some Structuralist technique quite helpful in understanding a text or a myth, and then why not use it? As Paul Feyerabend (*Against Method*) exhorted, the only principle that does not inhibit thought or research is "Anything goes!" We sightless gropers have experienced far too little of the surface of that great big elephant to start pontificating about which features it can or can't have. There is always more to the whole picture than we know, so we have to be modest in declaring contradictions, disqualifying this or that theory, because of an apparent collision with another that seems equally compelling. This is an embarrassing admission only if we imagine our task as theologians, philosophers, culture critics, as that of cataloguing and explaining *everything*. But if we have grown past that silliness, we can feel free, as Derrida and Levi-Strauss would, to choose whatever peculiar-shaped gadget will do the particular job at hand. In this book, you will see Tillich the handyman already producing odd gadgets which turn out to be oddly appropriate, and you will surely discover insights from this late, greater and greater, thinker, which you will feel compelled to put into your own eclectic tool kit, whatever judgment you may render on what is *not* contained here: the systematic theology of Paul Tillich. Here are fragments of Tillich that reflect a fragmentary world — the one we live in.

I owe very great thanks to R. León Santiago (a.k.a. "Quixie") for his indefatigable efforts in transcribing these essays. No book without Tillich or Santiago! ❖

Robert M. Price
July 22, 2002

WHAT IS WRONG WITH THE "DIALECTIC" THEOLOGY?

When I am asked, What is wrong with the "dialectic" theology? I reply that it is not "dialectic." A dialectic theology is one in which "yes" and "no" belong inseparably together. In the so-called "dialectic" theology they are irreconcilably separated, and that is why this theology is not dialectic. Rather, it is paradoxical, and therein lies its strength; and it is supernatural, which constitutes its weakness. All that follows in this discussion is devoted to the proof of these two statements.

I

To ask what is wrong with the "dialectic" theology presupposes the conviction that it contains something that is right. Only because this is presupposed, could I entertain the question proposed to me. It is, indeed, my conviction that there is not only something that is right in the "dialectic" theology, but something quite definitive for theology and equally fundamental for the church. Not until that fact is emphatically established does significant criticism become possible.

Perhaps it is worthwhile at this point to recall the historical origin of the "dialectic" theology. Karl Barth, its theological founder and head, with whom we are principally concerned in our exposition and criticism, comes from the Swiss religious-socialist movement. The most important advocates of this movement—Ragaz and Kutter and their Württemberg predecessors, the older and the younger Blumhard—worked out *one* determinative idea which, in spite of all variation through which it has passed, has remained decisive also for Barth. That idea is the notion that God stands as sovereign, not only over against the world, but also against the church and piety, and consequently he has the power to make more of his will known through a contemporary secular movement—even through an atheistic movement like that of social democracy—than through ecclesiastical activities and the churchly forms of piety. In so far as church and piety are of the world—and they *too* are always of the world—they take no sort of precedence over other forms of worldly existence. On the contrary, the significance of the church is more questionable and imperiled just because it pretends to be something other than a part of worldly existence. The Blumhards and the religious socialists taught that God's will is most clearly manifest not in subjective piety and the rescue of individual souls but in the administration of the world, the vanquishing of the demonic powers therein, the coming of the Kingdom of God. And for this purpose God can employ such instruments as seemingly are least his, even the enemies of the church and of Christianity—for example, the revolutionary laborers' movement.

There was power in this idea. In order to understand its significance one must bear in mind the fact that, on the one hand, from the point of view of ecclesiastical theory and practice the socialist laborers' movement was an abode of godlessness, agitation, and materialism, and that for this very reason it was impossible for a pastor to join the party. On the other hand, the leaders of the movement and the great masses who belonged to it fought the church and theology and perhaps even religion as their most dangerous enemy. The work of the religious-socialist movement that emerged in this setting had extraordinary theological significance notwithstanding the political shipwreck of the movement. It produced an awareness of the limitations of churchliness and piety; it weakened the church's Pharisaic attitude toward the unchurched masses. But there was also a danger hidden in religious socialism. Just as was formerly the case with the church and its secular activity, the will of God could now be identified with political and social forms of activity. The Kingdom of God could be understood as a mundane social reality, and the struggle to realize the Kingdom of God could be interpreted as a political struggle for social righteousness. But the sovereignty of God, denied to the church, was thereby surrendered to a political movement. The Swiss religious socialism did not entirely escape this danger. Therefore Barth withdrew from the movement and retained only the notion of the unconditioned sovereignty of God over against both the church and the world.

Barth laid hold upon this notion with the whole force of his theological thinking and volition. Fundamentally, his entire theology is contained in the first commandment, "I am the Lord thy God; thou shalt not have any other gods beside me." Every single sentence of his writings can be understood as the application of this notion to a particular phase of the relation between God and the world. Any teaching that draws God into the sphere of human possibility is rebellion against the first commandment. This is the theme of Barth's commentary on the Epistle to the Romans, which is his most radical and most strongly provocative book and is the one in which his prophetic spirit is most in evidence. God is "impossible possibility"; that is, he is beyond human possibilities. From the human point of view every statement about him is a paradox—a statement regarding that about which nothing can be said. Such statements as "impossible possibilities" have given rise erroneously to the name "Dialectic theology." For such statements are not dialectical but are paradoxical. They do not yield a process of thought in which "yes" and "no" are mutually involved, but they permit only a constant repetition in other words of the idea expressed in the paradox. The choice of words depends upon the particular sphere in which the fundamental paradox is to be used.

The relation between God and man is expressed in the sentence "God is in heaven and thou art on earth." Between God and man there is a hollow space which man is unable of himself to penetrate. If it were possible for him to do this, he would have power over his relation to God, and thus would have power over God himself. But no creature has such power. The contention that the creature possesses this power is idol-worship.

The claim to have inherent power to attain unto God can be made in various ways by theology and the church. From a Christian point of view it is perfectly understandable that this claim is made beyond the limits of Christianity, in Judaism, humanism, and heathendom. But the fact that such tendencies prosper in the theology and practice of Christianity, thereby causing a transgression of the first commandment, is the theological and ecclesiastical scandal that calls forth the indignation of Barth and moves him to passion.

This offense issues in two fundamental notions. One is the blending of the divine and human spirit; the other is the blending of the divine and human kingdom. The former constitutes the idol-worship of all mystical and humanistic theology, and the latter is the idol-worship of Catholicism on the one hand, and of the social and political aspects of Protestantism on the other.

These presuppositions enable one to understand the severity with which Barth, and all the theologians who follow him, assail mysticism. Mysticism assumes the identity of the human and the divine spirit. Naturally, this identity is to be sought neither on the sentient nor on the rational level of the human spirit. The divine element in the human spirit, upon which its identity with the divine really rests, lies at a deeper level, namely, at the point where the distinction between subject and object, between sense perception and discernment, between the conditioned and the unconditioned is eliminated. All mysticism seeks God in the depths of the human spirit. It seeks the deepest levels of the human in order to meet God, since where the speech ceases the divine in man begins. But to be Christian is to seek God in the Word and in the Word only. The Word stands over against us. It is spoken to us by another. It is outside of us and demands faith and obedience, not submergence and ecstasy.

The element of mysticism appears everywhere in theology since wherever a naturalistic theology is taught, it accordingly is maintained that man can know God from nature. Barth has carried his radical rejection of the naturalistic theology even to the point of opposing his disciple, Brunner. On this issue Barth recognizes only an "either-or." If man is at all able to recognize God as God from nature, then human activity is involved in the act of faith. But if the act of faith is purely a work of God, then man can be allowed no antecedent possibility of knowing God. Hence all naturalistic theology signifies in the last analysis a tendency toward the deification of man. This danger is concealed especially in teaching about the possibility of man's likeness to God. Barth holds that the likeness of God in man is a thing to be sought, a goal of salvation and perfection, but is nothing given, no natural equipment by whose help one can attain any knowledge of God. We can attain knowledge of God only by means of God himself, that is, through his spirit which is in us but not of us. The spirit alone makes possible man's likeness to God.

It is apparent that from Barth's standpoint all philosophy of religion is set at nought. In so far as it aims to be more than a description of psychological and ethnological phenomena, thus differentiating itself from psychology and history of religion, philosophy of religion attempts to say something about the truth of religion detached from faith. It speaks about God, but it does not say that the Holy Spirit determines its utterances as in the case of the authentic testimony of faith. Philosophy of religion seeks out knowledge about God and worship among all men and peoples, presenting the connection with God as a fact of the history of religion, instead of as an "impossible possibility," that is, a single occurrence of revelation and belief therein.

Every type of natural and cultural theology is condemned along with the philosophy of religion because it attempts to discover immediate knowledge of God from nature on the one hand, and from philosophy, science, art, and history on the other. Culture and history are the spheres in which man stands by himself alone; they express human concerns and are subject to human, not to theological, criteria. Nature also can be interpreted only in a human, not in a theological, way. Human and divine possibility are radically separated, for man is a sinner and the possibility of natural sinlessness is an abstraction that can have for us absolutely no meaning.

Therefore the liberal theology is heresy. In place of the sinner it substitutes the self-developing personality; in place of Christ, the self-developing man Jesus; in place of the word of God in Scripture, the self-developing religious consciousness of humanity. From these three positions Barth launches his attack against the liberal theology. For him the creatureliness of man is essentially an expression of his separation from God, an expression of the rigid contrast between the creator and the creation. Not the dignity but the nothingness of the creature is expressed in the doctrine of creation. And Barth does not concede that one can derive from the teaching about creation divine decrees, as a divinely ordered form of nature and of man and of society. Even if something of this were apparent in the original creation, it has become invisible through sin, for sin has

27

radically transformed nature and man. We are unable to derive from the natural laws of pre-human and human being any norm for natural and human perfection. Sin has made this impossible. Therefore, all human distinctions, from the most perfect to the most imperfect, are subject to the same judgment; they signify nothing before God. Perfection is an eschatological conception, a transcendental "impossible possibility."

The liberal theology's picture of Christ is accorded a like caustic treatment. This does not mean, however, that Barth rejects the historical work of the liberal school of theology. That is so far from true that even the most radical historical critic of the New Testament, Bultmann of Marburg, can be at the same time one of the most active advocates of the Barthian theology. Historical criticism is of so little concern to Barth that he can quite avowedly express his indifference toward the question of the existence or non-existence of the "historical Jesus." He does not reject the historical research of the liberals, but he treats it as a trifling matter, of which his Christology is independent. His Christology continues to rest explicitly upon the paradoxical formulas of the Chalcedonian council regarding the "inseparability and unmixed quality of the divine and human nature in Christ." For Barth Christ appears in history only in so far as he is above history; he does not participate in the development of human history and of human spiritual life, but is God's insert into history. Viewed historically and psychologically, Christ continues to be the "impossible impossibility."

From such a position, the third line of assault upon the liberal theology is capable of being understood. God speaks to us, not *by means of* our spirit and its cultural and historical creations, but he speaks *to* our spirit and that means *against* our spirit, since our spirit is dominated by the law of sin. The form in which God speaks is the word of the Bible. This is his only and his entire communication. But at this point it should be immediately affirmed that Barth does not intend to combat biblical criticism nor to revive the dogma of biblical inspiration. Whether the word of the Bible becomes for one the "word of God," and by what means, depends upon the working of the Holy Spirit. Not the letter of Scripture, not even the religious spirit of the men who wrote it, not the historical account as such, neither a world-picture nor a morality that might be found in the Bible, make it the word of God, but only the fact that it bears testimony to the revelation made in Christ. But no one is capable of understanding this testimony unless God himself makes it possible through the Holy Spirit. Beyond the word of God there is no disposing power. This understanding is mediated neither by the letter of Scripture, nor by preaching on Sunday, nor by theological study. It can occur, but where and when the event happens is not under our control. It is linked with the Bible, but we do not possess it when we possess the Bible. Like everything else that we can say and learn of God, it is "impossible possibility."

The same paradox holds also for the relation of the Kingdom of God to human action. The Kingdom of God is a purely transcendental quantum which is not constructed by men but which comes to men. It is a purely eschatological quantum entirely distinct from human culture and history. Culture is a human possibility, and in history man stands by himself alone. Therefore, culture and history can furnish us neither standards for Christian teaching nor norms for Christian conduct. Nor can any single procedure in culture and history lay claim to being entirely or partly a realization of the Kingdom of God. The Kingdom of God is never present in history, either in a utopian perfection, or in the real or imagined progress of history. Even the church is not the Kingdom of God. The church is commissioned to bear testimony to God and his kingdom, yet it is not identical therewith. The church is a historical reality, and as such it does not rank above any other historical reality. It, like the others, is a human performance subject to error and change and is not insured against the possibility of leaving its commission unfulfilled. Yet it has this commission; that is its truth. But just as having the Bible does not signify possession over the word of God, so no more does membership in the church signify dominion over the testimony of God. That testimony can happen within the church but it can also fail to appear. Yet when it does happen it is not the realization of the Kingdom of God but is only its announcement.

The same thing holds true for all of the church's activity. Even its instructional and charitable work is the announcement of the Kingdom and not the realization of its presence. Thus, indeed, obedience is rendered to the commands of God, but there is no Christian ethics in the sense of an anticipation of the righteousness of God's Kingdom. Paul's hymn to love is an eschatological hymn and does not furnish material for a system of Christian ethics. For love, like the word of God and the Kingdom of Heaven, is not a human possibility. The one like the other is "impossible possibility," the object of faith and not of sight.

The total result is, finally, that theology can be nothing but the exercise of a critical self-consciousness upon the content of the Christian pronouncement, in which the word of Scripture is the ultimate standard of criticism. Any mingling of philosophical ideas in this task is rejected. The use of any sort of natural theology as a preliminary to reflection on God, the world, or man is stoutly resisted. Philosophy, like religion, belongs in human culture and in the sphere of human possibilities. Theology rests on revelation, which is humanly impossible. And there is no bridge spanning the gulf between the divine and the human.

Thus the Barthian theology, from first to last, preserves the sovereign prerogative of God as expressed in the first commandment. God's sovereignty is not blended with any form of human existence and action. Unquestionably, this seems to me to be the truth that is preserved not only in the

Barthian theology, but in any theology that deserves the name. A criticism of this position would be not only a criticism of Barth, but of the Bible, the church, and theology in general.

II

If Barth must be criticized, criticism is possible only when it deals with that which escapes Barth when judged by his own standard. Does Barth's interpretation of the Christian paradox protect it from the distortion of its meaning? Or does not his interpretation directly weaken the paradox and restrict the sovereign prerogative of God? I believe that to be the case, and it results from Barth's attempt to establish the paradox by means of supernaturalism rather than by dialectics.

Again I would approach the subject by recalling history. When Barth's commentary on Romans was published, a wide circle of theologians of the same age attached themselves to the school for which Barth had prepared the way. Some did so publicly, and some — like the author of this article — in a "subterranean" group of fellow-laborers. In the course of a decade the situation has been completely changed. As the supernaturalistic trend of the Barthian thinking became more clearly evident, it became necessary for me to give up the "subterranean" fellowship. The same was true of Bultmann, who had taken his stand for Barth in a much more open fellowship but whose attachment to the "existential" philosophy brought about his separation from Barth. Gogarten also turned aside. He joined the political reaction and his theological justification for this move made clear the gulf between him and Barth. Finally, last year, a sharp controversy broke out between Brunner and Barth over the possibility of a natural theology. It is, of course, understood that these happenings in themselves prove nothing against the truth of the Barthian theology. But they constantly press home to us the question, What is it in Barth's elaboration of his fundamental idea that has forced these friends and fellow-laborers to seek other ways? What, in their opinion, is wrong with Barth's theology? We are asking about their opinions, not about the opinion of those who have never been gripped by the force of Barth's thinking and who have never understood the larger truth of his fundamental paradox. Therefore, the criticism that follows is to be understood as coming from the former "subterranean" fellowship and not from the originally antagonistic group.

The paradox of the "impossible possibility" is an impossibility from the standpoint of men but is a possibility from the standpoint of God. And it is not only a possibility but is also a reality. For only because it has become a reality can we speak of it as a possibility. Theology is the methodical form of speaking of the human impossibility, and of the divine possibility, which has become reality. Now, there are two ways of speaking of this event—of this reality—the supernatural and the dialectical. The supernatural way seeks to protect the divinity of the event being diluted with human possibilities, while attaching it to definite temporal and spatial procedures, persons, words, writings, societies, and actions, such as the events of the years one to thirty, the history of Jesus and the Apostles and their language, the writings of the Bible, the church, and preaching and sacraments. Barth never means that these procedures as such, as human and historical procedures, are the divine event. He does not even deny it as a possibility of thought that God could have happened to use other procedures for the realization of his action, but he does maintain that God chose only one of these procedures and no other, and has restricted revelation to this. He emphasizes in a genuinely nominalistic way the contingency of the divine activity.

It is otherwise with dialectical thinking. It denies, just as does the supernatural way of thinking, that what is a purely divine possibility may be interpreted as a human possibility. But dialectic thinking maintains that the *question* about the divine possibility is a human possibility. And, further, it maintains that no question could be asked about the divine possibility unless a divine answer, even if preliminary and scarcely intelligible, were not always already available. For in order to be able to ask about God, man must already have experienced God as the goal of a possible question. Thus the human possibility of the question is no longer purely a human possibility, since it already contains answers. And without such preliminary half-intelligible answers and preliminary questions based thereon, even the ultimate could not be perceived. Were an event only a foreign substance in history it could neither be absorbed by history nor could it continue to be operative in history. It is as far from right to call history purely God-abandoned as to call it simply God's revelation. Indeed, when speaking of revelation, one must say that history is always equipped with revelation because it always contains divine answers and human questions. Thus there can be a "fullness of time," a moment in history when history by means of preliminary procedures has become capable of realizing the ultimate—a moment when history has become ripe for the event, which does not originate from history and also is not injected into it as a foreign substance, but breaks out within it and is capable of being received in history. Liberalism speaks of this as an event arising out of history, and supernaturalism calls it a foreign injection into history. In his radical opposition to the possibility affirmed by the liberals, Barth has made his decision in favor of the supernatural rather than the dialectical interpretation. This is his limitation.

Criticism of the details of the Barthian theology follows from this fundamental criticism which, from the standpoint of the dialectical explanation, must be applied to the supernatural explanation of the Christian paradox.

Certainly God is in his heaven and man is on earth. But man can make this statement only in case heaven and earth have touched one another time and again, not only once, but in a process of history in which statements and then doubts have been expressed about gods who are thought to be on earth and men who are thought to be in heaven. That statement can be made and accepted only as the expression of a preliminary erring knowledge about God and man. Erring knowledge is not utter ignorance, especially when it begins to doubt its accuracy and to ask for true knowledge.

Since Barth does not recognize the dialectical value of erring knowledge about God, but makes it identical with ignorance, the whole history of religion is transformed by him into a "Witches' Sabbath" of ghostly fancies, idolatry, and superstition. A warning against the literary frivolities of religious syncretism was certainly appropriate; also religio-historical relativism is dangerous, indeed disastrous, and it is impossible to identify the history of religion with the history of revelation. Yet it seems to me to be just as certain that the church fathers' doctrine of the Logos, which has scattered its seed everywhere, giving answers and inspiring questions, is not only truer from the standpoint of dialectic but in the end signifies much more for every unbiased contact with extra-Christian piety than does Barth's de-divinizing of the history of religion. The liberal interpretation confuses history of religion with revelation; the supernatural interpretation makes them mutually exclusive; the dialectical interpretation finds in the history of religion answers, mistakes, and questions which lead to the ultimate answer and without which the ultimate answer would have to remain something unasked, unintelligible, and alien.

Certainly Barth is right when he measures nature, culture, and history by a human standard. In all three areas man stands apart—even though he is within nature. For nature can give man only that which it has in common with him and not some other thing that is eternally foreign to him. But the question arises, What is this human entity? Can it be thought of only as something without the divine, without the capacity for receiving answers from the divine and for asking questions of the divine? One thing is certain. Creations of culture in which none of these questions and answers are to be found we call superficial. The measure of a culture's depth and power is the measure of its sensitivity to such questions. Every unbiased contact with original cultural creations compels recognition of the fact that they concern themselves neither solely with God as a remote reality nor solely with human self-glorification, but with erring and questioning knowledge about God. I doubt whether there is any meaning in applying to this way of knowing God the term "natural" knowledge of God. As employed in this connection, "natural theology" has very little to do with natural human wisdom in the general and formal sense. Perhaps the conception "natural theology" is itself the product of a faulty supernaturalism.

Certainly culture is not revelation, as a naïve theory of culture assumes it to be. Culture is a human possibility, while revelation is impossibility, which means a divine possibility. Yet revelation would not be even a divine *possibility*—revelation is indeed revelation to man—if it could not be received by means of forms of culture as human phenomena. It would be a destructive foreign substance in culture, a disruptive "non-human" entity within the human sphere, and could have had no power to shape and direct human history. It would not convey any message to man, who is ever a historical and culturally sensitive being. It could communicate only with a ghostly and empty form of man, the content of whose being would have to be self-engendered.

Criticism of Barth's repudiation of philosophy of religion or so-called "natural theology" follows immediately from what has just been said. Barth is right in combating the identity in nature of God and man and in rejecting all attempts to find a point in man where he may be able to find and lay hold of God. He is correct in his resistance to all mysticism, which would permit union with God in the depths of man's own human nature. Apart from the Augustinian *transcende te ipsum* there is no access to God. But this precept contains within itself the demand to proceed *through* self *beyond* self. Therefore, the other statement, *in interiori anima habitat veritas*, is more basal in the dialectic of Augustine. We can find God *in* us only when we rise *above* ourselves. This transcendentalizing act does not signify that we possess the transcendental. The point is that we are in quest of it. But on the other hand this quest is possible only because the transcendental has already dragged us out beyond ourselves as we have received answers which drive us to the quest. The development of this dialectic is the proper aim of philosophy of religion and of the improperly so-called "natural theology." Only it should not be supposed that this can be a substitute for the theology of revelation. Theology is not anthropology and when studied as if it were it surrenders itself into the hands of Feuerbach and his psychological and sociological followers. But theology is the solution of the anthropological question, which is the problem of the finiteness of man. Again, the question itself is possible only because man has already received answers to it, and therefore can have knowledge about his finiteness.

But Barth will answer that finiteness is not sin. In so far as sin cannot be defined in terms of finiteness, he is correct. But guilt and despair belong to finiteness and are understood as sin in the revelation of God against whom they are guilt and for whose sake they are despair. Sin could never be experienced as sin without the anthropological possibility of guilt and despair. Otherwise they would be empty words, an unintelligible communication, and not a revelation of man's status before God. Therefore it is not correct to say that sin makes impossible any knowledge of God. On the contrary, in the experience of guilt and despair the question of perplexing knowledge about God is as radically presented as it ever can be apart from revelation. And only because of that fact is the answer "sin and grace" a real answer and not an utterly meaningless formula.

In so far as the liberal theology puts human development in the place of revelation, Barth's criticism also holds good for dialectic thinking. But when he deprives the human of any relation to the divine, as he does in his teaching about the God-likeness of man, about Christ, about God's word, and about the Bible, Barth's peculiar formulations are objectionable or wrong. On that account all these ideas become unintelligible. Assuredly the God-likeness of man is not an unfolding of personality independent of revelation; but it cannot be understood merely as a work of the Holy Spirit. The Holy Spirit bears witness to our spirit—a witness that we are able to understand, since this witnessing takes place not beyond our spiritual life, but in response to the quest for a relation to God. The answer is, that we are God's children not through our humanity but through grace; yet the demand for this answer, and the capability of asking and perceiving it, come through humanity. Without this antecedent God-likeness of man no consequent God-likeness would be possible. Without it the witness of the Holy Spirit to his spirit would not concern him. In general, Barth leaves unexplained how revelation can communicate anything to man if there is nothing in him permitting him to raise questions about it, impelling him toward it, and enabling him to understand it.

Barth quite properly makes his Christology and his teaching about the word of God independent of the results of historical criticism. Revelation can neither be called in question nor established by means of historical criticism. But the content and the manner of interpreting that which is called the occurrence of revelation in the New Testament are intelligible only for one who is informed about the questions which are implicit in the New Testament answers. The terms used by the authors of the biblical books were produced by the religious tradition by which they were determined, and the original meaning of these terms must first be understood. At the same time the fact that the ideas when applied to the Christian paradox instantly transcend both these traditions and the individual reworking of tradition by particular authors brings out the revelatory character of the ideas. Yet they would reveal nothing, but would be only alien conglomerations of words, if they did not carry along, so to speak, their traditional usage in the service of revelation. In this fact lies the great theological significance of historical and religio-historical criticism and interpretation of the Bible, and likewise the impossibility of divorcing the word of the Bible from cultural history. With that fact established, the genuinely supernatural notion of verbal inspiration is no longer a remote idea. And, actually, the younger disciples of Barth are moving in this direction. The consequences of this supernaturalistic tendency are evident. That has been true for a long time in the preaching of many pastors of this school who repeat the biblical text in the Barthian way without taking the trouble to treat in a vital way the higher problem to which the word of the Bible is the answer. Barth is right in protesting that preaching has been devoted to displaying religious experience, personal piety, cultural and social convictions. It ought to bear witness to God and not to man. Yet, it must witness for man, and it ought to take pains to vitalize the human means, not waiting for a miracle to enable the message to become God's word for the hearer.

Barthian teaching about the relation of the Kingdom of God to human activities is also subject to criticism. It is a fact of church history that Barth made an end of the naïve identification of the Kingdom of God with ecclesiastical activities, social programs, political reconstruction, or human progress. Thus, and only thus, was he able to save German Protestantism from dissolving into a worldly political movement embodying strongly extra-Christian elements. That outcome would scarcely have been possible without Barth's radical and one-sided emphasis upon the separation of the divine from the human. But an instrument that is a mighty weapon in warfare may be an inconvenient tool for use in the building trade.

According to the supernatural way of thinking the Kingdom of God as an eschatological phenomenon is absolutely non-existent in the present world. But dialectic thinking seeks to derive the nature of eschatology from the words of Jesus, "the Kingdom of God is at hand." "At hand" means that it is here and not here, it is "in your midst" but it cannot be seen and handled. It is qualitatively different from everything that is known to us. But, with this distinctly qualitative difference, it breaks into our world. Therefore, we can never say that it is present in this or that ecclesiastical and social activity, form of human progress, charitable deed, or conception of truth. When we would lay hold upon it, we find that everything is always under the dominion of the demons and never does the dominion of God alone come into realization. Yet we cannot say that the Kingdom of God is not present at all, as though only the dominion of the demons and not the dominion of God prevailed. What we can say is that in this or that act of the church or of society there is a hint at what is meant by "Kingdom of God," namely, "righteousness, peace and joy in the Holy Spirit." Now hints of the Kingdom of God can occur only where the power of this kingdom has broken through into human existence. Because Barth is not acquainted with this dialectic method of interpreting the presence and absence of the Kingdom of God, he would have to conclude that without the insert of revelation as a foreign entity, the world must stand exclusively under the dominion of demons. But he does not draw this conclusion, for the forceful New Testament and early Christian thinking about demons has remained undeveloped in Barth's Calvinistic theology. He believes in a godless objectivity of human action ravaged by sin and without any relation whatever either to the divine or to the demonic. This seems to me to be one of the weakest points in Barthian teaching; and on this ground his refusal to recognize a theological ethics is also based. Now belief as an objective existence, indifferent with respect to both divine and human dominion, is an illusion. We never live merely in the first and second dimension of our existence (in dead matter and in the form we give to it), but we also live constantly in the third dimension (on the divine mountain-top and in the demonic abyss). That holds true of all our activities, even of those that are apparently the most secular. One who does not recognize that fact and who, mistakenly holding to the belief in a two-dimensional reality, renounces the religious conflict against psychical, social, and spiritual demonic forces, does in truth forward demonic interests. In this respect the Barthian theology is in effect undeniably guilty. But the liberal theology is liable to the same condemnation, for it, too, through its belief in progress, has obscured the power of the demonic element in human existence. But while liberalism arrives at this erroneous conclusion by identifying a continuity of humanly valuable activities with the realization of the Kingdom of God, Barth arrives at it by the severance of human activities from both divine and demonic powers. Both deny the realism of dialectic, that is three-dimensional, thinking.

By his mighty proclamation of the Christian paradox Barth has saved theology from forgetting the deity of God and has saved the church from lapsing into secularism and paganism. This positive value is more important than all the objections that may be urged against Barth. But there is this defect: although he has been called a dialectic theologian, he does not think dialectically, but supernaturally. ❖

THE KINGDOM OF GOD AND HISTORY

INTRODUCTION

1. THE TASK

The task with which I have been entrusted is that of giving a religious interpretation of history from the standpoint of the Christian belief in the Kingdom of God. Christian theology, under the influence of Greek thought, has taken almost incredible pains over the problems of the natural and the moral sphere seen in the light of the Christian faith in God. In the sphere of the Christian interpretation of history, however, in spite of some outstanding individual conceptions, the problem of the *Kingdom of God and History* has received far less attention. This is partly due to the pressure of an ecclesiastical conservatism, which has regarded history as practically consummated in the existence of the Church. The opposition of the revolutionary sects, in all the various periods of Church history, was not sufficiently strong to break down this barrier. It is only during quite recent years that the question of our biological existence has become central for all vital theological and philosophical thought and discussion. The Churches can evade this question only at the cost of a complete withdrawal from the life of the present day. They are summoned to reflect upon the great solutions of their past and to seek for a new solution, expressed in some powerful symbol, which will meet the need of the humanity of the present day in its questionings and its despair.

2. THE WAY

The way to this goal leads through a threefold process of reflection. First of all we need a philosophical and theological clarification of the concepts used. It is obvious that this preparatory stage is of more than merely formal significance. Even the most abstract conception of history, and the most formal presentation of the categories which constitute it, includes ultimate philosophical decisions. These, for their part, are dependent on ultimate religious decisions, consequently on religious faith. Thus the preparatory work on the concepts contains, in abstract form, the whole solution.

The second step is the general presentation of the relation between the Kingdom of God and history according to theological principles. Here the task of theology proper outweighs that of philosophy, which is relevant for the first step. Here too, however, it is true that the whole is included in the part. For since theology has to do with the Logos and with practical life at least so far as its form and its material are concerned, it is also determined by philosophical and practical decisions.

The third step is the concrete attitude to the historical forces of the present day. Since the only entrance to the interpretation of history is historical action, there is no serious grappling with the problem of history which has not been born out of the necessity for coming to a present historical decision. Philosophical idealism and theological transcendentalism try to conceal this state of affairs. But it comes out clearly in every single interpretation of the historical process, and indeed in every category of interpretation, however abstract it may be. It is therefore more honest and more fruitful to include in the interpretation of history itself the fact that such interpretation is rooted in historical action and, on the other hand, to justify this by means of the actual interpretation.

3. THE STANDPOINT

The practical standpoint presupposed in the following outline and at the same time to be confirmed by it is that of so-called "Religious Socialism." It starts with the insight that the bourgeois-capitalistic epoch of occidental development has reached the stage of a most radical transformation which may mean the end of this epoch altogether. Religious Socialism links the insight, which is being more and more widely acknowledged by people of historical consciousness, with the special conviction that the coming form of human society must be a socialist one if it is to be adequate to the actual necessities as to the moral demands of the situation. The religious interpretation of history explained in this article consequently has two roots — a religious-transcendent root, the Christian message of the Kingdom of God, and a political-immanent root, the socialist interpretation of the present. The former supplies the principles and criteria, the latter the material and the concrete application. This bi-polar method is essential for any religious interpretation of history. It does not, however, mean that the theological decisions are subjected to the political ones, neither does it mean that political decision acquires theological dignity. It rather means that the divine claim over the world is not kept within an abstract transcendence but is used for evaluating and moulding actual reality. Religious interpretation of history is "applied theology," and therefore necessarily bi-polar. Any attempt at eliminating the concrete, political pole entails either the destruction of a true interpretation of history, or a concealment of the latent political attitude which in this case becomes effective unconsciously and without criticism. Interpretation of history is subjected to the same methodological demand as the production of a Christian "world-view" or of Christian ethics; there must be the quest for a bi-polar beginning.

Part I: CONCEPTUAL PREPARATION

I
The Concept of History
(i)

History is the totality of remembered events, which are determined by free human activity and are important for the life of human groups.

History is *remembered* history. Both in German and in English the word "history" has a twofold meaning: subjective and objective. This suggests the fact that history, in the strict sense of the word, begins as soon as historical consciousness arises, which creates historical tradition. But the converse also is true. Historical consciousness and historical tradition arise as soon as history in the strict sense of the word begins. The subjective and the objective element, memory and event, are inseparable.

History is dependent upon free human activity, but it is not dependent on this *alone*. Nature too has a share in the making of human history, in so far as it creates the geographical, biological, and psychological bases for it, and also exercises a constant influence upon human action. But nature itself has no history because it has no freedom. In all nature the existence of things is a necessary result of their essence. Upon the basis of existence new things happen, which do not follow from essence, but are due to human freedom. Here is the difference between mere becoming and history. (Biological spontaneity may provide a transition from the one to the other, but ultimately it belongs to nature, not to history.)

Among the countless events in which human freedom participates those alone constitute history which stand in relation to the life of human groups. The action of the individual only gains historical significance through his relation to the life of a social group. This is true even when his action takes the form of *separation* from the social group. Even the hermit in his denial of society is related to society. And only through this relation does the life of a hermit as a whole gain historical significance.

(ii)

Historical groups are all those human groups which on the one hand have the power to exist and to maintain their existence, and on the other hand are the bearers of a definite system of values for the establishment of which the historical group feels responsible. This sense of responsibility is expressed in the form of consciousness of a special vocation.

Every human group may become a "bearer" of history: from the family, by way of the tribe and the nation, perhaps up to a united mankind. Yet mankind as a whole has not hitherto become a "bearer" of history, since it has not achieved a uniform group existence supported by power, nor has it gained a common sense of values.

Historical existence presupposes power, at least the power to exist. Since, however, life only exists while it is growing, the *power of growth* also belongs to historical existence. A group only has the power to exist and to grow in this way if, as a group, it is *united*, that is, when it has the possibility of forming a united political determination. Every living form of power realizes itself in constantly changing discussion with other powers, natural or historical, and out of this the impulse to historical movement is born.

Human freedom implies the consciousness of meaning and value. Accordingly, every historical group feels its existence to be in a special way meaningful and filled with value. No Imperialism could develop apart from such a sense of value or of vocation. The nationalism of the Western nations is absolutely bound up with a definite consciousness of vocation.

(iii)

Historical time is directed time—time with an end, a beginning, and a centre, and is consequently *qualitative* time, developing in different periods.

Historical time must be distinguished from physical and biological time. In nature the cyclic movement of time predominates; the end returns to the beginning; nothing essentially *new* takes place. In history directed time breaks through the cyclic movement. Something new takes place and replaces the process of mere repetition. Emergent evolution in the biological realm may be considered as a limited anticipation to the historical newness, limited first by the lack of freedom of decision, second by the fact that with the creation of "man historical" biological evolution seems to have reached its summit and end.

From this it follows that history is not merely a continually flowing stream which can be measured by quantitative standards, but that every historical period has a special quality whose character is dependent upon its significance for the total historical process. Thus for the Christian consciousness the time before and after Christ does not only differ quantitatively but qualitatively. The understanding of the total direction of history is decided by the event in which a human group perceives the meaning of its history. We call it the *centre* of history. The character of this centre then determines the conception of the *aim* of history, and the centre is at the same time decisive for the fixing of the beginning of history, that is, that point in time in which a human group for the first time becomes conscious of its historical character. Thus, for instance, from the Christian point of view, *Christ* is the *centre* of history, the realization of His Kingdom is the *End*, and the first expectation of the Kingdom is the *Beginning* of history.

Historical time cannot be measured in terms of physical time. Billions of years before and after man appeared on the earth neither continue nor frustrate the meaningful direction of history. Neither the end nor the beginning of history can be designated on the plane of physical time.

(iv)

The meaning of history can be found neither in the final stage of historical development — the ultimate fulfillment of all historical potentialities — nor in an infinite approximation to a fulfillment which can never be reached, nor in a continuous change of historical growth and decay as found in nature, nor in a transcendent supra-nature unconnected with history.

The idea of a final stage in which history has, so to speak, fulfilled its aim contradicts human nature, since in historical man existence is necessarily contrasted with essence. (This is not a natural necessity, but is made necessary by freedom and fate.) Further, the idea of a final stage would exclude all other stages and all generations of men living in them from the meaning of their historical existence.

The idea of progressive approximation to a final fulfillment can only be applied in three directions. First, in the sense of technical progress, which is the original and adequate meaning of this concept; second, in the sense of a progress in political unification, which is to be considered as a consequence of the technical control of mankind over the whole earth; thirdly, in the sense of the gradual humanization of human relationships. But there is no progress with respect to the creative works of culture or with respect to the morality of mankind. The first is impossible because creativity is a matter of grace, not of growth; the second is impossible because morality is a matter of free decision, and consequently not a matter of delivery and tradition. Education can only communicate the standard and level on which moral decisions can be made, not the decisions themselves. Further, it must be said that an infinite approximation to the final fulfillment would replace the fulfillment by the way towards it; and this is ultimately self-contradictory.

The naturalistic interpretation of history, as for example Spengler's theory of cultural circles which grow up and decay, or the nationalistic interpretation of history from the point of view of national growth and decay, reduces history to the level of nature. In both these cases the distinction between what is and what ought to be, between true and false, between good and bad disappears in favour of self-realization, self-repression and power.

History loses its meaning when it is presupposed that its meaning and value are fulfilled in an eternal world of essentialities, which is either entirely severed from historical development or is only accidentally connected with it. Both in the thought of Plato and in that of Neo-Platonism history is thus emptied of content. Both interpret the relation between time and eternity in such a way that what happens in time has no meaning for the eternal at all. Both make nature the pattern of history either in an idealistic or in a mystical form, and both miss the significance of history.

(v)

The ultimate meaning of history is the supra-historical unification and purification of all elements of preliminary meaning which have become embodied in historical activities and institutions.

The category of the supra-natural is used to express a closer relationship of the transcendent, ultimate meaning to the immanent, preliminary meaning than the categories eternal and temporal are able to do. The supra-historical is beyond history but it is essentially related to history, while eternity is the mere opposite of time. It is meaningless to speak of the supra-historical in terms of a stage of being, or a form of existence, or something future which is not yet but will be sometime. The transcendent cannot be expressed in terms of being but only in terms of meaning. We understand what is meant by "unconditioned meaning" — for instance, unconditioned good or truth — but we do not understand what is meant by "unconditioned being" because all our thinking is limited to the realm of conditioned beings and its categories.

From this point of view we can affirm only two characteristics of the ultimate meaning of history: it is unification and purification. Unification means that the dispersed embodiments of meaning in historical activities and institutions have an invisible, supra-historical unity, that they belong to an ultimate meaning of which they are radiations. And purification means that the ambiguous embodiment of meaning in historical realities, social and personal, is related to an ultimate meaning in which the ambiguity, the mixture of meaning and distortion of meaning, is overcome by an unambiguous, pure embodiment of meaning.

In so far as this unity and purity lie beyond history we have to state that the meaning of history transcends history. In so far as nothing is contained in this unity and purity, which does not belong to real history and its dispersion and ambiguity, the meaning of history is to be found in history. Both statements are true, but they are true only in connection with each other. In this way historical activity acquires ultimate importance without becoming Utopian, and the supra-historical acquires content without becoming mythological.

II
The Concept of the Kingdom of God
(i)

The Kingdom of God is a symbolic expression of the ultimate meaning of existence. The social and political character of this symbol indicates a special relation between the ultimate meaning of existence and the ultimate meaning of human history.

It is a symbolic expression for the relationship of the unconditioned meaning of existence to actual existence. It must be symbolic since it is impossible to grasp this relationship directly and unsymbolically. It is, however, a true symbol, *i.e.* a symbol which irreplaceably stands for what is symbolized. It expresses the majesty, controlling power, and distance of the unconditioned meaning of existence with respect to the realm of conditioned meanings. There are other possible symbols for the same relationship taken from different realms of experience. So, for instance, Paul speaks in a more ontological way of the final stage of existence in which "God will be all in all." In John there are more mystical symbols, such as Eternal Life in Christ, Friendship with God. All these symbols have in common the presupposition that being as being is meaningful, while the doctrine of Nirvana sees the ultimate meaning of existence in the dissolution of being.

"Kingdom" is a symbol taken from the social and political sphere. It points more than the other symbols mentioned to the overwhelming importance of human historical life for the ultimate meaning of existence. It suggests that human personality, freedom, and community constitute the centre of existence, its development and its fulfillment. Consequently this symbol has to be the main tool for a Christian interpretation of history.

The historical relation of the symbol "Kingdom of God" is obvious in the latent contrast implied between the Kingdom of God and the kingdom of this world. The

Kingdom of God is expected to triumph over the kingdoms of this world; it is a dynamic power acting in history, materializing itself in history although never becoming identical with history.

(ii)

The contrast between the Kingdom of God and the kingdoms of this world is expressed most clearly in the assertion that there is a demonic opposition to the Kingdom of God within the realm of human history. History in this way becomes a battlefield of the divine and the demonic.

The "demonic" is a category which was used for the religious interpretation of history in Persia, in Jewish Apocalypses, in the New Testament, and in the ancient Christian Church up to the time of Augustine. Later this category emerged again and again in periods of great historical tension. The loss of it in modern times is connected with the rise of the idea of progress and the destruction of the original Christian interpretation of history. It is understandable that the breakdown of the idea of progress amid the historical catastrophes of the present and recent past has given a new significance to this category. Religious socialism was the first to rediscover and use it. This was possible only because the mythological or ontological sense of the demonic, in which demons are a kind of beings, was sufficiently destroyed, and so the term could be applied to that destructive, blind, chaotic element which is implied in all powerful creating movements and drives them towards final dissolution. While the word "demonic" has this positive and creative connotation, the word "satanic" points to a purely negative principle. The satanic can only be understood as absolute contradiction, while the demonic participates in the divine creative power. Therefore the satanic cannot exist in itself; it needs the positive of which it is contradiction; it has reality only in the demonic powers which control existence generally, and human existence especially.

When Augustine equates the Kingdom of God with the Church and the Kingdom of Satan with the great world empires, he is partly right and partly wrong. He is right in asserting that in principle the Church is the representative of the Kingdom of God; he is wrong in overlooking the fact— which as a Catholic he could scarcely help overlooking—that the demonic powers can penetrate into the Church itself, both in its doctrines and institutions. He is right to the extent in which he emphasizes the "demonic" element in every political structure of power. He is wrong to the extent in which he neglects the creative significance of the political power for historical existence.

(iii)

In the symbol of the Kingdom of God the final victory over the demonic powers in existence generally and in history especially is implied.

The Kingdom of God is a dynamic conception. It designates the necessity that the ultimate meaning of existence is never given; it acquires reality only in overcoming meaninglessness and the distortion of meaning. "Righteousness, peace and joy," the characteristics of the Kingdom, enclose a possible opposition which is overcome in them. It is not completed but always becoming; not present, neither immanently nor transcendentally, but always "at hand." It expresses that "God is a living God," entering history, struggling in history, fulfilling history and is not the unity of eternal essences.

Therefore it is wrong to conceive of the Kingdom of God merely as the restoration of the original order which has been destroyed by sin. We know nothing of such an order. It is an abstraction whose roots lie in a static conception of transcendence. The Kingdom of God is, however, not a system of eternal essentialities, whose realization was given in the Creation, was lost at the Fall, and was regained in Redemption. The Kingdom of God is the dynamic fulfillment of the ultimate meaning of existence against the contradictions of existence.

****

Part II: THE GENERAL CHRISTIAN PRINCIPLES

I

The Kingdom of God as the Meaning of History
(i)

For the Christian consciousness Christ is the centre of history. His appearance is interpreted as the "fullness of time," that is, as the fulfillment of all historical preparation.

In calling Christ the centre of history we do not apply a category to a special case, but we apply a category which is found through the analysis of the significance of Christ (in Christian faith) to Christ; we return to Christ what we have taken from Him. For in Christ, namely in the reality which is contained in different original interpretations in the New Testament, Christianity sees the appearance of ultimate meaning of life in history. The fact that the Christian nations speak of a period before and a period after Christ shows how deeply Christian consciousness is penetrated by belief in Christ as the centre of history.

The centre of history is decisive for the beginning and the end of history. From the Christian point of view history has a supra-historical beginning—the Fall; and an intra-historical beginning—the rise of the expectation of a redeeming event. History has also a supra-historical end—the final consummation or the parousia of Christ; and it has an intra-historical end—the victory over the anti-divine powers which arise in history, or the Reign of Christ. Neither this beginning nor this end can be determined in terms of physical time. We can express them only in symbolic records of the past (Gen. i–xii) and in symbolic interpretations of the future (millenniums).

A specially important category of the New Testament interpretation of history is *Kairos*. It designates the fulfillment of the period of expectation or preparation, and the beginning of the period of reception or fragmentary actualization. The Greek word *Kairos*, which originally only meant without discrimination the "right time," is used in a prophetic interpretation of history for *the* right time in which all time gains its meaning and qualification. The predominance of the logos-doctrine within the Greek Church prevented the development of a *Kairos*-doctrine, *i.e.* a Christian interpretation of history.

(ii)

The Christian interpretation of history considers the history of mankind ultimately as history of salvation.

The belief that Christ is the centre of history, and that in Him the reality of salvation has appeared in history, implies the belief that human history is ultimately to be interpreted in terms of salvation. Salvation means the fulfillment of what existence ought to be by overcoming the destructive, meaning-defying, powers of existence. As in Christian doctrine, Christ is saving man in temporal life as well as beyond temporal life, so the history of salvation is going on in history as well as beyond history. Salvation is actualized in history whenever a demonic power in social or individual existence is overcome by the divine power which has become visible in Christ. And salvation is actualized beyond history in the ultimate unification and purification of meaning.

The human mind is not able to conceive salvation beyond life and history in terms taken from world experience which are technically called "ontic." It can be conceived only in terms of meaning. If ontic terms such as resurrection, immortality, new earth and new heaven are used, they have a symbolic character, since they point to some elements of the ultimate meaning of existence. The symbol of a new earth points to the truth that the natural basis of history is not excluded from the ultimate meaning of existence. Hence it follows that the choice of symbols is decisive for truth or error.

Salvation is related to individuals as well as to groups, to mankind as well as to nature, to personalities as well as to institutions. For the problem of history the salvation of groups and institutions is of special importance. It means that the demonic perversion and destruction of groups and institutions is overcome, partially in history, completely beyond history. While the Christian Churches in the Catholic period dealt with the salvation of individuals and with the salvation of groups and institutions only with respect to the Church itself, and in Protestantism the salvation of groups and institutions is neglected altogether, the post-Protestant period of Christianity probably will deal predominantly with the ultimate meaning and the salvation of groups and institutions. The fact that a religious interpretation of history has become a very urgent problem of applied theology testifies to this.

II
The Kingdom of God in History
(i)

The realization of the Kingdom of God within history is determined by the history of the Church, in part directly through the historical growth of the Church itself, and partly indirectly through the conscious or unconscious relation of all history to the history of the Church.

If the meaning of history is salvation, then all history must be related to that course of history in which redemption is prepared and received. The Church is the "bearer" of this course of history, both in the stage of preparation and in the stage of deception.

Hence we are justified in calling the Church the "bearer" of history. Of course this does not mean that the events of world history have been determined, in a historico-empirical sense, by the synagogue and the Christian Churches; only a very small part of mankind, from the point of view of space and time, has any contact with the Churches at all, and even where there is contact, or even very close touch, it is truer to say that the secular powers have far more influence on the outward destiny of the Churches than the other way round. But the Church is more than the Christian Churches and their precursors. The Church is the community of those partly visible and partly invisible, who live in the light of the ultimate meaning of existence, whether in expectation, or in reception. The Church, understood in this way, is the power which gives meaning to historical life as a whole.

The meaning of Christian Missions is based upon this truth. It is the task of the Christian Mission to gather the potential, divided Church out of all religions and cultures and to lead it into the actual Church, and in so doing to transform potential world history into actual world history to give humanity a unified historical consciousness. This also means that all over the world expectation is to be transformed into reception.

(ii)

Through Christ as the centre of history, history is divided into two main periods: the period of preparation and the period of expectation. In each of these two main periods, however, this division is repeated, in so far as history always has the basic character either of expectation or of reception and fragmentary actualization of a new principle of meaning. The transition from one to the other may be called a special *kairos*.

From the standpoint of its ultimate meaning all history is either the preparation for or the reception of the centre of history. But the preparation is never merely preparation; it is always also anticipating actualization. If it were not so, all pre-Christian history would be devoid of meaning. But this would be true neither of the prophetic Hebrew stage of preparation nor of the general "sacramental" preparation within paganism.

The vital force of both is drawn from their anticipating reception of the centre of history; the Jewish development in direct preparation for its appearance, and the pagan development in indirect preparation create the parallelity of understanding. On the other hand, the post-Christian development is never only reception, since it always contains pagan and Jewish elements of expectation and preparation.

The fundamental division applies also to the two main periods themselves. Each period is subdivided into shorter periods, each with its own centre which gives it meaning, its own beginning and end. Periods which seem to be controlled by expectation are succeeded by periods which prove to be a fragmentary actualization. From the sociological point of view this has been described as the rhythm of "critical" and "organic" periods. Even the history of the Church often follows this course. But no age is completely lacking in "reception" and none is without an element of "expectation."

For the Christian interpretation of history the centres of particular periods are dependent upon the centre of history. This gives the criterion for the interpretation of each centre and for historical universal action from every particular centre. If the New Testament idea of the *kairos* is applied within a definite period, it expresses the conviction that that which has appeared once for all in the "fullness of time" has reappeared in a special way as the centre of a particular historical period. The unique, non-recurring *kairos* remains the standard for all the particular forms in which it reappears. For instance, the period preceding the Reformation may be called a period of expectation and anticipating actualization. The appearance of the new interpretation of the centre of history by Luther may be called a special *kairos* (as Luther himself felt), and the Protestant materialization after him may be called a period of reception and fragmentary actualization. In the same way the present period of the decay of liberalism and secularism may be called a period of expectation which perhaps may be followed by a period of reception after the turning-point, the *kairos*, has occurred. It is exactly this feeling which gave rise to the renewal of the doctrine of *kairos* by the "Religious Socialism." It is impossible to give criteria abstracted from the actual situation by which the existence or non-existence of a special *kairos* can be judged. It is a matter of the faith of those who act in a special situation; it is a venture which may fail because faith and spiritual power may not be strong enough. The "will of God" in any given historical situation cannot be recognized by general criteria but only by daring faith.

III
Salvation and World History
(i)

For the Christian interpretation of history salvation is the meaning of world history. But salvation is not the same thing as world history. Primarily and above all salvation is judgment passed upon world history.

The negative presupposition of world history is human freedom with which the Symbol of Temptation deals, and the emergence of the contradiction between essence and existence which is expressed in the Symbol of the Fall. From this presupposition of history there follows the contradiction in which it stands to salvation: salvation is the actual overcoming of the contradiction between essence and existence upon which world history is based.

A direct expression of the contradiction in history is the abuse of power. Power in itself is a structural principle of historical existence. But it is not only in accordance with but also in opposition to the meaning which is to be realized through historical power. It not only fulfills historical vocation but it also betrays it. In so far as all history is a history of struggles for power, salvation is judgment passed on world history. The external expression of this judgment is the destruction of power by power. Hence in the Kingdom of God, the goal of world history, power is only found in absolute unity with love.

(ii)

If world history were only opposition to salvation, it would directly destroy itself. It can only exist at all because it is not only judged by salvation but is also supported by it.

Power cannot exist without a meaning, in the name of which it is power. The values with which power must unite itself are realizations of the meaning of history, moments in the fragmentary actualization of salvation upon which the possibility of power, and therefore of history, are based. The sociological expression for the fact that power needs a meaning, in order to be able to exist, is "ideology." The word "ideology" has acquired a negative sense, challenging the deliberate or unconscious misuse of ideas for the preservation of a power whose existence is threatened. But the thing itself, the combination of power and value, should not be estimated in a merely negative manner; it is the positive foundation of history as a whole.

History is carried by those groups and individuals who represent in their existence a meaning which belongs to the ultimate meaning and is unified and purified in it. As far as salvation is the latent meaning of history those are its real bearers who incorporate and represent in themselves this meaning, either in expectation or in reception. The spirit of salvation radiating from those personalities and groups is the power which again and again overcomes the demonic self-destruction of historical existence. If we call the latent community of those people the invisible Church, we must agree with the New Testament in asserting that the Church is the real bearer of history. This is not a claim for the empirical churches, but a demand upon them.

It is a general experience that in the moment in which the divine breaks into the temporal and a new *kairos* is approaching the demonic acquires increased power. It is, however, impossible to derive from this experience a general law of progressive regressive development of universal history. Both judgments, the optimistic as well as the pessimistic, should be avoided.

(iii)

As salvation is carrying world history so, on the other hand, world history is the fragmentary actualization of salvation.

The seriousness and the gravity of human history depend upon the fact that world history is the fragmentary actualization of salvation. Each particular act which is related to the ultimate meaning which has appeared in Christ has infinite significance, because it is the "coming of the Kingdom of God." It is a logical result of their point of view that those who interpret the Kingdom of God in a purely transcendental manner finally come to regard history as a meaningless occupation of man with himself, while the concept of salvation falls away altogether.

The fragmentary actualization of salvation in world history does not mean that salvation can be fulfilled within history. For salvation within history is opposed by destruction; the divine is opposed by the demonic. Salvation is actual within world history to the extent in which the destructive forces are overcome, the power of the demonic is broken, and the final fulfillment of meaning appears. Thus salvation within world history does not remove the conflict between the divine and the demonic.

Accordingly, the doctrine of the millennium should not be interpreted as a static final condition, and certainly not in Augustine's sense of the sovereignty of the hierarchy. The millennium should be interpreted as the symbol of the victory over concrete demonic forces within history. The demonic is subdued in actual victories from time to time— but it is not extirpated. When the power of a particular form of the demonic is broken the *kairos* of a particular period is fulfilled. To expect not only that the power of concrete demonic forces will be broken at definite periods in history, but that in some future age the demonic as a whole will be utterly destroyed, is a religious "Utopianism" which should be regarded as quite untenable. The relationship of the fragmentary actualization of salvation in history and its fulfillment in the transcendent unity and purity of meaning cannot be expressed in terms of time and history. Every attempt to do so makes the ultimate meaning a section in the totality of meanings, a history after history, a time after time. History itself can define the supra-historical only in negative terms. Every positive expression is a symbol and has to be understood as such in order to avoid that "transcendent Utopianism" which belongs to the distortions of religion and Christianity.

****

Part III: THE PRESENT TASKS OF THE CHRISTIAN INTERPRETATION OF HISTORY

I

The Significance of the "Present" for the Christian Interpretation of History

(i)

Historical interpretation is self-reflection on the part of one who is acting historically about the meaning, the purpose, and the presuppositions of his historical action. The Christian interpretation of history is the reflection of the Christian who acts as a member of the Church about the meaning, the purpose, and the presuppositions of his action as a member of the Church.

Historical interpretation is self-interpretation, that is to say, the historical interpreter must himself be living and acting historically. History cannot be understood from the outside, from the non-historical point of view of the spectator. All historical interpretation contains a concrete historical decision; that is, the spectator's point of view has been abandoned. Historical action is not confined to political action in the narrower sense of the word. All action which aims at the formation of community, however theoretical it may be, is historical action; in the broadest sense of the word it is "political."

The purpose of this process of reflection on the part of one who is acting historically is to help him to perceive the spiritual presuppositions on which his action is based and further, by the "give and take" of discussion with those who hold other views, either to justify, or, if necessary, to alter his own basic principles, and thus to give spiritual weight and the power to create community to historical action.

All this also applies to the Christian interpretation of history, which is self-reflection on the spiritual presuppositions of the action of the Church; for Christian-historical action is Church action. Reflection on the part of one who is acting as a member of the Church is reflection upon his spiritual presuppositions, that is, the spiritual principles, the essential philosophical and theological ideas, and the present reality from which his action springs.

Church action flows in two directions: along one channel it seeks to influence the Churches which now exist, as historical facts; along the other channel Church action is directed towards the historical existence of an epoch as a whole.

(ii)

All Christian historical action is determined on the one hand by the universal centre of history, and on the other by the centre of the particular period in which the action takes place. Accordingly, in all Christian historical action the sense of the unique *kairos* is combined with the sense of a special realization of this *kairos*; this also implies that the struggle against the "demonic" forces in general becomes concrete in the struggle against the particular "demonic" phenomena of the present day.

Christian historical action or Church action, in the universal sense of the word, is bi-polar: the one pole is the unique (*einmalige*) centre of history, the *kairos* in which in principle the ultimate meaning of history has appeared, in which the demonic destruction of history has in principle been broken. The other pole is the actual situation from which the action of the Church springs, whether such action is related to the Churches themselves or to historical existence as a whole. "Church action," in this sense, may take the form of ecclesiastical politics or the politics of the State, it may be theological or philosophical, artistic or liturgical work, or it may take the form of constructive work in religious or secular communities, education in Church or school. Every actual situation from which Christian historical action proceeds contains a negative and a positive element: the negative element is the special "demonic" phenomenon which is characteristic of a period, and especially of a period of transition, and against which the prophetic struggle of the Church must be directed; the positive element is the special promise and the special demand which this situation carries with it, an element which was described by the term *kairos*.

The bi-polarity of Christian historical action, as well as the difference between its two tendencies, is the cause of a whole series of tensions and problems which arise out of a one-sided emphasis on one of these poles or on one of these tendencies. If the unique *kairos* excludes every other, that is, if it denies bi-polarity, then all Christian historical action becomes meaningless: the reality of the Kingdom of God is independent of such action, for it belongs to a sphere beyond and above history (*dialectical theology*). If the individual concrete forms of the *kairos* destroy the unique *kairos*, then the criterion for Christian historical action disappears, and in place of the struggle against the "demonic" we see Christian theology falling a prey to changing forms of the "demonic" (*nationalistic theology*). If one-sided emphasis is laid upon the tendency to concentrate action *within* the Church, then world history itself is abandoned, uncivilized, to the dominion of that force which destroys all meaning (*orthodox Lutheran theology*). If one-sided emphasis is laid on Christian historical action outside the Church, then Church history loses its independence, and in so doing its critical power to give meaning to history as compared with world history (*liberal-reformed and denominational theology*).

Christian historical or ecclesiastical action is carried out either by the Church as such, that is, by its official representatives (synods, bishops, clergy, lay people who exercise official ecclesiastical functions), or by members of the Church (under some circumstances also outside the organized Churches), who act as members of the Church but not as representatives of the Church. Representative ecclesiastical action may be directed both negatively and positively towards the Church itself (creation of confessions or creeds and of constitutions, fight against heresies and wrong conditions), but it can only influence historical existence outside the Church negatively, not positively (by revealing the "demonic" forces and their destructive consequences, by forming a critical estimate of ideas and plans in the light of ultimate standard, but not by fighting for definite philosophical, artistic or political solutions). The positive aspect of historical action outside the Church can only be achieved by Christians who are either entirely or in certain definite functions not representative of the Church, and who are willing to incur the risk of falling into philosophical and political errors, and of being disowned by the Church (Christian philosophers, educationists, politicians, artists, etc.). The Christian interpretation of history which issues from the sphere of concrete historical decisions of this kind has no ecclesiastical or dogmatic significance, but it may have prophetic or theological significance.

II
The Actual "Demonic" Forces of the Present Day
(i)

The fundamental "demonic" phenomenon of the present day is the autonomy of the capitalistic economic system, with all its contradictions, and the mass disintegration and destruction of meaning in all spheres of historical existence which it produces. This "demonic" force has been unmasked in the main by the prophetic spirit outside the Church, but this discovery may, and indeed must, be absorbed into Christian historical categories and developed still further;

we should also note that the Christian interpretation of history given in this article owes some of its own vital impulses to this discovery of capitalism as a "demonic" force.

The autonomy of the economic sphere, which is the result of the doctrine of economic liberalism, has had two fundamental results: first of all, it has caused the class struggle which arises inevitably out of the mechanism of an industrial system, which like all other "demonic" forces is quite independent of the moral will of the individual and causes destructive divisions within society, and even within the Church. Secondly, the economic sphere, which has become autonomous, has brought all the other spheres of human historical life into subjection to itself and has deprived them of independent meaning; thus it has set in motion a great process of mass disintegration, the movement of which is subject to destructive laws.

The Socialist Movement, and primarily theoretical Marxism, has opened the eyes of Western society to the working of these laws. The vitally prophetic element in Marxism, under the pressure of the spiritual situation of the nineteenth century, has clothed itself in anti-religious materialistic forms, which are inadequate for what is meant by the idea of Socialism. Under the name of "Religious Socialism" the Christian interpretation of history has set itself the task of expressing the anti-"demonic" criticism of Marxism in the categories of the Christian interpretation of history; the impulse to the discovery of such categories came essentially out of the presence of a socialistic movement with a Marxist interpretation of history: the categories which are expounded in this article have been brought into the sphere of the theological thought of the present day by the urge to unite Christianity and Socialism in positive criticism.

The content of the categories of the Christian interpretation of history springs from the prophetic and sectarian tradition and its reflection on the philosophy of history throughout the centuries. Christian theology, which makes these categories its own, does not support a special political party, but by making use of the intellectual tool which a sociological theory has placed at its disposal it has reformulated Christian thought on history. The implicit political decision which has been made in Religious Socialism cannot become an ecclesiastical decision in the formal sense of the word. It must remain a venturesome decision of some individual members of the Church, a decision which may possibly contain error. The Church, however, is under obligation to bear formal witness against the destructive consequences of the "demonic" forces of the present day and their heretical foundations.

(ii)

The "demonic" force of *nationalism* is dependent on the "demonic" element in the economic system, yet at the same time, as a means of mass reintegration, it is to some extent opposed to it. At the present time nationalism is the most evident and the most dangerous incarnation of the "demonic" principle in general, especially where, as in various places, it has assumed an explicitly religious form. It represents the modern variety of polytheistic bondage to space and division, and it drives that section of mankind which has fallen under its sway to historical self-destruction.

Nationalism means that the natural and historical reality known as the "nation" is posited as an absolute, that is, it constitutes the Supreme Good to all who belong to it. This also means that all who do not belong to this nation are excluded from a share in this Supreme Good. To the prophetic view of history the Supreme Good and the criterion of all historical existence is the Kingdom of God, in which all national divisions have been removed, but to nationalism the self-assertion of the nation over against every other is the Supreme Good and the criterion by which human historical existence is measured. Thus in nationalism the emphasis upon space, characteristic of polytheism, has been restored, in contrast to the emphasis on time in prophetic and Christian monotheism.

Nationalism must therefore be described as neo-paganism even when it assumes no explicitly religious form. In the countries in which it has assumed a religious form the Christian and the nationalistic views of history have come into open conflict, and the Church has formally condemned nationalistic neo-paganism as heretical and "demonic." The Christian interpretation of history, however, must go further and reveal the heretically "demonic" character of the nationalistic system of values as such; above all it must show that with the elevation of a definite space, of a definite race, and of a definite nation to the rank of the Supreme Good, history as such has been abandoned, spatial co-ordination and division have triumphed over temporal direction towards a goal.

The development of nationalism in the Christian West is made possible by the division and disintegration introduced by capitalism. Once the nation had been substituted for the Church, as a unifying centre, it appeared to affront the first and the most natural principle of reintegration; this process was hastened by the fact that the Church was utterly incapable of providing such a principle, since she was weakened by her own divisions and by the fact that she too was entangled in the net of widespread disintegration. But this nationalistic form of reintegration, when regarded from the Christian and the humanistic point of view (which indeed overlap), actually represents the most advanced stage of disintegration. Nationalism must be unmasked and attacked by those who hold the Christian and prophetic view of history as a kind of false "prophecy" in the sense of the Old Testament.

(iii)

The necessity for the reintegration of the masses has led to dictatorial forms of government, in which the "demonic" force of an unrestricted exercise of power drives men into presumption towards God and to destruction of the human values which belong to the Kingdom of God: formal justice, truthfulness, and freedom. This is also true of that form of government which, in the name of material justice, has rejected the "demonic" forces of capitalism and nationalism. Unrestricted exercise of power is a "demonic" temptation which none who possess it can resist. The Early Church expressed this in its condemnation of the Roman Empire. Henceforward tyranny has always evoked the opposition of Christian historical thought. Tyranny is presumption towards God and oppression of man. Hence it falls under the condemnation of that combination of love and power represented by the idea of the Kingdom of God.

This is the case, in the first place, when dictatorship is surrounded by a halo of an almost religious kind, or when it proceeds to attack the Church. The deification of the dictator, whether as the representative of the ruling power or as an individual, the interference of the state, with its totalitarian claims, with the sphere of religion, the quasi-religious character of its decrees imposed like taboos, the enforced conformity of the Church to the state, or its destruction, and the creation of martyrs in the narrower sense of the word; these are the anti-Christian implications of the exercise of absolute power. They force the Churches into a campaign of direct resistance, and they provoke those who hold the Christian and prophetic view of history to make a vigorous protest against this "demonic" exercise of power.

But there is another series of results of the unrestricted exercise of power which also comes under the condemnation of the idea of the Kingdom of God, *i.e.* the destruction of human values by tyranny. The Christian doctrine of man, as having been created in the image of God, as well as the doctrine of Christ as the Logos, means that Christianity is responsible for the human values, *i.e.* formal judicial justice, which is the prophetic standard for the estimate of a political power: truthfulness, to deny which the New Testament regards as an evident sign of the satanic principle and freedom, that is, the recognition of human dignity or, in Christian terms, the fact that every human being is potentially a child of God. To the satanic principle also the New Testament ascribes all actions which injure this human dignity, whether they touch man's mental life (by putting a "stumbling-block" in his way) or his physical life (by murder).

The deliberate renewal of these "demonic" forces whose power has already been broken by Christianity in principle, and is being hotly contested by Christian humanism in practice, constitutes the third outstanding "sign of the times." Even the Bolshevist dictatorship, in spite of the fact that it is fighting against capitalistic and nationalistic disintegration in the name of material justice, is of this "demonic" character. Thus the protagonists of the Christian view of history are called to bear their testimony in the name of the idea of the Kingdom of God, in the midst of their present historical existence, against capitalism, from the point of view of its content; against nationalism, on account of its content and its way of exercising authority, and against Bolshevism on account of its way of exercising authority.

III
The "Kairos" of the Present Moment
(i)

The "demonic," in a threefold form, threatens to destroy our present historical existence. From the human point of view the tragic element in this situation drives those who study history from the Christian point of view to inquire into the positive meaning of these events, that is, the *kairos* immanent within the present moment in history. In accordance with the double direction of ecclesiastical action a double answer is required: one which is given within the Church and one outside the borders of the Church.

A situation is tragic in which the very elements which are most valuable by their very value drive it to self-destruction. This is the case with the humanistic element contained in capitalism, as well as with the purpose of reintegration which is contained in nationalism, and with the expectation of judgment which is contained in Bolshevism. All three in a tragic fate contradict their own original intention and are driving society as a whole, in the Christian West, towards self-destruction. The protagonists of the Christian view of history cannot prevent this tragic fate, but they can and should show clearly the *kairos* which is being fulfilled within this process of self-destruction, that is, the positive principle which is giving meaning to this development. In so doing they will provide the present action of the Church with a concrete criterion and a concrete aim for the future.

(ii)

The fact that our present historical existence is menaced means that the Church is called to reformulate the universal reintegrating principle which Christianity contains, the centre of history as a whole and as a present centre. This means *negatively* the freeing of the Church from her entanglement with the disintegrating powers of the present and the past; positively it means the preparation of a new historical existence through the action of the Church.

It is impossible in this connection to point to all the consequences which spring from the Christian action of the

Church within her own borders. Some points only can be mentioned here.

First of all we must understand the radical nature of the present process of historical self-destruction, in which the Churches are also involved. This applies to Protestantism in particular, with its lack of power to provide a reintegrating principle to the masses. We must reckon with the possibility that, in the narrower sense of the word, the Protestant period of the Church may already be ended, in order to make way for a new post-Protestant form of Christianity. In this time of change in her own life and in historical existence as a whole the Church must strengthen her own life and must also transcend it. She strengthens herself by a deep and thorough union with that centre of history which she proclaims and by which she lives. It is at the moment that she makes room for historical change that she needs the criterion by which all history is to be judged. The act of transcending herself is based upon the knowledge that there is an invisible history of the Church, for which the visible Churches are also responsible, and by which at the same time they are determined.

For the action of the Church from within her own borders the special *kairos* of this period will consist in the preparation of a historical existence of her own after the self-destruction of the present structure of historical existence. This process of preparation includes three elements: being set free from entanglement with the disintegrating "demonic" forces of present history, fresh consideration of the ultimate criterion as compared with history as a whole, and the application of this criterion to ecclesiastical action both inside and outside the Church.

(iii)

So far as the action of the Church outside her own borders is concerned the present menace to historical existence summons her to represent the unity of the Kingdom of God in face of the divisions caused by the "demonic" forces. Where capitalism is concerned this means the application of the criterion of material justice. Where nationalism is concerned it means the application of the criterion of the unity of the human race. Where dictatorship is concerned it means the application of the criterion of the finite character, and yet at the same time the dignity of every human being.

The application of the criterion of justice to the present social situation means the destruction of the capitalistic class-contrast and of the autonomous supremacy of economics over life as a whole. The use of the word "Socialism" to describe this process does not mean a decision for a special party, but it does mean the concrete character of the demand for justice in the historical situation of disintegrating capitalism.

The application of the criterion of the unity of the human race to the present international situation means the removal of the dominating political sovereignty of the individual states. The use of the word "pacifism" for this demand does not mean the support of the present pacifist organizations, but the concrete character of the demand for peace in the historical situation of self-destructive nationalism.

The application of the criterion of the finite character and yet dignity of every human being to the present political situation means the introduction of anti-dictatorial corrections into the structure of government. The use of the expression "the rights of man" for this demand does not mean the support of a liberalistic structure of society, but the concrete character of the Christian-Humanistic demand, in a situation in which tyranny dominates the masses.

(iv)

It is in accordance with the idea of the *kairos* that that which the ultimate criterion requires is a promise and therefore an object of hope. And since, from the point of view of history, every promise is connected with the condition of human free activity, the hope of any historical realization remains doubtful. The only unconditional prospect is the promise and expectation of the supra-historical fulfillment of history, or the Kingdom of God, in which that which has not been decided within history will be decided and that which has not been fulfilled within history will be fulfilled.

The phenomenon which is described in the New Testament as interpretation of the "signs of the times" — the judgment on the "tendencies" of the present which is always presupposed in action — this is meant by the unity of demand and expectation in interpreting history. In every period there are symptoms which show what is going on under the surface. The perception and the interpretation of these symptoms is the task of the prophetic spirit, which may appear either in a more intuitive or in a more rational form, but is never wholly without either the one or the other. The words of Jesus, "Repent, for the Kingdom of Heaven is at hand," represent in classic form that combination of demand and expectation which arises out of the interpretation of the *kairos*. The most magnificent theoretical interpretation and the most effective practical interpretation of an historical period was the Marxist analysis of capitalist society. It too united summons and demand with interpretation and expectation.

Historical interpretation from the point of view of the *kairos* must resist the temptation to separate demand and expectation. Mere demands lead to Pharisaism and moralistic Utopianism. Just as the Jew who was loyal to the Law found it impossible to bring in the day of the Lord by force, so in our own day pacifists and Utopian socialists have found it impossible to enforce world peace and social justice by means of moralistic propaganda. Only that which at least potentially exists as a reality can be realized historically. The Kingdom of God only comes at all because in Christ it is already "amongst us." World peace will only come in so far as the actual union of humanity has in principle removed the divisions caused by nationalism. The classless society will only come when the inward power of society has already been concentrated in *one* class. But all this does not imply any inevitable course of events. The Kingdom of God "tarries" in the process of drawing mankind together, new "confusions of tongues" break out, the class in which all classes are to be removed may fail, or may fall a prey to new divisions.

Neither prophetic promise nor historical dialectic speaks of things which *must* happen. It is not the prophet but the diviner, not the dialectician but the mechanist who tries to predict the course of history and thus tries to turn it into a natural process.

The certainty that these elements of demand and promise which a *kairos* contains will be fulfilled points to the supra-historical unity of the ultimate meaning. Here, and here only, all that is undecided in history is decided, and all that is unfulfilled is fulfilled. Therefore historical action can remain sure of itself, and the religious interpretation of history can defend its rights, even in face of the disappointment provided by unfulfilled expectation and fragmentary actualization. The question of history has a final answer: the Kingdom of God.❖

THE GOSPEL AND THE STATE

If the dialectical method has any field in philosophy and theology where it must be applied, it is the relationship between the Gospel and the State. All relations of the Gospel to the State contain a Yes and a No, an affirmation and a negation, a likeness and a contrast. But not only this. Both concepts, the Gospel as well as the State, are dialectical in themselves. They contain immeasurable tensions, contrasting possibilities, paradoxical elements. This is the reason for the tremendous amount of possible interpretations of each of these concepts and of their relation to each other. Therefore, if the word "dialectic" has still any meaning and methodological value, if this main discovery of Plato which has been used by the Greek philosophers as well as by the Christian theologians, is still important to us, the dialectical method must be applied to our problem.

I know that the word dialectical today is suspect to many people, partly because they connect it with the so-called "dialectical theology" of our day (which in reality is not dialectical at all) partly because the kind of thinking which rightly is called dialectical is strange to those who are accustomed to mere empirical and statistical methods. Therefore it is significant to realize that the whole New Testament is dialectical in its explanation of the relationship of God and man, of sin and justification, of the Kingdom of God and history, in its attitude toward the State, expressing different sets of Yes and No.

But, obviously, it is not only the complexity of the concepts and the necessity of applying the dialectical method which makes our problem so difficult. It is also the great variety in the interpretation of the Gospel through the different churches and denominations, and the abundance of forms and self-interpretations of the State in the course of history. In order to limit our task we shall concentrate our interest on the recent developments of the State in the totalitarian countries. But in order to understand them we must understand the State itself and its main characteristics, and we must, first of all, have a clear concept of what the Gospel means.

I

THE DIALECTICAL INTERPRETATION OF THE GOSPEL

The Gospel is a message coming from *beyond* man and coming *to* man. In order to be Gospel, Good News, to me it cannot be *from* me. What I already have is neither new nor message to me. "Me" means human existence generally, and, since man is the center of his world, it means the world universal. The Gospel is by its very definition transcendent, from beyond the world. But at the same time it is a message *to* me; I must receive it; it must concern me in my very existence and in my world. I must understand it, my existence must be transformed by it. Therefore it is immanent, it belongs to my world.

The Gospel pronounces the transcendent fulfilment which cannot be found on earth, the Kingdom which is beyond the historical kingdoms, which is "not of this world." Here must be found the reason for the complete detachment from all the affairs of State, law, politics, culture which we find in Jesus. Here is the root of the eschatological flavor in all sayings and actions of Jesus; for his complete unconcern for Jewish nationalism as well as for Roman imperialism; for Pilatus as well as for Herodes.

No Christian doctrine of the State is possible which does not start with this radical detachment. The Gospel comes from another realm and leads to another than that in which the State is powerful. But the Kingdom of God is not only of another world; it is also *in* the world. It has appeared in it through Christ; it is struggling in it against the kingdoms of earth and their demonic power; it is represented in the history of the Church, and our hope is that it may "come to us." It is an immanent reality although it is not of this world.

Therefore, the detachment in principle must be followed by a concern in actuality. In the New Testament we find two main affirmative attitudes toward the State — the Paulinian and the Apocalyptic. Paul acknowledges the State as a divine order for the sake of suppressing the social evil and of preventing complete chaos. He demands, from this point of view, that the Christian acknowledge the legality of State-power by subjecting himself to it — a word which implies the refusal of enthusiastic anarchism (a danger of primitive Christianity) but which does not imply any support of conservatism and bad government, as it was abused in Church history. The other attitude is the struggle against the Roman Empire because of the persecution of the Christians by it and because of its demonic arrogance in making itself God and commanding divine adoration. This attitude is expressed in the Revelation of Saint John and means something quite different from detachment and unconcern.

Beyond mentioning these two attitudes (in which all problems of later Church history to the present are anticipated) we may point to the fact that the use of symbols like "Kingdom of God," "the Reign of Christ and his apostles," as well as the demand for order and leadership within the Church itself, indicate that the idea of some statelike structure even in the perfect community is maintained. But all this does not mean an explained doctrine of the State. The situation of early Christianity made a complete affirmative attitude toward the State impossible.

What we can learn from the New Testament with respect to our problem is first and mainly the complete detachment of Jesus himself; secondly, the very limited and hesitating affirmation of the State by Paul and, thirdly, the radical criticism of a demonized State by John.

II
THE FIRST DIALECTICAL TENSION OF THE STATE AND THE GOSPEL

The State is an institution which creates social unity by power and law. Both elements, power and law, belong essentially to the State. It is the ultimate power and therefore the bearer of law. Consequently the first dialectical tension in the State is that between power and law. The naturalistic interpretation, most radically explained in orthodox Marxism, considers the State essentially as power, namely as the power which is necessary to establish class rule. Laws are laws only for the subjected groups or classes. The ruling class adapt themselves to it as far as it is necessary in order to maintain order and through order their power. The idealistic interpretation, on the contrary, considers law as a reality in itself which, unfortunately, needs power and compulsion in order to be realized but which is self-sufficient and which should become more and more independent of power. This is the main ideal of the democratic interpretation of the State.

The Christian attitude toward this tension is dependent on the following points: As far as the transcendent character of the Kingdom of God is emphasized, as far as its realization is seen beyond human possibility, as far as the cleavage between God and man is recognized, as far as the realities of sin and tragedies are taken seriously, Christian theology must be inclined to share the naturalistic and even materialistic interpretation of the State. So Augustine has explained in his *City of God* that States are the name for the successful groups of pirates and burglars. The demonic will to power is connected with everything which has State character. Therefore, the earthly kingdom necessarily is a demonic kingdom. Here as in many other points Christian and Marxian realism are much more in agreement than Christianity and some types of an ideological bourgeois idealism.

On the other hand Christianity asserts that the Kingdom of God is appearing and struggling in history. From this point of view Christianity must emphasize the idealistic element in the nature of the State. Augustine agrees with Cicero that Justice is the special quality of the State and he includes the State in his universal idea of peace which insists on unity, order and justice. "The peace between men consists in the ordered concord: and especially the peace in the family in the ordered concord of its members with respect to commanding and obeying; the peace in the State in the ordered concord of the citizens with respect to commanding and obeying; the peace of the heavenly city in the perfect and united fruition of God and the mutual fruition of each other in God, the peace of all things in the quietness of order. Order means the division of equal and nonequal things which gives to each of them its proper place." In positioning the State between the family and the Kingdom of God, Augustine attributes to it an essential perfection which, of course, is completely distorted in the existential actuality of the earthly State.

Considering these two qualifications of the State, the essential and the existential, we have to ask what is the judgment of the Gospel about the real State in which both qualifications are united. Augustine has two answers, corresponding to the two poles of the tension between power and law. He answers much as did Paul, that the State even in its demonized reality is better than chaos. The compulsory action of the State, which in itself is sinful, at the same time suppresses sin and makes possible all social life, even that of the Church. "We too use the peace of Babel." This was the answer also of Luther, who, however, gave a more positive meaning to the State in teaching that its compulsory acts are an expression of the love of God, although indirectly, in a veiled and paradoxical form. And the same is the attitude of the present Reformed theology which emphasizes (for example in Brunner) that the State must suppress human arbitrariness by compulsion. It was and is the prevailing attitude of the Greek Orthodox Church. The danger of this attitude is that it prevents any critical judgment against the State. If in any case the State has demonic qualities and if just this character, namely its unrestricted power, makes it, although paradoxically, the tool of God, then no criticism of the State is meaningful. For the sake of realizing *some* order the *just* order is neglected. But order without justice finally defeats itself. The unchallenged demon is a bad servant of God. The tragedy of European history and the servility of the Christian churches toward the State-powers in Central and Eastern Europe is rooted in this attitude.

The other element in Augustine has become predominant in Catholicism and Anglo-Saxon Calvinism: The State can be sanctified by its subjection to the will of God which, in Roman Catholicism, is represented by the Church; in theocratic Calvinism, by the Bible. The divine law, imposed on the Christian States, must be enforced by Christian rulers. American denominationalism has not much changed this attitude since sectarian and Calvinistic theology agreed to a great extent on this point. And even secular democracy has maintained the same attitude. The law of the State must represent the divine law. The State-powers have to serve this law or must be overthrown. Order must be *just* order. The State must realize as much as possible the justice of the Kingdom of God. The danger of this attitude is that the Christian detachment disappears, that, therefore, a relatively democratic and peaceful state of things seems to be the Kingdom of God; that the depth of sin and tragedy in any human power, especially State-power, becomes invisible and that the height of the justice of the Kingdom of God becomes lowered. The same problem exists in the relationship of States to one another, and the same principles are valid for the Christian interpretation of world politics. There is no possible world peace without a law to which all nations are subject. And there is no possible international law without a power beyond the nations which is able to enforce this law. World peace is dependent on a world-State, and no other form of world peace can be imagined. This means that from the point of view of the Gospel as long as there are sovereign nations which act according to their natural will to power, it is idealistic utopianism to assume that those States could be subjected to law without an embracing power strong enough to enforce the law. On the other hand, there is no reason for denying the possibility of a development toward an embracing power in which the sovereignty of the single national States is transferred to the sovereignty of a united State for all nations. Only in such a final unity of universal power and universal law the political goal of human history is reached—to become, not the realization, but the representation of the Kingdom of God.

III

THE SECOND DIALECTICAL TENSION IN THE STATE AND THE GOSPEL

The State is a unity of human beings, who are individuals. This leads to the problem whether each individual is the purpose of the State or whether the State is the purpose of each individual belonging to it. Whether the individuals who are united in the State or the State as the unity of those individuals is decisive for the structure and activity of the State. The modern liberal and democratic State has chosen the first way. The main task of its theory of the State is to determine the limitations of the State. The liberal State tries to give as much independence as possible to every individual. It is more interested in giving rights than in requesting duties. The philosophical background of this theory is medieval "Nominalism," namely, the doctrine that the only reality is the reality of the individual and that universals are mere names or terms for institutional tools to be used for the satisfaction of each individual.

The opposite answer also is dependent on medieval thought, namely on the mystical realism in medieval philosophy. It considers the individual as a merely contingent bearer of the universal. The State as a universal has more reality than any individual belonging to it. Therefore its power and growth are more important than the happiness and improvement of the individual. There are no "rights of man" as the rights of individual man. Justice is the expression of the needs of the State or the group united in the State. In modern times the idea of organism was used in order to describe the superiority of the State as a whole over each of its members. The so-called "State-reasons" became a weapon in the hands of ruling groups for suppressing justice and personal rights for the sake of the assumed happiness of the whole. In State-totalitarianism this tendency has reached its most radical expression, unbroken by the religious restrictions of medieval realism.

Christianity never has admitted a complete mystical realism and universalism, not even in a period in which the State was supposed to be a Christian State. The idea of personality and of the infinite value of each individual soul before God makes the submerging of the individual in a totalitarian community, even a Christian one, impossible. The Kingdom of God is a community of personalities who have a direct relationship to God. This separates Christianity from any kind of pagan mysticism and totalitarianism. God has appeared in a personal life. The idea of the God-man is the idea of a personal reality. Love in the sense of "Agape" is a personal relationship in distinction to love in the sense of "Eros" which means mystical identification. The individual personality stands directly before God, subject to his judgment, his salvation or damnation. A State which attempts to create a representation of the Kingdom of God on earth, must acknowledge the infinite value of each individual personality as a potential image and child of God. In this respect Christianity and humanism are in full agreement. Both, for example, have worked together toward the abolition of slavery, humanism more directly in the political sphere, Christianity more indirectly in destroying the pagan assumption that the slave must be considered as a thing and not as a person. The same prophetic presupposition and the same humanistic demand are effective in the protest of Marxism against a social order which uses human beings as working power to be calculated and measured instead of being considered as the real purpose of collective work. This also can be expressed in terms of freedom; the freedom of the individual in a state is not, of course, identical with the "freedom of the children of God." This transcendent freedom is possible even in chains. But this is the exception and should not be considered as the rule. Man as the image of God must be able to participate in God's creative freedom. Not an abstract, merely negative, idea of freedom can be derived from the interpretation of man in the Gospel. But a freedom for everybody to share the creative work of the State is an unmistakable demand of the Christian doctrine of man. It is the fundamental right of man to be considered as personality. And all especial rights must be derived from it. The denial by a state of the rights of man in this sense is tyranny and must be attacked as tyranny by Christian prophetism. It must be challenged as a demonic destruction of justice. Hobbes was right in calling this State by the name of the mythological portent "Leviathan."

But Christianity never has and never should neglect the other pole of dialectical tension. The Christian churches, in long periods of history, have formed authoritarian forms of the State. Catholicism even today favors fascism although it is threatened by it. Greek Orthodoxy has supported Czarism. Lutheranism favors absolute monarchy, the Anglican church is allied with aristocracy. The authoritarian form of church administration in Catholicism and to a certain extent in Lutheranism makes those churches inclined to support State-authoritarianism. The idea that the eternal order of things has hierarchical character is an expression of the demand for an hierarchical order in Church and State. For Augustine, even in the genuine creation and in the final fulfillment, hierarchical differentiations exist. No beings are equally near to God and therefore equal in power and grace. The Kingdom of God and the Reign of Christ are monarchic symbols and have consequences, consciously or unconsciously, for political theory.

Another impulse in this direction comes from the sacramental character of Christianity: First the divine gift, then human activity; first the assembly of God which as such is holy, then the individuals who belong to it; first the people of God, then those who are elected to it; first the body of Christ, then the single members and organs. All this works strongly in the direction of mystical realism. This feeling is deepened by the evil in human existence, in the lack of actual personality in the majority of men, in the arbitrariness and disintegration of souls and groups. The Christian pessimism with respect to human nature has helped a great deal to bring about the alliance between Christianity and authority.

So the second dialectical tension in the State becomes very important for the relationship of the Gospel and the State. A solution must be sought in the direction of a doctrine of the State, in which community is the first and individuality is the second, but in which not the State as such and not the individual as such are the ultimate goal of history but the honor and glory of the Kingdom of God.

IV

THE THIRD DIALECTICAL TENSION IN THE STATE AND THE GOSPEL

The State appears as an external form of life; but no external force can exist without something which gives meaning to it, without a content in which its power of being and growing is rooted. This leads to a tension between the interpretations of the State from the point of view of form and content. Where the State is considered as a mere form, its task is to protect the real life which is independent of it. Where the State is considered as a meaningful life in itself, its task is to create life by its own activities. In the extreme form of this latter interpretation the State is called the "God on earth" embracing and fulfilling all sides of human life. The "God-on-earth-State" against the mere "Police State" — this is the tension with which we have to deal finally and which leads us into the center of the State-Church problem in our present situation.

There is no doubt that any State needs a spiritual substance, an ultimate meaning of life on which it is based. No devotion to a State is possible without it. Even the liberal State has such a substance: the national idea. It never could exist without it. And this substance has always religious or semi-religious character. It is connected with the ultimate meaning of human existence. This becomes manifest by an historical survey of the different stages in which form and content of the State have developed in relationship to each other. We can distinguish four great periods of this development. In the first, pre-Christian period of the relationship between religion and State there are three main stages. The primitive tribal stage in which State and religion were completely identical, king and priest had the same function, State-activities were, without distinction, religious activities. In the second, polytheistic stages mythology as well as rites are the expression of the State-life and are serving the State-purpose. The priests are cult officials in the service of the State. The latest and highest development of this pre-Christian period is the abstract State of the Roman Empire which is beyond the concrete life of its subjects and at the same time an object of adoration in the personality of the emperor. Here the form of the State itself has become sacred.

The second period in the development of State and religion in relation to each other is marked by the prophetic protest against any identification of State and religion. Religion in the prophetic message is related to any personality without mediation of the State and, consequently, has universal character without limitation by any national State. The great Jewish prophets, making the distinction between God and national politics, created an entirely new relationship between State and religion. This line was followed by Christianity in its absolute detachment from the State, in its message to each individual in all States and nations and consequently in its supernational universalism.

The third period of the development of State and religion in their relationship to each other begins with the foundation of the Christian State by Constantine. Three lines of development must be mentioned in this period. First, the Greek which is nearest to Constantine's interpretation of his function as Christian emperor and which is not very far removed from the State-religion of the pagan emperors. This form of a Christian State must be characterized as Caesaro-papism. The emperor as emperor is at the same time representative of the Church; so it was in the Byzantine

Empire and in Czarist Russia. The second line of development is the Roman-Catholic, which must be characterized as Papo-caesarism: The pope as the successor of Christ is at the same time the universal monarch, from which all other monarchs must receive their power. The medieval history can be considered as a struggle between these two lines: On the one side the pope aspiring to be emperor, on the other side the emperor of the Holy German Empire aspiring to have papal powers. The third line of the idea of the Christian State is expressed in both main groups of Protestantism, namely the demand for a Christian government but for a government which has no direct religious functions. This demand was directed to the Christian prince in the period of absolutism as well as to the elected governments in democracy. The Christian State in this manifold sense of the word was a reality, not because the authorities were personally Christian but because there was no other substance of life in these States. Even the humanistic epoch did not change the situation because modern humanism was Christian humanism.

The fourth period of the development of State and religion in relation to each other began in this twentieth century only. Christian humanism became more and more secular and empty. It lost the power of giving a meaning and a spiritual substance to human life. A feeling of complete meaninglessness conquered the souls of many groups of people, first of all the younger generation. The Christian Churches were not able to show a new meaning and to give a spiritual substance to State and society. This, in connection with the tremendous growth in nationalism, led to the rebirth of the old tribal powers of the first period. Nation, blood and soil became the real content and the spiritual substance of many States. The fundamental identification of religion and State in the pre-Christian period was resumed. And the final outcome of all this was the totalitarian tribal State as represented first of all by National Socialism.

This historical survey has shown that the Gospel is the fundamental and everlasting protest against tribal religion, religious nationalism and State adoration. There is no possible compromise between Christianity and the religious philosophy of National Socialism; there is no possible compromise between Christianity and the religious glorification of race, soil and blood. Therefore, the struggle between Church and State in Germany must be considered as the renewal of the struggle between the Roman Empire and the old Christian Church. The struggle cannot be solved by a clear-cut separation between State-power and Church-power. When the State itself assumes Church character the fight becomes inescapable. The demand of the National Socialist State-authorities that the Church restrict itself to the transcendental realm, is only a method of replacing the Christian Church by the German racial community, its creed and its cult. Neither is there a possible compromise with the National-Socialist State, since the alternative is exclusive: either nation and race are the ultimate values for which the sacrifice of soul and body is duty, or the salvation of the soul is the ultimate duty and meaning of human existence, equally in all nations and races. Therefore only the third way is left, the way used by the old Church in the days of persecution, to become an underground Church in order to save the Christian message for its members and for coming generations. This way is used today by the radical wing of the Confessional Church in Germany. It is unavoidable but it also is dangerous. It works in the direction of a sectarian seclusion, of dogmatism, Pharisaism, and hierarchical dictatorship. These dangers already have become visible in the life of the Confessional Church.

The democratic countries cannot remain neutral in the long run in this struggle. The more secularized the democratic States become, the more danger of an entire loss of Christian substance is imminent. But since any State needs a spiritual substance nationalism would more and more replace Christianity, thus assuming a semi-religious character itself. And whenever the national idea has become the ultimate meaning of life, racial fanaticism, the adoration of blood and soil, the hatred of the foreigner and the adoration of State power are the final outcome. Nationalism as the substitute for Christianity necessarily leads to some form of State totalitarianism. Only a few people in the present democratic countries realize this tremendous danger. The insight into the dialectical tension between form and content in every State may force the realization upon all. If Christianity is no more able to give spiritual substance to the State and an ultimate meaning of life to its subjects, other powers will break into this vacuum, powers which always are dwelling in the depth of the human soul, which are overcome in principle by the Gospel, but which may rise again and wage a life-and-death struggle against the Gospel.❖

FREEDOM IN THE PERIOD OF TRANSFORMATION[1]

I

The question of the quality of freedom in a special historical period has meaning only if freedom is subject to historical change. Such an assumption, however, is difficult. Of course, every historical period creates different forms, institutions, and ideas in which freedom is realized. This kind of change is so obvious that it need not be mentioned. But the problem is whether the historical change of the forms of freedom also entails an essential change in the nature of freedom. Furthermore, if freedom is considered to be an essential, perhaps the most essential, characteristic of man, a change in the very nature of freedom would involve a change in the very nature of man. It would mean that man not only has history but that human nature as such, the very essential character of humanity, is subject to history and to historical transformation. Is such an assertion tenable?

In order to answer this question we must first understand the unique nature of freedom. Freedom has an ambiguity in its very nature by which it is distinguished

---

[1] The term "transformation" is taken from Karl Manheim's book **Man in the Period of Transformation**

from every other reality. Everything except freedom is determined by its own nature. Its actualization follows its nature by necessity. But it is the nature of freedom to determine itself. Freedom is the possibility of transcending its nature. This utterly dialectical character of the nature of freedom makes the doctrine of freedom both fascinating and dangerous. A philosophy which ignores the fundamental ambiguity in the nature of freedom is a philosophical attack on freedom; and in being an attack on freedom it is an attack on humanity. For freedom makes man man. Even those who deny it presuppose it. Even those who attack humanity by attacking freedom can do so only in the very name of humanity and freedom. In the act of deciding against freedom one is a witness for it, since one's decision pretends to be true, and this means that it is not dependent on one's individual or social nature, but on objective norms which one is able to accept or reject. This situation has been darkened by the traditional problem of the "freedom of will," a problem which cannot be solved because the form of the question itself is fallacious. Man and not a section of man is free.

From this it follows that it is impossible to formulate a definition of human nature in the ordinary sense of "definition." For man has the possibility of changing the nature which has been defined in such a definition. Man is able to break through the limitations of every definition of man, except that definition which refers to man's ability to change his nature. Therefore, all definitions of human nature and freedom which try to establish a human nature or a nature of freedom above history are impossible. Man's historical existence makes them impossible. No historical definitions of the nature of man deprive man of his freedom, namely, of his power to determine his nature in history and to become something new through history. Consequently, if we attempt to formulate a definition of man we should say: Man is that being who is able to determine his being in freedom through history. And if we attempt to formulate a definition of freedom we should say: Freedom is that faculty of man by which he is able to determine his being through history. And if we attempt to formulate a definition of history we should say: History is that happening through which man determines his own being, including his freedom.

Freedom is the condition of history, history is the condition of freedom; they are mutually interdependent. There is no history without freedom. There are natural processes, going on with natural necessity. Denying freedom of history means making history a natural process, depriving it of its uniqueness and its meaning. Conversely, there is no freedom besides history. Freedom which has ceased to be the power of determining itself in history has ceased to be freedom, and men who have lost this power have lost their full humanity. They are dehumanized. They have mere ideology, designed to cover up the lack of real freedom in the interest of enslaving groups if "freedom above history" is praised. Freedom must *appear* in history, must *embody* itself in history, or it is not freedom.

II

If man is that being who determines his being in freedom through history, only those can be called men who posses this freedom and participate in the self-determination of man through history. Ancient political philosophy agrees with this view: man is he who is free, and free is he who participates in the self-determination of the historical group to which he belongs. Citizenship, freedom, and humanity are identical.

The slave is a "human being" but not a "man" in the full sense of the word because he is not free. The decision as to whether someone is a god or a human being or an animal depends on fate. And whether a human being is *man* in the full sense of the word or is excluded from full humanity is a matter of destiny. Freedom is a quality of human nature and, at the same time, a fact of historical destiny. These two aspects can contradict each other. He who is free by nature can become a slave by destiny. This was a very practical philosophy: the entire social system and the entire foreign policy of classical Greece were dependent on this idea. It was the justification of slavery, and it was the justification of the contempt for the "barbarians." For man is he who is free; free is he who is citizen; citizen is he who is Greek; consequently the Greek citizen alone is man in the full sense of the word. Outside of Greece are human beings. The Greeks alone represent humanity. In this attitude the one great solution of the problem "freedom and history" is given.

The later ancient development, represented by Stoicism and Epicureanism, brought about another solution. When the political self-determination of the Greeks was destroyed by Alexander and the Romans and many of the Greek citizens became slaves of the conquerors, the historical element in the concept of freedom became weakened. Freedom was considered a natural characteristic of man generally which cannot be lost by fate, although fate excludes the majority of men from political self-determination. The Epicureans even suggested that freedom could be maintained only through retirement into a completely private life. But at the same time the Roman emperors, influenced by Stoic philosophy, extended freedom and Roman citizenship more and more, to the point that it became a kind of universal citizenship. Those who were considered essentially free as human beings should receive historical freedom as Roman citizens. Stoicism tried to approximate freedom by destiny and freedom by nature. But this, of course, did not mean the political self-determination for the overwhelming majority of people. The government was in the hands of a few. A non-political citizenship developed, implying equality before the law and the acknowledgement that all human beings have a natural claim to become man in the full sense.

Even less political was the Christian idea of freedom. Political freedom was considered as irrelevant to the state of being a Christian, and that means to having the "freedom of the children of God." This freedom is the only possible fulfillment of man's natural freedom. It is the liberation from man's transcendent servitude, from the servitude under sin, guilt and demonic powers. Political freedom cannot provide this liberation and enslavement cannot prevent it. It is a work of God and God alone. But even this transcendent freedom has historical implications. The work of God is realized in history, in Christ and in the Church, that is (as the original Greek word indicates), in the "assembly," namely the "assembly of God" which replaces the city—assemblies of importance and dignity. Therefore freedom and active "citizenship" in the assembly of God are identical. The free citizen of the Greek city state is replaced by the free member of the universal Church. And the Church is not only a mystical body, but is also a historical community. He who belongs to it as a true Christian has not only transcendent freedom but also historical freedom. For as a member of the Church, he participates in determining history, not directly but indirectly, through the regenerating power of Christians in all secular communities. As a member of the Church he is equal to any other member even if the hierarchical order excludes him from leading functions within the Church.

In this respect Protestantism carries through the original Christian impulses. It puts the layman, not only before God, but also in the actual life of the Church, on an equal basis with the minister, or more exactly, it makes the minister a layman and the layman a minister, giving the actual freedom of determining the history of the Church to every member. So the hierarchical limitations of historical freedom in Catholicism are overcome in Protestantism. Freedom before God involves historical freedom, although within the boundaries of the Church.

Further development removed even this limitation. Freedom before God, which was originally freedom from guilt by salvation, became more and more identified with the natural freedom of every human being, the freedom of self-determination through history. The "rational" man of Stoicism and the "saved man" of Christianity were merged into each other. The democratic doctrine of freedom emerged. Modern democracy combines the classic ideal of political freedom as the actualization of natural freedom with the Stoic doctrine of freedom as the general character of human beings and with the religious universalism of the Christian idea of freedom. It implies elements of all these and makes something new of their combination. This comes out very clearly in a document such as the Bill of Rights. In the democratic constitutions the identity of natural and political freedom is apparently complete. The freedom of man cannot be separated from his freedom to determine his historical fate politically. Every human being, that is, every one who has reason, is naturally and, consequently, politically free. He belongs to those who determine the nature of man and the nature of freedom by determining human history in political acts. Those who are deprived of their democratic rights are deprived of the human characteristic to be free.

From this life-and-death struggle for the "rights of man" in many countries, the religious enthusiasm for democracy, for instance, in the United States, the unrestricted affirmation of democracy by the churches in some democratic countries, are incomprehensible. This struggle is felt as the struggle for essential humanity, for the maintenance of man as man against the distortions of humanity and human freedom. The World War as a "crusade for democracy" was a consequence of this kind of thinking; it was a consequence of the radical identification of natural and political freedom and of both of these with the freedom before God.

It is doubtful whether the present war will create the same ideology. It may be that the criticism of these identifications during the period between the two wars has destroyed the possibility of their revival.

This survey shows that the interdependence of natural and political freedom always has been acknowledged, directly or indirectly; it further shows that there is a trend in history to enlarge the realm of political freedom towards its full identification with natural freedom or towards universal democracy. The fact that man is free by nature makes him restless until he has become free in history.

But this trend is contradicted by another which idealizes the aristocratic and hierarchical systems of the past and tries drastically to limit those who are free to determine history by political actions. Political freedom shall be reserved to a comparatively small number of leaders, to the so-called élite, to privileged classes, to educated persons, to landowners, to military or bureaucratic powers. In these theories, of which the élite doctrine is the most recent expression, and all kinds of fascism, its most important application, a condition is established beyond natural freedom on which political freedom shall depend. Political self-determination is permitted only to those who have superiority in natural gifts, heredity, tradition, environment, in brief, in historical fate. Freedom needs something beyond freedom in order to become political reality. The democratic identification of natural and political freedom is denied. As in some religious doctrines transcendent predestination determines the eternal fulfillment of the eternal destruction of man, so in these doctrines historical predestination decides whether a human being is destined to be a man in the full sense of humanity or not. The consequence of this doctrine is that the natural freedom of the majority of men never becomes actual as political freedom. And this has led in all human history to the dehumanization of the masses, to a situation in which the natural freedom of man is destroyed by the lack of historical freedom. Nevertheless, this theory has arisen again and again. It has not only been powerful in the past, before the democratic development began, but it became powerful again at the very moment when the democratic idea of freedom seemed to be victorious all over the world. And it is pathetic to see that not only ruling groups and new "élite" supported this tendency but that the masses themselves helped to destroy their own political freedom. The democratic identification of natural and political freedom seems to be inadequate to human nature.

Religion as well as idealism very often has supported this view by making a strong distinction between external and internal freedom which everyone is able to maintain, even as a slave. Free is he who acts as a moral personality or as a saved child of God, even if he is in chains. "Freedom in chains" is possible in every political system, in democracy as well as in tyranny. Only the interior freedom is ultimately significant. One can live under a bill of rights or in a totalitarian and collectivist system, one can be free in both of them, one can be free in chains or without chains. There is no historical circumstance in which one could not develop one's natural freedom to full humanity.

And arguments from the historical and political realm are added to these religious and ethical arguments. It is emphasized and it cannot be doubted that human history is shaped in a much more profound way by nonpolitical men than by any kind of politician. There are innumerable proofs of this. These proofs exist not only among those who are considered the great creative men in human culture but in every man who participates in shaping human history. Political creativity is a special gift, embodied in a few people who under favorable conditions become political leaders and who determine history in their special way. But it is as much nonsense to demand that everyone participate in political creativity as it would be to demand that everyone participate in mathematical or musical creativity. Therefore political responsibility should be reserved for those who are able to carry it. And it is by no means a deprivation of freedom and full humanity if the large majority of people are excluded from political self-determination.

These arguments must be taken very seriously. They establish a simple identification of natural and political freedom, such as modern democracy has assumed to be impossible. *The freedom of historical self-determination is not identical with the freedom of political self-determination.* There is a direct relationship between them but not a simple identity. Political self-determination is a special and extremely important section of historical self-determination; but historical self-determination goes far beyond it. Historical freedom is not bound to a system of voting, of majority, parliamentary representation. It is not bound to democratic institutions in the technical sense of the word. But historical freedom is bound to a realm of free creativity by which history is shaped and transformed. They are not excluded from full humanity who are excluded from participation in direct political activity, but only those who are excluded from any realm of creative freedom and, therefore, from historical self-determination. If this is taken for granted, if the distinction between historical and political freedom is established, the aristocratic and idealistic arguments can be answered in this way: Man's natural freedom, his complete humanity, does not exist except in different forms of historical freedom. Any attempt of religion and idealism to restrict freedom to the so-called "inner-freedom" must be rejected. Inner freedom cannot even be imagined without historical freedom. Of course, the "free man in chains" may represent human freedom better than a mass of voters. But in order to represent freedom he must have experienced freedom, he must have lived under a political system which makes freedom a subject of possible experience. There is a political suppression which dehumanizes nations and generations in such a way that not even the free man in chains can be found. The freedom in chains is dependent upon the experience of the freedom without chains; even the freedom of the "children of God" is a meaningless phrase if freedom never has been a subject of historical experience. As the religious and idealistic language is derived from the concrete language of daily life which gives the realistic basis for even the highest and most removed symbols, so the experience, expressed in these symbols, must keep its roots in the concrete experiences in which they first appeared. Inner freedom without historical freedom is an abstraction which, taken for a reality, surrenders historical freedom and, finally, destroys itself.

III

Historical freedom is not political freedom. But the question is whether historical freedom is possible without political freedom and, if not, what kind of political freedom is necessary to guarantee historical freedom. In order to answer these questions we must qualify the nature of historical freedom. Freedom exists only if there is a realm of free creativity, a realm within which everyone is able to determine history and to transform human nature through history.

Creative freedom has three conditions: Freedom for *meaningful* creativity, freedom for *autonomous* creativity, freedom for *self-fulfilling* creativity.

The first condition is the freedom for meaningful creativity, that is, the freedom to decide about the meaning and purposes of one's creative actions. No one has historical freedom who acts for a purpose, the meaning of which he denies. It is not necessary that he himself discover and set up that purpose, but it is necessary that he agree with it. If he does not agree with it and must work for it in order to maintain his physical existence, he is enslaved. Large masses of people are enslaved in this way. They are not enslaved because they are working for the profit of someone else. One can work for the profit of another without losing one's freedom, if the meaning and the purpose are accepted and the other elements of freedom are guaranteed. And one can work for one's own profit and feel at every moment the meaninglessness of one's work. Working for oneself can be the slavery of toiling for infinite profit and infinite economic power without any meaningful purpose beyond this. It is more than a nice phrase when socialists emphasize that the salvation from capitalism is not only the salvation of the exploited masses but also the salvation of the exploiting rulers who are deprived of this freedom of meaningful creativity by the tyrannical laws of competition. No romantic glorification of the freedom of competition should conceal the dehumanizing and enslaving consequences it can entail. The important question is not whether man works for himself or for someone else or for the group to which he belongs. The problem is whether his work is supported by the freedom of meaningful creativity, the first condition of historical freedom.

The second condition is the freedom for autonomous creativity (autonomous in the traditional and only meaningful sense of following the laws embodied in things themselves without any encroachment either by authorities or by one's accidental nature), that is, the freedom to follow the objective demands involved in the nature of one's work, unrestrained by heteronomous demands coming from outside. Every creative work has its structural necessities which follow from its special nature. An artist, for instance, has the freedom for autonomous creativity only if he is free to follow the structural demands, first of his material, second of the forms of his art, and third of the special style he represents. In the same way the scholar must be able to follow the methodological demands of his material without restriction by religious or political powers. And the technical worker must be able to follow the principle of the greatest effect with the smallest means and must not be obliged to suppress or to disturb creative possibilities under the urge of political interests. Wherever this freedom is denied, man is deprived of his self-determination through history. He is enslaved and dehumanized. A judge who is not able to follow his judgment about the law and the special case to be judged has no freedom. He becomes a dehumanized tool of political tyranny. He has lost his historical freedom by losing his autonomous creativity.

The third condition of historical freedom is the freedom for self-fulfilling creativity. Freedom is destroyed if the vital power and joy which belong to creativity are lost. The freedom of the self-determination of human nature through history cannot be separated from self-fulfillment in the sense of the Greek word *eudaimonia. Eudaimonia*, or happiness, is that stage of man in which the potentialities of his nature are fully actualized. *Eudaimonia* is self-fulfillment. It is distinguished, although not entirely separated, from *hedone*, pleasure, which is a secondary consequence but not an essential element of happiness. Ordinarily it should be connected with happiness but it can be lacking. Happiness is possible even in pain and suffering. But pleasure alone can never create happiness. The fact that in the course of occidental thought the Greek principle of *eudaimonia* has been confused with the principle of *hedone*, that happiness and pleasure have not been strictly distinguished, that Christian ethics denied not only pleasure but also happiness in the sense of *eudaimonia*, has greatly disturbed personal as well as social ethics in the ancient and modern world. When socialism demanded happiness for everyone, the foes of socialism attacked it as the establishment of the pleasure principle and used the religious or idealistic arguments against the pleasure principle as arguments against socialism. And since creative self-fulfillment is essential for human nature, the process of the dehumanization of the masses in industrial society was supported by this kind of argumentation. Freedom of self-fulfillment cannot be maintained if the joy and the vital courage of creativity are destroyed. There is no historical freedom if the vital condition of creativity is undermined by insecurity, anxiety, fear, and suppression of the most vital impulses by the lack of means to satisfy them. There is no historical freedom if happiness through creative self-determination is extinguished by a social structure and technical procedures which make man a part of a machine or a quantity of working power, to be bought and to be sold. This means that freedom is dependent not only on political forms but also on social structure in which the self-fulfilling creativity or the creative happiness of everyone is guaranteed in order that complete fulfillment of man and society may be achieved.

Summing up we can say: Human nature demands the freedom of historical self-determination. Historical self-determination demands a realm of creative freedom. Creative freedom presupposes the freedom of meaningful creativity, the freedom of autonomous creativity, the freedom of self-fulfilling creativity.

Political freedom is a status of human society in which this historical freedom of human self-determination is guaranteed to everyone by political institutions. Political freedom is the guardian of historical freedom. A political system is free in the measure in which it is able to guarantee and to promote the free creativity of everyone in determining human history. The question whether in a political system freedom is embodied cannot be answered by the legal character of its constitution and its laws. Legal and constitutional freedom does not necessarily imply historical freedom. The form of freedom does not necessarily involve the content of freedom. Democracy is that system which from a constitutional point of view embodies more freedom than any other political system. The participation of everyone in the government in voting and the equal right of everyone before the law are the strongest expression of the will to freedom which can be imagined in a world in which government and power cannot be avoided. But even such a system can become a tool for suppressing free creativity. The very dialectical history of liberalism, the system which bears the name of liberty, shows clearly that the constitutional form alone is not able to guarantee historical freedom. It may be necessary to transform the legal form of liberty into something which appears to be a strong restriction of freedom in order to save historical freedom. This is the present situation in all countries in which liberalism has become predominant! *And this is the reason why we face a long and catastrophic period of transformation in which constitutional freedom probably will be doomed to a certain extent and in which historical freedom, free creativity, and the right of man to determine his own nature through history will be, and even is at present, utterly endangered.*

Facing this situation we must ask ourselves how far historical freedom is dependent on constitutional liberties. If it were entirely dependent, no hope would be left for historical freedom in the period of transformation. But there is such hope because historical freedom is not identical with a special form of political liberty and consequently with a special form of constitution and law. There were situations in human history in which historical freedom was comparatively safe in authoritarian systems. Monarchy, for example, in some cases can balance the contrasting class interests better than highly developed forms of democratic capitalism. This is possible but not necessary. And monarchy always has the disadvantage that the lack of constitutional correctives may lead to an arbitrary use of power by which the largest number of people are excluded from the realm of historical self-determination. From this point of view democracy provides more guarantees against the abuse of governmental power. But on the other hand it makes a situation possible in which private groups, without public responsibility, control the masses by their economic power to such an extent that historical freedom is doomed, under cover of democracy. Therefore neither an authoritarian system in itself nor democracy in itself can offer a guarantee for historical freedom. No system in itself can do this. Nevertheless, a "synthetic system" in which a strong, uniting, and determining governmental problem is checked by democratic correctives must be considered as the ideal form of political freedom.

But there is not much probability that such a system will be the outcome of our present situation. It seems to be an inescapable law of human history that the historical existence of the ideal form of political freedom is only a favorable accident, a chance which sometimes occurs but which has a very transitory character. *Historical freedom, guaranteed by an ideal form of political freedom, is as rare as all great things in human history.* Therefore our actual task is to find a way in which man's historical self-determination is saved in the period of transformation. This period which in economic terms is a period of mass collectivism, in intellectual terms a period of heteronomy, in political terms a period of unrestricted authority, affords for us an ideal constellation. Freedom in this period must have the character of "in spite of," namely, meaningful creativity in spite of superimposed purposes; autonomous creativity in spite of collectivistic authority; self-fulfilling creativity in spite of destructive social conditions. How is this possible, if it is possible at all?

It is my task to analyze the present economic, sociological, and intellectual conditions which inescapably lead either to another creative period of history or to chaos and the rebarbarization of large sections of mankind. There are three interdependent reasons for this development: first the self-destructing tendencies in the economic structure of later capitalism; second the dehumanizing force of all controlling nationalism, third the disintegrating power of a mechanized and secularized technical civilization. Each of these causes would be strong enough to enforce a fundamental transformation of the structure of human life. Together they are irresistible. It could be said that every period in history is a period of "transformation." This is true if transformation is used in the superficial sense of mere change, but if it is used in the sense of a fundamental structural disintegration in all realms of human life, it must be applied emphatically to our period. It is a transformation through catastrophes and revolutions but it is more than catastrophe and revolution. Something really new is forthcoming, something new which can be utterly creative but which also can mean the end of any creativity in many parts of the world. It is not necessary to argue further for this interpretation of the present situation. The arguments for it are known to everyone and have become cheap slogans, used and abused in daily life. Things which some decades or even years ago were treated as esoteric wisdom, venturing prophecy, and audacious radicalism, have become normal articles, bought and sold at every market. Cassandra's prophecies, voiced through Spengler's mouth, have become a matter of routine for newspaper editorials. But even so, what was true of esoteric wisdom is still true as exoteric talk. A period of transformation, in the most radical sense of the term, has begun; we are in the midst of it, asking whether its outcome for our generation and for those following will be creation or chaos.

What is the place of freedom in this stage of society?

First, what is the place of freedom of meaningful creativity in spite of purposes forced upon individuals and groups by foreign powers or by the trend of historical development? An outstanding example of the former is the subjection of the industrial masses to the arbitrary purposes of the economic rulers, while the destruction of the middle classes and their proletarization is an important example of the latter. In both cases people are deprived of their freedom of meaningful creativity, of historical self-determination and consequently of their full humanity. The period of transformation will increase the loss of meaningful creativity. A few people — economic or political leaders, civil or military dictators, newspaper, radio, or movie czars, members of the inner cabinet in so-called democracies — will determine the purposes of hundreds of millions of people. The concentration of power which is rooted in a mass society, its technical means and its social and national contracts will make meaningful creativity more and more difficult and even impossible. Very often, of course, the subjection to foreign purposes is voluntary and requires no coercion. The subjection can be outspoken or silent, it can express itself in noisy praise or in silent acceptance of the purposes established by the ruling group. As long as this is the case, the freedom of meaningful creativity is not lost. But in a system in which democratic outlets are lacking, a situation must unavoidably arise in which the purposes of the ruling group and of the ruled masses become opposed to each other. In such a situation, meaningful creativity is severely endangered. There are only two ways to maintain it, the religious and the revolutionary, and both must be adopted at the same time. The religious way can save the consciousness of man's essential freedom, of his humanity and dignity, even in an epoch in which the process of dehumanization has gone very far and historical freedom has almost disappeared. The religious question is the question of the ultimate meaning of life, expressed in religious or in philosophical terms. Whether the consciousness of man's natural freedom is saved in Christian or in Stoic concepts, whether the "freedom of the children of God" or the "freedom of the wise man" is the symbol in the name of which humanity is maintained—if it is maintained—does not depend on the religious way alone. If historical freedom disappeared completely, man's essential freedom would perish in spite of faith and heroism. But there is a way in which historical freedom can be maintained even in a period of its suppression: the way of revolutionary resistance. This does not necessarily mean actual revolution. Generations of revolutionaries may wait for it in vain. But it *does* mean the way towards revolution, it *does* mean the latent resistance before and manifest resistance when "the day" comes. In the period of the suppression of historical freedom the revolutionary attitude is the refuge for meaningful creativity and humanity. The second question is: What is the place of the freedom of autonomous creativity in spite of collective authority, forced upon every realm of life by totalitarian claims? There is no doubt that the period of transformation, at least in its first part, must lead to collectivistic and authoritarian systems with more or less totalitarian claims. The example, laid down by the Fascists, and—on the basis of the opposite principle—by the Soviets, will be followed (although with important variations) by the democracies. The tremendous task of a fundamental transformation of the world, politically and socially, will permit no other way. The consequences for the freedom of historical self-determination, especially for the freedom of autonomous creativity, will be very grave. An outstanding example of what will happen is the suppression of the freedom of the universities and of many other institutions of science and learning in the totalitarian countries. Men are deprived of their right, and in the long run of their ability, to ask for the objective structure of reality and to act in accordance with their knowledge of things. A process of deterioration in all realms of cultural creativity is initiated, which finally endangers the totalitarian systems themselves.

How can the freedom of autonomous creativity, the second condition for historical freedom, be saved in such a situation? Two answers, again, must be given, a suprahistorical one on the one hand, and an historical one on the other. These are of vital importance in considering the problem of freedom. Starting with the second we suggest: *In a totalitarian period the freedom of autonomous creativity can exist only in an esoteric form.* In order to explain this proposition it is necessary to mention the different types of esoterism and to ask what bearing they may have on cultural creativity in the period of transformation. There is a *natural* esoterism which always has existed and always will exist because it is rooted in the differentiation of human abilities. This natural esoterism is entirely compatible with the most liberal management of intellectual freedom. The esoterism of higher mathematics or of the knowledge of foreign languages or of the work of the physicians or industrial leaders is not exclusive in principle; it is a natural, not an intentional, esoterism. Everyone who is able to understand the material is a potential member of the esoteric group, which is not a group in any sociological sense. There are no protective measures to safeguard this esoterism because it is protected by its very nature.

Another kind of esoterism is just the opposite of the first; it is entirely *artificial* and is not grounded in the material itself. It can be found in groups which create a mystery around themselves in order to be more attractive or in order to maintain exclusiveness and social prestige. Ruling classes often protect themselves by esoterism of this kind in order to keep down the controlled masses. Religious and non-religious sectarians use esoterism as a means to enhance their own self-consciousness and their esteem by those excluded. Priests, scholars, physicians, sometimes abuse the natural esoterism, implied in the difficulty of their material, by augmenting this difficulty artificially in order to increase the superiority and exclusiveness of their profession.

The third type is the *mystical* esoterism. It is rooted in the fact that some religious and psychological experiences are impossible without strict preparations. In this instance, mystical esoterism is related to natural esoterism. But since the initiation into the mystery group is often dependent on some more or less arbitrary rules, the mystical is related to the artificial esoterism. In many cases it is difficult to draw the line between the two.

The fourth type of esoterism is the *educational*. It is rooted in the idea that not everything can be said to everyone at every moment, that some things can be said only at the right time and in the right place, and some things cannot be said at all to some people. There is a truth which ceases to be truth if it comes to people who necessarily misunderstand and abuse it. This is the reason why educational esoterism is used practically by every educator at all times and can never be omitted. Even the most autonomous method in education must adapt itself to the different degrees of maturity in the object of education. The fact that many educators intensify educational esoterism in order to enhance their authority over their pupils does not refute the essentiality of educational esoterism.

Very close to educational esoterism, and to a certain degree identical with it, is the fifth type, the *political* esoterism. We exclude from this term all kinds of revolutionary movements which are forced to conceal themselves in order to escape persecution by the ruling powers. In such "catacomb groups" esoterism of the mentioned types may develop. But the fact of flight from persecution is not esoterism in itself.

Political esoterism is the attempt to keep in some kind of seclusion knowledge or ideas which are considered to be dangerous for a political and social system. The problem, faced by every government, even the most democratic, is:

How much truth and how much error can be admitted, without dangerous consequences for the group, as a matter of public knowledge and public discussion? Truth is dangerous for people who are not able to understand the whole truth, namely, the totality of implications in a special truth. Therefore the pronouncement of a special truth can lead to actions that contradict the whole truth and entail destructive consequences. The danger of error is obvious. But the difficulty is that there is no truth without possible and even unavoidable error. Truth lives in the process of finding truth, and this process involves error, often extremely dangerous error. If everyone participates in the process of finding the truth, it can happen that the masses are grasped by an error strong enough to destroy a whole system of life. In former centuries natural esoterism prevented the uneducated masses from participating in political, social, and intellectual decisions. The problem of esoterism was actual for only narrow groups. And even within the small stratum of educated people, only esoteric groups were allowed or allowed themselves to discuss the fundamental problems of religious and political life. Public discussions of these problems involved the danger of inquisition and condemnation of Church and State. In the later Middle Ages the doctrine of the "double truth" was an attempt to enlarge the esoteric groups without surrendering the principle of esoterism. First with the rise of Protestantism and enlightenment, esoterism as such broke down. Liberalism, supported by the new means of mass education—newspapers, popular magazines, radio, movies, etc.—narrowed down more and more even the realms of natural esoterism. Today esoterism in every form seems to have disappeared. But actually it has not. Those who control mass education and mass propaganda are protected by a new type of esoterism—the esoterism of political power without public responsibility. It was easy for the totalitarian systems to take over this esoterism and apply it to the dictatorial form of government.

Dictatorial esoterism is determined by the political interests of the ruling groups. It can and must admit some freedom of autonomous creativity within the limits of this interest. But it can never go beyond these limits. Therefore, dictatorial esoterism necessarily creates revolutionary esoterism. Not the fact that it has to conceal itself makes it esoteric, but the fact that only small groups are able to participate in the creation of something which is able to stand the test of the future. Only people with courage and patience, vision and rationality, at the same time, can constitute this "esoterism of political vanguards." It seems that these groups will be the main bearers of the freedom of autonomous creativity in the period of transformation. It would be necessary that they remain esoteric even if there were no persecution, because the dictation of truth into slogans while the generation of the truth is still going on destroys its creative power completely. But at the same time it is obvious that esoterism is not purpose in itself for these groups. Revolutionary esoterism, as directed against hidden or manifest dictators, has the tendency to make itself unnecessary by creating a fundamental conformity on the basis of which free discussion and the freedom of autonomous creativity are possible. The aim of revolutionary esoterism is democratic esoterism.

People who belong to the political vanguard need a faith that cannot be destroyed, either by a force from without or by skepticism from within. Everyone who belongs to such a group needs a realm in which he is beyond his own skepticism and his own weakness. This realm is not necessarily a special religious doctrine or a special philosophic principle. It is faith and heroism with respect to truth in whatever terms truth may be expressed. In some epochs it is not a disadvantage that only people who are willing to stand sacrifice and persecution are able to maintain truth and autonomous creativity. The creative spirit after a period of practically unlimited freedom, may need the hardships of suppression and persecution in order to become more serious, profound, and vital than it was in the period of safe and unhindered self-expression. Nevertheless, the freedom of autonomous creativity and self-determination must be the final aim of revolutionary esoterism.

Finally we ask: What is the place of freedom of self-fulfilling creativity in spite of the destructive social conditions that will prevail in the period of transformation? These conditions are unavoidable because of the heavy losses connected with radical changes, because of the catastrophes inescapably resulting from these changes, and because of the pressure, exercised by the dictators, those hidden as well as those manifest, on all groups of people. There is and there will be a tremendous amount of suffering and destruction of vital power in large masses. Self-fulfilling creativity will become more and more the reservation of a few leading groups while all the others must toil as parts of a mechanism, unable to reach happiness in their work and continually threatened by insecurity through the possible loss of work. How can the freedom of self-fulfilling creativity, how can happiness, be saved in such a situation? Again two answers must be given. It is the greatness of religion and the reason for its power over the human mind in all periods of history that it can provide a happiness of a different type, called, by religion itself, "blessedness." Religion as well as those who attack it has very often distorted the meaning of blessedness by interpreting it as the promise of a happy life after death! But this is only its mythological expression. Its real meaning is the presence of blessedness in a situation of deepest distress and in the extinction of normal happiness. The religious concept of "eternal life" points to a freedom of self-fulfilling creativity which is dependent on an ultimate source of happiness beyond the contrasts of normal happiness and normal unhappiness. Therefore religion and philosophy as far as they maintain the idea of "eternal life," as present in the temporal and transitory existence, are able to give the first answer to the "quest for happiness." It is an answer which in some situations of human life, and certainly in many situations in the period of transformation, will appear as a mere paradox. It is a paradox, but nevertheless it is true and witnessed by philosophers and prophets.

But the suprahistorical answer alone is not sufficient. It must be completed by an historical answer. Happiness as a paradox alone is impossible. It must also become an actuality. How is this possible in the period of transformation? It is possible only if the transformation is taken in a revolutionary sense. The happiness which cannot be drawn from the present reality must and can be drawn from the anticipation of a future reality. *Freedom of self-fulfilling creativity in the period of transformation can be saved only through anticipating creativity.* There is a happiness of anticipation without which the life of the masses would be utterly meaningless and desperate. It is probably the greatest achievement of the socialist movements in the nineteenth and twentieth centuries that they have provided "happiness by anticipation" for those who struggled with them for a new order of life. Today the active power of these movements is almost broken. But it does not follow that the creative impulse is broken! It can be renewed in small groups which are able to anticipate future fulfillment, to struggle for its realization, and to maintain happiness by anticipation. Although the weapon of these groups in the period of transformation is not aggression but resistance, it implies creativity, self-fulfilling creativity by anticipation.

Many aspects of the problem of freedom are not even mentioned in this essay. The problem of national freedom in a world which becomes narrower every day and urgently needs some form of supernational unity is not considered.

The freedom of economic liberalism is only implicitly considered. Its breakdown in all countries is one of the three fundamental causes for the period of transformation. No utopian description of the freedom after the period of transformation is given. The possibility that this "after" will be the "chaos" has prevented such an attempt.

Our question was: How can freedom be saved in a period in which it is becoming more and more a matter of defense and retreat? A tyrannical collectivism denies man's essential freedom. But freedom, historical freedom, must be saved if humanity is to be saved. Servitude is dehumanization. What we have tried to show is the way in which freedom can be saved in the coming period. It is a narrow one, not spectacular, but profound.❖

EXISTENTIAL THINKING IN
AMERICAN THEOLOGY

When I spoke the other day about the book[2] of Richard Niebuhr to a colleague—with great enthusiasm on both sides—he asked me to make two statements in my review: Firstly, he asked me to say that Niebuhr's book, although strictly scientific, shows an astonishing amount of almost poetic beauty; and secondly that the book, although popular in style and easy to read, has a tremendous profundity and ranks in the first line of advanced thinking. Since I fully agree with both assertions, especially with the second one, I make them herewith my own.

Niebuhr's book—in order to use a more difficult term than he himself does—is the successful attempt to interpret the idea of revelation in *existential* terms. Existential thinking is confronted in all sections of the book with theoretical thinking. Existential thinking, for instance, interprets history as "our history" while for theoretical thinking history is the "history of things." Revelation can only be understood from an existential point of view, as "revelation for us." Only he who has received revelation as a reality for himself understands what it means and knows its content.

In this way Niebuhr gives expression to a theological and philosophical development foreshadowed by Kant's separation of practical and theoretical reason. It has been carried further by Marx's protest against a theory not linked

---

[2] *The Meaning of Revelation*

to social practice, by Kierkegaard's protest against a theory which is not linked to the ethical situation of the individual, by the attempts of the philosophers of life to understand truth as a function of life—a development which was reinforced in recent years by the theologies and philosophies of existence as represented by Barth and Heidegger.

Niebuhr starts his treatment of revelation by historical relativism, the necessary correlate of revelation. Historical relativism, while destroying the illusion that one's concept can be universal, does not necessarily create scepticism:— "one who understands how all his experience is historically mediated must not believe that nothing is mediated through history" (p. 18). Historical reason is not the negation of reason, but the only way in which reason can work. Historic truth is not the denial of truth, but the actuality of truth for man. In this sense revelation is "historic faith" and theology has its home in the Church as Schleiermacher and Ritschl have seen. "Theology of revelation" is existential theology, meaningful only for those who share the life of the Church.

Historical relativism is associated with religious relativism, the insight namely "that one can speak and think significantly about God only from the point of view of faith in him" (p. 23). But this does not mean, as religious liberalism has assumed, that faith can take the place of God. If *religion* becomes the "enhancer of life—the redeemer of man from evil, the builder of the beloved community" (p. 28), then God disappears, even if the idea of God is maintained. For he becomes a necessary (or even a not necessary) auxiliary and instrument. But this is not an unavoidable consequence of an existential doctrine of God. It is an aberration of religious relativism, as scepticism is an aberration of historical relativism.

The existential attitude towards history is clearly performed in the method of the Biblical writers, who have not merely formulated some general doctrines about God, man and the moral law but who speak of events they have seen and heard of. And they speak of them as participants in the same history out of which the records came. Therefore it is obvious "that we cannot know a historical Jesus save as we look through the history and with the history of the community that loved and worshipped him" (p. 51). In order to make this clearer Niebuhr introduces the difference between "history as lived" and "history as seen." Through a splendid example taken from a highpoint of the American history, the difference between the "history of things" (external history) and "our history" (internal history), becomes evident: In external history "past events are gone and future happenings are not yet. In internal history our time is our duration. What is past is not gone—what is future is not non-existent" (p. 69). In this way the realm is discovered in which revelation is to be found: "Internal history, the story of what happened to us, the living memory of the community" (p. 90). Niebuhr ably shows that this does not exclude, but strongly demands external history. Existential thinking does not deny but postulates theoretical thinking; it is not a second sphere of truth beside the theoretical truth. It is a qualification of it. Therefore existential and theoretical thinking cannot conflict when they rightly understand each other.

In the central chapter of his book, "Reasons of the Heart," Niebuhr develops first the relation between the (wrong) imaginations and the (right) reasons of the heart: "The heart must reason" (p. 108). The interpretation of religion in terms of irrational emotions is entirely mistaken. The contrary is true: "The revelatory moment is revelatory because it is rational, because it makes the understanding of order and meaning in personal life possible" (p. 109). "By revelation in our history, then, we mean that special occasion which provides us with an image by means of which all the occasions of personal and common life become intelligible" (p. 109). The description of the way in which revelation, understood in this way, interprets the past, the present and the future, destroying the wrong imaginations of the heart, is the most beautiful and one of the profoundest chapters of the book. What the author of this review has called the "center of history" is expressed by Niebuhr in the following words: "Through Christ we become immigrants into the empire of God which extends over all the world and learn to remember the history of that empire, that is of men in all times and places, as our history" (p. 116). Revelation in this sense is not the illustration of the "uniformities of divine and human behaviour—though it does that also—but it exhibits a unique, unrepetitive pattern" (p. 127). Historical revelation is unique and universal at the same time.

The last part is called: "The Deity of God." It deals firstly with the nature of the knowledge of God. It is not a knowledge of things in which "the object is a passive and a dead thing" (p. 144), (a "knowledge of control" as I would call it), but it is a knowledge of the knower, presupposing the knowledge of ourselves. "To know a knower is to begin with the activity of the other who knows us or reveals himself to us by his knowing activity. ... Knowledge of other selves must be received and responded to" (p. 145). This is the model of the knowledge of God. Knowledge of God is possible only though this "self-disclosure of the infinite person" which we accept in an act of commitment, not as a belief about the nature of things (p.154).

The question arises how revelation in this sense is related to the moral law and to the whole of human insights in nature and history. The answer in both cases is obvious: Revelation does not give a new law and a new knowledge. But it is "the beginning of a revolutionary understanding and application of the moral law" (p. 172). And it involves "the radical reconstruction of our beliefs, since these always reflect both human provincialism and concern for self with its idols as well as objective knowledge" (p. 172). Revelation nether augments nor removes the moral law and the objective knowledge, but purifies and transforms them from an ultimate point of view. It is illoyal to God, *not* to develop scientific knowledge.

A very important question remains: The relation of revelation to the religious life of mankind, including the philosophical idea of God. Niebuhr answers in the same way in which he has answered the question of the relation of revelation to the moral law and the objective knowledge. "Revelation is not the development and not the elimination of our natural religion; it is the revolution of the religious life"; (p. 190) and: "This conversion and permanent revolution of our human religion through Jesus Christ is what we mean by revelation" (p. 191). Although I fully agree with these formulations I cannot help saying that they must be developed in a system of theology in order to receive a real meaning. They are the expression of a program which must be carried through as the test of the method indicated in them. As they stand they must arouse the question: What happens in this revolution, if neither new laws nor a new knowledge, nor a new religion is created by them? What is the difference between a revolutionary transformation and the positing of something new? And beyond this a very special question must be asked. If revelation is the conversion of human religion, and if—as it is obviously the case—out of this conversion a new religious life grows—which again must be converted—is the pre-Christian religious life itself a result of earlier revelations or not? In the trend of Niebuhr's thought it seems to me an unavoidable consequence that it is. But he does not say so as far as I can see. On the contrary: By calling the religious life of mankind "Natural Religion" he prevents himself from drawing that consequence. Of course: Revelation is always revelation for us. But are we justified in excluding that there is revelation for others that is not revelation for us? We cannot! This does not mean that we can say affirmatively, as liberalism did, that the history of religion *is* history of revelation. But, on the other hand, we cannot deny that there might be revelation *in* it.

This is a book with which I find myself in an agreement, as it rarely happens between theologians of a very different background; a book which is *the* introduction into existential thinking in present American theology. ❖

"FAITH" IN THE JEWISH-CHRISTIAN TRADITION

My task in this article is a double one: (1) to give as much material as possible about the meaning of faith in Prophetism and classical Christianity, and (2) to show the consistency with which the basic religious impulse in the concept of faith has lasted through the different periods of history and has emerged again and again after moralistic or intellectualistic distortions.

It is almost impossible to use the word faith today in Christian teaching and preaching without saying in great length what it does not mean and without stressing that it means just the opposite of "opinion" or a lower degree of certainty, and that daily-life-beliefs have nothing to do with faith. From this point of view this article may have some practical value although it does not contain original research. Faith in the sense of Isaiah, faith namely in God's paradoxical action in history will be needed very soon by every thinking American, as it was needed by Messiah and given to him.

I

THE BASIC CONCEPT OF FAITH IN THE OLD TESTAMENT

The basic relationship of man to God in the Old Testament is awe. Religion is "fear of God," not a fear which makes man flee from God, but the kind of fear which has been called "numinous," an awe that unites horror and fascination. God is, above all, the overwhelming power, different in quality from everything which belongs to the realm of normal experience, transcending any human possibility. Ontological and moral qualities in God are not yet distinguished. Therefore the word for holy, *qadosh*, is not identical with "good" in a moral sense: it points rather to the unapproachable Divine majesty. The "holy" is what produces that numinous fear that man cannot endure. "Who is able to stay near Jahveh this majestic God?" (I Samuel 6:20). Isaiah in his vision (Ch. 6), describes the identity of the holiness and unapproachable majesty of God in classical words. People tremble when they hear the voice of Jahveh. But this trembling, this fear of the holiness of God is, at the same time, the foundation of justice. Without the fear of God there is no guarantee of righteousness. The judges must fear God, otherwise they would not give judgments. The realm of values and the realm of power are united in the holiness of God. It is obvious that on the basis of such an idea of God no identity between God and man in any mystical or ontological sense can be imagined. Biblical religion maintains the distance between God and man, even when mystical elements appear. There is a Christ-mysticism in Paul, but never a God-mysticism. Fear of God remains the basic note of Biblical religion.

The experience of this majestic God and his numinous presence could be called "faith." But if *we* call it so, we must understand that it is not a special psychological act, distinguished from unbelief. It has no theoretical meaning. It is the living in a reality, as real as the life in nature or society. The fool who, according to the psalm, says that there is no God, has no theoretical doubt about the existence of God; but he acts as if there were no God, namely without the fear of God.

The original idea of faith in the Old Testament developed on a quite different basis, namely in connection with the idea of "the covenant." God commands and promises at the same time. Confidence in his promising benevolence becomes an element of the fear of God. The unity of numinous awe and confidence is clearly expressed in Exodus 20:19: "And they said unto Moses: Speak thou with us, and we will hear, but let not God speak with us, lest we die. And Moses said unto the people: Fear not! For God is come to prove you and that his fear may be before you that ye sin not." Those words contain the two elements of the relation between God and man, implied in the idea of "the covenant": "Fear not," that is, Do not flee, have confidence! "His fear may be before you," that is: Don't forget his unapproachable holiness. The feeling of confidence as expressed in the Hebrew word, means finding one's security in something, holding something worthy of confidence, assuming that something is certain. But this confidence contradicts all probabilities, all visible events and calculations based on them. It is "paradoxical" in the strict sense of the Greek word; against opinion. This appears most significantly in the famous word said about Abraham (Genesis 15:6): "He believed in Jahveh, and he reckoned it to him for righteousness." Abraham was confident against all human possibilities, when God told him that he would become a great nation, although he had no heir and his wife was in her old age. Such a faith, hope against hope, acceptance of the paradox, is not only a matter of religion; it is, at the same time, the source of righteousness; it determines all personal and social life.

In Isaiah this idea of faith is related to history. Any non-religious interpretation of the political situation of his time must lead to despair. Clever alliances and shrewd diplomacy will not succeed in saving the nation. Only faith in the transcendent power and paradoxical action of God can give confidence: "If ye will not believe surely ye will not be established." The people must turn away from the earthly powers — which are "flesh," transitory, giving no security and ultimate hope—to God who is "spirit," that is the eternal, meaningful and creative power. Isaiah demands the paradoxical faith in an ultimate meaning of history against all immanent standards of meaning and power. *The transcendent order of God's action reverses the immanent order of human possibilities. The acceptance of and confidence in this transcendent order is faith.* This is the idea of faith in Prophetism and classical Christianity.

In the Second Isaiah a special element is introduced into this basic idea, the demand to "wait for Jahveh," not to become tired, not to doubt, although the empirical situation, the situation of the nation as the "suffering servant" contradicts completely the tremendous promise. These poor remnants in captivity shall become the saving force in world history. This is utterly paradoxical and its acceptance is "faith." In the later development of Judaism the idea of faith became more individualized. In Job the pious individual fights against the rationalistic moralism of his friends in behalf of the inscrutable majesty of God and his paradoxical action. Job sticks to his faith although he is the victim of the action of God in which God reverses the moral standards of ordinary legalism. The same feeling is expressed by the psalmists' belief in the forgiveness of their sins and the final self-manifestation of God in his victory over all enemies. At the end of the development of the Old Testament, the paradox of faith transcends the whole realm of finiteness and from the divine promise to the nation derives the promise to the individual, that he will participate in the final salvation of nation and world. Faith in the resurrection of the martyrs and then of all righteous is not a rational conclusion from the nature of man, but is the acceptance of the transcendent divine order, which turns about the immanent order of finiteness, death and sin, in history as well as in individual life. The development of the idea is consistent throughout the Old Testament.

II

THE DEVELOPMENT OF THE IDEA OF FAITH IN THE NEW TESTAMENT

It is worth noticing that in the picture of Jesus given by the Gospels he does not use the word faith (*pistis*) for himself. For him God's action has not the paradoxical character of an "in spite of" as it has for Isaiah and Job. His will is united with the will of God; his fight is not a fight for faith but for obedience. His natural desires contradict the will of God, because God's will is that he suffer and die. But even in his struggle the unity with God is never disrupted — an observation which alone is sufficient to prove that the Catholic and liberal Protestant doctrines of the "imitation of Christ" or of Jesus have no ground in the Biblical picture of Jesus as the Christ. In contrast with him, his followers need faith. His first word is strictly in line with the prophetic idea of faith: "The time is fulfilled and the Kingdom of God is at hand. Repent ye and believe in the Gospel." Repent ye, that is, change your mind, leave the order of finiteness and sin, and receive the transcendent order which has become present in him who *is* the Kingdom of God. This new order reverses everything: the smallest in this order is greater than the greatest in the other order; sinners are admitted and the righteous excluded. Pagans and children and Samaritans and peasants receive what the privileged descendents of Abraham, the pious and moral people, do not receive. These do not receive it because they reject the attitude of mere receiving, namely, faith; they want to *show* something, their piety, morality, noble birth as members of the selected nation. But faith is the acceptance of a gift which contradicts all human standards and human possibilities. In the Fourth

Gospel Jesus appears as the all-embracing gift, which must be accepted by faith. The resistance of the Jews against him is not due to a theoretical difficulty but is the resistance against the divine order in the name of the order of the "world" which is demonic in its basic structure.

In Paul the general line is still more apparent. Faith is not a theoretical assent but is the acceptance of the paradoxical judgment of God which calls the sinner righteous while he is still sinner. Faith is the acceptance of the divine act which contradicts all Jewish and Greek conceptions of the nature of God's action. The Jews expect "power," the Greeks "wisdom"; but God acts through the weakness and foolishness of the Cross. Again he reverses the human order and establishes his power and his wisdom for those who accept it—in faith. Therefore our reconciliation with God, with the ultimate meaning of life, and consequently with ourselves and the others is not a matter of our striving and running, but rather the acceptance of a gift by which we are made "gracious." Faith is not an emotional act, artificially created by ourselves, and it is not an intellectual act which takes uncertain things for certain; but it is an internal readiness which is given and not produced.

Faith implies the element of trust, but it is not identical with trust. *Pistis* is the state of being convinced. Therefore the element of acceptance in the idea of faith cannot be eliminated. But it is never a doctrine, it is always a reality which is accepted, a divine, paradoxical act. Faith, including conviction and trust, is the adherence to the transcendent order. The eleventh chapter of the Epistle to the Hebrews sums up different elements of the idea of faith. "Now faith is the assurance of things hoped for, a conviction of things not seen." "Things not seen"—this is the transcendent order, to be accepted in faithful conviction; "things hoped for"—this is the paradoxical action of God in the individual life and in history generally to be accepted in faithful trust. The Epistle, showing this in numerous examples, brings to a conclusion the Biblical development of the idea of faith, a development of a surprising consistency from its earliest beginning to its final maturity.

III

DISTORTION AND PRESERVATION OF FAITH IN CHURCH HISTORY

When Christianity spread in the Greek world it had to adapt itself to a strange spiritual atmosphere. The unbroken life of the Biblical tradition did not connect with Greek culture. Here rational thinking prevailed. Knowledge was considered as the main function of the human mind in the form of *gnosis*, even as the saving function. Thus, only a hundred years after the end of the Apostolic period, an apologist could reduce the creed of the Christians to the following points: "They know God as the creator and maker of everything, they have the commands of their Lord Jesus Christ carved in their hearts and safeguard them, they expect the resurrection of the dead and the life of the coming aeon" (Aristides 15:30). Faith is replaced by the intellectual acceptance of different elements of a doctrine, on the one hand, by moral subjection to a new law, on the other hand. Of course, Christians in reality had more than these words indicate, but they had lost the paradoxical power of the Biblical idea of faith. This becomes evident in a man like Tertullian who emphasizes again the paradox: "The Son of God has died; it is credible because it is inadequate. And the buried has resurrected; it is certain because it is impossible." This is the intellectual form of the paradox: Christianity has become a logical instead of a real paradox. It negates reason in a rational form. This Tertullian type of interpreting faith has appeared again and again in Church history up to our time. Neo-supranaturalism largely uses this method which claims to be Biblical but is not. And because it is not Biblical it cannot escape a heteronomous subjection to Bible or Church. Tertullian says: "To know nothing against the rule of faith is knowing everything." Neo-supranaturalism could subscribe to this sentence after having changed "rule of faith" into "Biblical word." But this is simply not Biblical.

If the authority of faith is derived from something outside of itself the realm of autonomous thinking comes in to stand beside faith,—according to the Greek mind, above it. So in Clement and the school of Alexandria, faith is acceptance of the authoritative tradition. Beyond faith *gnosis* interprets tradition "according to the true philosophy." Faith is the acceptance of a philosophy, to be interpreted by reason. In Augustine two elements in faith are distinguished: first the acceptance of the doctrine on the basis of the authority of the Church. Without this authority, Augustine declares he would not have believed the Gospel. From this must be distinguished the understanding faith, in *intelligere* which is identical with the "believing in the truth itself." In the same way he distinguished between "believing Christ" and "believing in Christ," the former pointing to the subjection to Christ as authority, the latter to the mystical adherence to Christ as living reality. But the former precedes: "Believe in order to understand!" With the demand of "faith in the truth itself" Augustine renews (although with a more mystical emphasis) a basic element of the Biblical idea of faith. But he maintains, at the same time, the authoritarian element of Catholicism.

The medieval schools follow the Augustinian lead with respect to the supranatural character of the real "formed" faith (*fides formata*), as they call it. For the earlier Franciscans faith in this higher sense is an immediate unity with the ultimate truth, that is with God. It is a tasting and touching of the transcendent reality, as immediate and as certain as any sense experience. It is felt as sweetness and joy. From this "formed faith" must be distinguished the "unformed" faith (*fides informis*). It is a psychological reaction to the hearing of the word or to rational arguments. It is a preparation for the real faith, namely to the mystical adherence which implies love.

In Thomas Aquinas intellect becomes the real organ of faith: "The act of faith essentially consists in knowledge and its perfection." But perfect knowledge is dependent on two conditions. The supranatural objects cannot be reached by the intellect alone. The intellect must be moved by the will to accept them—with the assistance of grace. But—this is the second condition—perfect, namely explicit, faith can be reached only by a few learned people. The masses, even of the lower clergy, can reach implicit faith only. They believe what the Church believes, and that is enough. The supranatural habit which is necessary for a faith, becomes more and more a subconscious inclination to believe the contents of the Bible and its ecclesiastical interpretation. Here we have all the elements which in our times have made the Biblical idea of faith entirely incomprehensible: Subconscious inclinations, produced by the Christian tradition, intellectual acts which do not lead very far and which are completed by the will to believe what the authorities say. In the Middle Ages this was still carried by the reality of a religious substance in which everybody lived as in a natural atmosphere. Therefore the sceptical elements implied in the given description did not become dangerous until the rise of autonomous thinking. But in modern humanism the description of faith as a combination of a traditional disposition, a lower degree of intellectual conviction and a supporting act of will has led to the disruption of these three elements and the complete loss of the Christian idea of faith.

IV

THE REDISCOVERY OF THE BIBLICAL IDEA
OF FAITH BY THE REFORMERS

Luther rediscovered faith as the center of religion. Faith is rooted in the totality of our person. It moves our personal center towards God. Faith is the revolutionary act in which God gives himself to us, person to person, and in which we have nothing to do, but everything to receive. Believing is not an act of imperfect thinking, completed by an act of will, but believing is receiving something before any act of intellect or will. And faith is not a subconscious, supranatural habit, but it is a living, restless power. The right faith is a strong, powerful, and active thing: nothing is impossible to it, it does not rest and stop. It makes the personality, not conversely: "Faith creates the person, the person creates the works, not the works the person" — whether they be sacramental, or moral or intellectual works. They are consequences, not conditions, of faith. Faith is adherence to God and his promises. Faith is religion itself. Therefore the theology of the Reformers has no place for the "implicit faith." Community with God either exists or does not exist. Since it is a personal relationship it can not be divided into doctrinal pieces.

The rediscovery of the personal character of faith entails the rediscovery of its paradoxical character. For Luther, more than anybody else since Isaiah and Paul, God's acting has a paradoxical character. This is manifest — and at the same time hidden — in the nature of God's revelation in Christ. "He who believes in Christ must recognize wealth under poverty, honor under blame, joy under sadness, life under death." This is the way God acts wherever he acts. Therefore, the believer is "crazy and a fool" for ordinary reason. It is difficult to believe that the powerful God who is acting, in nature and history, in the most astonishing, creative and at the same time destructive way, is in his innermost heart the God of love; the God who makes himself small and powerless in Christ; or, in another expression of the idea, who forgives our sins. Righteousness, impossible in the human order and by human endeavor comes to us, if we accept it—that is, by faith. There is only *one* sin: the refusal to accept God when he gives himself to us, disregarding our guilt and despair, our immorality and error. Unbelief is the sinfulness in all sins because it is the negation of the transcendent order which reverses, judges and saves the order of finiteness and sin and death.

In Calvin the emphasis on the objectivity of the content of faith is stronger than in Luther, so that he can say: "Faith is certain and sure knowledge of the divine mercy towards me." At the same time, his Biblicism and his systematic interest reduce, to a certain extent, the enthusiasm in Luther's words about faith to more of a doctrinal soberness. Nevertheless the idea is the same. He especially attacks "implicit faith" as the complete destruction of a living, personal faith. He stresses the eschatological character of faith, the element of hope, and he knows as much as Luther about its paradoxical character: "The spirit of God shows us hidden things of which no sense experience is possible."

"We are promised eternal life—we the dead. We are told of resurrection surrounded by decay. We are called righteous—and sin dwells within us. We hear that we are blessed—and in the meantime we are oppressed by infinite misery. We are promised abundance of goods—we are rich only in hunger and thirst. God cries that he will be with us soon—but he seems to be deaf to our crying." In these words the whole development of the Christian idea of faith is summed up once again. Faith is the acceptance of the transcendent order which contradicts the order to which we belong. This is true of our personal life, of history and of the world as a whole. Faith is the triumphant paradox of life. ❖

KIERKEGAARD IN ENGLISH

I

Walter Lowrie has added to his translation of Kierkegaard's *Fear and Trembling* an account of "how Kierkegaard got into English." This report brings the good news that practically all important works of the Danish thinker can be read in English—now, one hundred years after their appearance. While Kierkegaard himself remained unknown to the English speaking world for a century, his opponent, the Danish Bishop Martensen, was translated during his lifetime. This is grotesque; however— it is tragic that Anglo-Saxon thinking was practically excluded from the tremendous impulses which Continental theology and philosophy have received for at least a generation from the German translation of Kierkegaard's works. But this situation has now come to an end. Thanks to the restless activities of Walter Lowrie—which he himself describes with much humor in his report—thanks to the help he has received from the late Professor David F. Swenson and now from Mrs. Swenson, thanks to Mr. Alexander Dru who has selected and translated *The Journals of Kierkegaard*, and to Professor Eduard Geismar, the author of the important *Lectures on the Religious Thought of Søren Kierkegaard*, thanks to the three publishing houses which have published by far the greatest part of the translations, the Oxford University Press, the Princeton University Press, the Augsburg Publishing House, thanks to the financial support of the American-Scandinavian Foundation, and thanks again--and never enough--to Walter Lowrie, who has taken upon himself not only the greatest amount of translation work but also the writing of his introductory book *Kierkegaard* — thanks to all of them the English speaking public has become able to read *Kierkegaard*. Thanks to them the American professor of theology can announce seminars about Kierkegaard, the minister can find more ideas for sermons than he can use even in a long lifetime, the religious layman can read a Christian thinker who proclaims that he is not a Christian but that he wants to show how difficult it is to become a Christian. American religion and theology have received a gift which hardly can be overestimated. And so has philosophy. The main source of what is called today "philosophy of existence" has become accessible for those American philosophers who did not want to use the German translation of Kierkegaard, many of them because that translation (by Schrempff) was rather subjective. This danger — rooted in the subjective character of Kierkegaard's style--seems to have been avoided in the English translation. Even the German student of Kierkegaard who cannot read Danish will have to consult the English translation.

The immediate occasion of this article is the appearance of the translation of Kierkegaard's largest work: *Concluding Unscientific Postscript* translated from the Danish by David F. Swenson, Professor of Philosophy at the University of Minnesota, completed after his death and provided with introduction and notes by Walter Lowrie, and published by the Princeton University Press for the American-Scandinavian Foundation, 1941. The book first appeared in February 1846 as a postscript to *Philosophical Fragments*, published in June 1844 and translated by Swenson for the American-Scandinavian Foundation, 1936. These two books, the *Fragments* and the *Postscript* to them represent the most systematic and philosophical works of Kierkegaard. They contain a continuous attack upon Hegel's system and upon his method of treating Christianity. In the course of this discussion Kierkegaard's idea of "existential thinking" becomes more and more apparent and at the same time its importance for theology and philosophy is emphasized. Kierkegaard gives a new meaning to the concept of "existence," not through a systematic development but through an ever repeated attack upon different forms of non-existential thinking. The result of each of these attacks is an enrichment of the idea of the "existential." But Kierkegaard not only attacks. He also points to his predecessors, the greatest of whom is Socrates; another, the half-forgotten classical representative of German Enlightenment, Lessing. The chapters on these two men belong to the most impressive Kierkegaard has written.

II

Before giving some hints about the meaning of "existential thinking" in Kierkegaard I must express a warning: You cannot get anything out of Kierkegaard without reading him in his own works, without subjecting yourself to the power and aggressiveness of his style. Thinking and speaking are united in him as in very few philosophers before or after him. Kierkegaard was afraid that his ideas some time would be transformed into a paragraph in a "history of philosophy." He knew that in such an excerpt of his thoughts nothing of their real meaning would be left; on the contrary, everything for which he stood would be turned into its opposite. His thinking which wanted to grasp individuals in their "existential situation" would become a doctrine amongst other doctrines. Perhaps it is providential that Kierkegaard actually did not appear for decades in the philosophical textbooks, so that his challenging power was preserved for the moment when his time had arrived.

According to Kierkegaard all his books deal with one question: How may I participate in the eternal happiness promised by Christianity— or in other words, how can I become a Christian? This question seems to be a merely practical one without relationship to a philosophical or theological method. But actually it has given rise to a powerful attack on the ordinary ways of modern thinking and has created a methodical discussion in the midst of which we are living. The existential thinker is the thinker who is interested in his subject infinitely, personally, and passionately, while the non-existential thinker, scientist, historian, or speculative philosopher tries to cultivate an attitude of objectivity and disinterestedness. Kierkegaard does not challenge the solid scholar who works for the enlargement of our objective knowledge with scientific detachment and self-sacrifice. But he denies that such an enterprise can be of more than finite interest. The eternal happiness is not at stake, as it is at stake when the question of Christianity is asked. Consequently, the attitude of the thinking individual in the case of Christianity cannot be that of speculative contemplation as it is in Hegel's system, nor can it be one of historical curiosity which never leads beyond an approximate certainty. If the eternal happiness of the individual is at stake the only possible attitude is an infinite, personal, passionate interest which never can be satisfied with historical probabilities or metaphysical possibilities. The objective thinker pretends to be above the sphere of decision; but as a living individual he is in it; and if he tries to forget his situation and resolves the existential question of his eternal destiny into a speculative question about the meaning of world history and the nature of God and the immortality of the soul, he becomes "comical." The actual existing subjective thinker constantly reproduces this existential situation in his thoughts, and translates all his thinking into terms of process. In connection with Socrates as existential thinker Kierkegaard says: "Existence is the child that is born of the infinite and the finite, the eternal and the temporal—and is therefore a constant striving. This was

Socrates's meaning." Therefore Socrates did not give results, no system, no scientific achievements. But through his irony he was and still is one of the most disquieting, most dialectical figures in spiritual history. In the same line lies the refusal of Lessing to accept the full truth, even if God would offer it to him. For, the full truth, the final system, is only for God. System and finality correspond to one another, but existence is precisely the opposite of finality—and men are in existence, between finiteness and infinity. This situation is called by Kierkegaard the ethical situation, the situation of decision, of subjective concern, of infinite, passionate interest. In his earlier book *Either-Or* he distinguishes it from the esthetic realm, the realm of contemplation and possible detachment. He shows the necessary breakdown of the esthetic as a sphere and challenges the system which has no place for ethics, because it avoids the element of subjectivity and decision. This leads to the famous definition of truth: "An objective uncertainty held fast in an appropriation-process of the most passionate inwardness is the truth, the highest truth attainable for an existing individual." Kierkegaard says a few sentences later that this is an equivalent expression for faith.

III

Innumerable consequences following from this fundamental distinction of objective and existential truth are developed by Kierkegaard in the *Postscript* as well as in his other books and in his religious discourses. The question I want to raise at the end of this short review is: Has this distinction and all that has been and may be derived from it a significance for the present theological and philosophical situation in this country? Kierkegaard wrote against Hegel in a special moment of the development of German philosophy. He belongs to a whole group of thinkers who emphasized man's existential situation against Hegel's idealistic *Rationalismus*. Schelling in his last period was one of them and there are many similarities and even identities between Schelling's and Kierkegaard's attack on Hegel's philosophy of mere possibilities (negative philosophy). Feuerbach's materialism is another expression of the emphasis on existence—a word used by him against Hegel. Schopenhauer's analysis of the individual life process anticipates the interpretation of existence as life in the later "philosophy of life." Marx, in his earlier writings, uses formulations in his attack on Hegel's non-existential system which remind us of Kierkegaard's terminology, only transferred from the inwardness of the individual to the outwardness of the social process. Are all these ideas merely German quarrels, Continental provincialisms, or is something more involved in them? History has already given the answer: The ideas of these revolutionary, anti-Hegelian philosophers of existence have determined in connection with the social-economic process the destiny of all nations and churches in the Twentieth Century. They have world-historical significance. This refers also to Kierkegaard.

Although the empiricistic and positivistic trend of the Anglo-Saxon mind has prevented the domination of a speculative system, the question of existential and objective truth is by no means solved by it. American theology still believes that the approximative historical truth can become the basis of the faith in Christ as our ultimate concern and does not realize the contradiction involved in this attempt. It still confuses systems of ethical abstractions or metaphysical possibilities with the ethical and religious existence of the individual before God. It has not yet accepted existential materialism as the great corrective to the Christian-bourgeois idealism. And contemporary philosophy has either—as logical positivism—extinguished every trace of existential passion and interest within philosophical thought—or it has—as metaphysical naturalism—removed the individual "existenting" man who stands between the infinite and the finite and never can be understood as a part of the whole of natural objectivity. And even pragmatism which is more closely related to existential thinking than the two other groups — because it acknowledges the fragmentary and dynamic character of truth — has surrendered itself as "instrumentalism" to the objective process of nature and society, producing means for ends which are finite and, consequently, not a matter of infinite, passionate concern.

So theology as well as philosophy needs the Kierkegaardian corrective — he gives correctives, not results or methods. The younger generation is longing for a philosophy in which an ultimate meaning of life is admitted — at least as a Socratic problem. Kierkegaard can become a guide in this direction. He can be studied now, in comfortable translations and with the uncomfortable seriousness demanded by an existential thinker.❖

VERTICAL AND HORIZONTAL THINKING

The first statement I want to make about the future of religion is the expression of a profound discomfort about the phrase "the future of religion." For this phrase conveys the idea of a product of history which may or may not have a future, whose future may be shorter or longer, which may be destroyed or merged with something else and disappear in one way or another. Such a view is logically possible, as it is logically possible to look at a man as a stimulus-response mechanism and to treat him accordingly. But the man will raise a furious protest; he will denounce this view as a denial of his human nature, of his dignity as a person. In the same way those who identify themselves with religion consider the phrase "the future of religion" as an implicit denial of its true nature, of its transcending of the modes of time.

Religion as a living experience does not ask the question of its own future. It is only interested in its content, the eternal and our relation to it. Religion cannot imagine any past or future in which man has lived or will live without an ultimate concern, i.e., without religion. Man is that being which by his very nature is ultimately concerned and therefore essentially religious. He may not accept this situation; he may fight against it. He may try to escape the shaking experience of being grasped by an ultimate concern. He may express the ultimate in mythical, theological, philosophical, poetic, political, or any other terms. He may avoid "religious symbols" in the narrower, traditional sense of the word. But he cannot avoid religion in the larger, more profound and more universal sense. Religion lasts as long as man lasts. It cannot disappear in human history because a history without religion is not *human* history, which is a history in which ultimate concerns are at stake.

This is the first reaction of religion to the question of its own future. If this reaction has been expressed religion can accept the question of its future development. Indeed, religion itself asks this question, whenever a religious interpretation of history is attempted, or the contemporary situation is religiously analyzed, or the theoretical and practical needs of the Church are discussed. Without some anticipation of the future no acting in the present is possible.

The relation between the temporal and the eternal takes on two basic forms, the "vertical" and the "horizontal" one. Both belong to every religion. But it makes a great difference whether a religion emphasizes the vertical or the horizontal element. It is the thesis of this article that religion (in the sense of "ultimate concern") will return towards the "vertical" element after it has been horizontalized in the preceding period.

Vertical and horizontal are spatial metaphors for qualities of our religious experience. "Vertical" points to the eternal in its presence as the ground of our being and the ultimate meaning of our lives. It points to our ability to elevate ourselves over the inescapable anxiety of finitude and over the destructive despair of guilt, in our personal and social existence. The religious cult, including prayer and meditation, the aesthetic intuition and the philosophical *eros*, mystical union and the "quiet of the soul" in face of the vicissitudes of existence, are expressions of the vertical element in religion. "Horizontal," on the other hand, points to the transforming power of the eternal whenever it manifests itself. "Horizontal" is the prophetic fight for social justice and personal righteousness, the struggle against the structures of evil in our souls and our communities, the work for the formation of men and the world. Sacred and secular ethics, education and politics, healing and the control of nature are expressions of the horizontal element in religion. Wherever an ultimate concern expresses itself, both elements — the vertical and the horizontal — do appear. For we are ultimately concerned about what has ultimate being, and, consequently, is the ultimate good for those who participate in being. What is and what ought to be are united in the ground of all being. A religion which relates itself to the "ultimate" in terms of "being" only results in a world-defying, static mysticism, without ethical dynamics and without a world-transforming will and power. A religion which relates itself to the "ultimate" in terms of "ought to be" only results in a world-controlling technical activism, without a spiritual substance and a world-transcending will and power.

The five hundred years of Western civilization which we usually call the modern period — ending in the first half of the twentieth century — are characterized by man's largely successful attempt to gain the control over nature and society through rational analysis and construction. The more man dedicated himself to this attempt and the more actual control he gained, the more he lost the vertical element in his interpretation of life; he moved horizontally from one conquest of reality to the other. The ultimate concern of man expressed itself in terms of scientific and technical progress, of moral imperatives, educational norms, and social ideals. The eternal became the background of man's horizontal activities; God was degraded to a "boundary-concept" and removed from the realm of real existence. The ultimate, that which gives meaning to life, is ahead and not above. This was a great and courageous attempt, especially in the fighting period of the modern mind. Prophetic wrath rings in the passionate words of Voltaire and Marx against the demonic distortion of the established churches, who used the vertical element in religion for the conservation of social injustice and tyrannical power, who used the eternal as a brake against the progress of the temporal, who identified the vertical element with conservatism and reaction. In this situation the horizontal protest was not only justified, but necessary for religion itself; it was a religious protest though it often appeared in antireligious terms. It was prophetic, even when it attacked the belief of the churches.

But the prophetic spirit disappeared from the secular mind when the victory was won. It was replaced by a self-complacent immanentism which produces means without ultimate ends, which sets purposes without an ultimate meaning, which has innumerable concerns without an ultimate concern. The expulsion of the vertical element (though historically understandable) deprived the horizontal element of its depth and its spiritual foundation. An atmosphere of unconquerable anxiety, a feeling of meaninglessness, of cynicism about principles and ideals, a despair of the future developed. Often this was covered by a normalized, conformistic existence in routine work and routine pleasure; sometimes it was alleviated by remnants of the optimistic expectations of the past. But it could not be removed any more; it became more and more typical for individuals and masses. The fact that the smashing victory of the Allied Nations and the discovery of the atomic power have not created anything like the enthusiastic hopes of the years after the first World War, but just the opposite, shows the change of the spiritual climate during the last twenty-five years. A tragic feeling about the limits of man's spiritual power—in contrast to his almost unlimited technical power—has spread all over the Western world. The transformation of our existence has ceased to be our ultimate concern and is replaced by the foundation of our existence as the content of our real concern: the pendulum has started swinging back to the vertical element in religion.

Not everything, of course, which seems to prove this movement is a real proof. The fact that the immediate presence of death for millions of people during the war has turned their minds towards the eternal does not necessarily mean a change of the basic trends in religion and culture. More significant may be the increasing influence of the Christian churches on the social and political life of the nations, as in the case of the churches of resistance in Europe, of Roman Catholicism, especially in the United States, and even (though with great restrictions) of the reestablishment of the Orthodox church in Russia. But these events could be explained either in terms of the natural reaction which follows revolutionary catastrophes, or in terms of political expediency. They do not give a clear evidence of a religious trend towards verticalism. Neither does the increase in enthusiastic groups which try to return to old mystical traditions. Things like that have always happened in periods of great insecurity and deep-rooted anxiety.

But there are genuine symptoms which give evidence that a trend towards a more vertical expression of our ultimate concern does exist in all realms of life. Much could and should be said about these symptoms and their significance for the understanding of our time. Here I can only point to them.

The vertical element in religion appears in two main types, the mystical type and the faith type. Although they do not exclude each other they must be distinguished. Both of them have reappeared — long before the world wars — with new power and meaning. Theology as well as philosophy of religion have rediscovered the meaning of the mystical experience, partly in connection with a deeper understanding of the Asiatic religions. It has become obvious that mysticism is not darkness and irrational emotion, but that it is a special way of looking at world and soul, which has its own right and its own perfection. Faith as a possible and meaningful attitude has been rediscovered by the prophetic-revolutionary movements of our period as well as by recent interpretations of religion by "Existential" philosophers and radical Protestants. It has become obvious that faith is not the belief in something which has a low degree of evidence but that faith is the state of being grasped by the eternal when it breaks into the temporal, reversing the expected course of things.

The mystical and the faith experience belong to the vertical element in religion. In correlation with them a new understanding of man has emerged. It has become visible that man is largely dependent on unconscious, individual and collective forces of an ambiguous character, that his conscious decisions have roots in preconscious levels, that he is not free for good and evil, but dependent on universal structures of evil and good for which he is the battlefield. It is not only theology but even more depth-psychology and sociology which have opened our eyes to this predicament of man. They have shown the tragic structures in human existence which refute any kind of utopianism, progressivistic as well as revolutionary. There is no doubt that the new emphasis on the vertical element in religion is very much strengthened by such a self-interpretation of man.

Symptomatic of the same trend are some changes in the doctrine of the Church. Its nature is not so much understood in terms of its purpose—the horizontal line—as in terms of its foundation—the vertical line. It has become obvious that receiving (the eternal) must precede acting (the temporal). Liturgical forms in Protestantism, as well as in Catholicism, are expressions of this feeling. The "Ecumenical" movement tries to find the common principles on which all activity in all Christian churches must be based. The question of the foundation begins to over-shadow the questions of operation.

The problem of the future of religion is not the problem of its relation to science, as it was in the "modern period" which also in this respect has come to an end with the beginning of this century. Historical criticism, natural sciences and recent psychology have been accepted without restriction by the predominant forces in Protestant theology. The sciences, on the other hand, have learned to distinguish their prescientific presuppositions and philosophical visions from their scientific insights. Both sides have recognized that the symbols in which our religion, i.e., our ultimate concern, expresses itself do not lie on the same level of statements about the existence or non-existence of beings or a highest being. The religion of the future will be free from the more and more sterile conflict between "faith and knowledge."

The pendulum is swinging back to the vertical element in religion, and the danger is that it will swing too far. That this may happen is the justified fear of many liberal Protestants and Humanists. They are afraid that Protestantism as well as humanism may disappear in this process of "verticalization." They certainly will disappear if their leaders do not understand the longing of the man of today for the eternal, from which he has been more and more cut off by the exclusive emphasis on the transformation of the temporal. The future of religion is dependent on a new, creative union of its vertical and its horizontal element.❖

REDEMPTION IN COSMIC AND
SOCIAL HISTORY

I

This paper is the *beginning*, not the end, of an investigation which seems to me of great importance to the present theological situation. There is a group of central Christian concepts which, in Protestantism, with some remarkable exceptions (especially in modern Protestantism), have lost much of their original power. To this group belong, besides others, redemption, regeneration, and the most embracing and most basic of these concepts, salvation. All of them are predominantly, and often exclusively, understood as describing the religious situation of the individual, his needs, and the fulfillment of these needs by the Christian message. In this way these concepts are deprived of their fuller meaning, namely, their cosmic significance and their relation to nature, mankind, and history. If we look at their interpretation in former periods of church history and at their meaning in the Bible, we find that, for instance, salvation is primarily a cosmic event and that the individual is an object of salvation only insofar as he is called to participate subjectively in the objective and universally valid salvation. The philological evidence for this statement has become the stronger the more the biblical scholars have used the overwhelming material provided by the history of religion for the interpretation of the early Christian terminology. This refers especially to the Hellenistic religions and their Asiatic and Greek sources. Philological investigation, though not equipped to answer by itself theological questions, can reveal the original, often very profound and often almost forgotten, meaning of basic religious terms. Following this method, I was drawn into an immense body of material, each aspect of which is as fascinating as it is revealing of man's religious existence and the connotations of many New Testament expressions. An infinitely small part of the material elaborated by philologists and historians could be studied and an even smaller part of it could be used for this paper.

But it might be asked, is the method sound? Have these materials digged out of the sand covering past cultures (physically and spiritually) any real meaning for us? Three answers may be given to this question: First, the New Testament is the classical document of the message of Jesus as the Christ, and, consequently, every way to understand its genuine meaning must be used by theology. Second, Christianity could not have used the most important concepts of post-biblical Judaism and Hellenistic syncretism without receiving, though transforming, their content. Third, the basic concepts of the history of religion everywhere have some fundamental elements in common. They are, as C. G. Jung has called them, archetypes (after Augustine's circumscription of Plato's "ideas").

It is useful to consider this latter point for a moment. Jung says: "The history of the development of Protestantism is one of chronic iconoclasm. We all know how the alarming impoverishment of symbolism that is now the condition of our life came about. The power of the Church has gone with that loss of symbolism."[3] The de-symbolized world of the Protestant has produced first an unhealthy sentimentality

---

[3] *The Integration of the Personality* (New York, Toronto: Farrar & Rhinehart, 1939), p. 61.

and then a sharpening of the moral conflict, leading logically, because of its unbearableness, to Nietzsche's "beyond good and evil."[4] Jung recommends the way into the collective unconscious, where the archetypes grow. It seems to me that the task of Protestant theology today is to acknowledge the situation as described by Jung and to reinterpret the lost symbols in such a way that their archetypal character becomes transparent again and their Christian transformation meaningful on the ground of their universal signification.

The following is an attempt to carry through this method, in a very tentative way, with the interdependent concepts of salvation, redemption, and regeneration, each of which, originally, stands for infinitely more than the average Christianity of today realizes and, perhaps, than any of us is able to receive existentially.

II

Salvation, redemption, and regeneration are eschatological concepts. They point to something which contradicts the present stage of the world and everything within it. Cosmical eschatology creates most of the symbols through which those concepts are interpreted. This makes it imperative to explain the method in which eschatology is understood in their reinterpretation. I understand it in the sense of a sentence from my book, *The Interpretation of History*, that nothing is in the *eschaton* which is not in history. This means that the transcendent symbols of eschatological imagination are prolongations into the absolute of realities appearing in history. These prolongations indicate that there is only fragmentary and anticipatory fulfillment on the plane of history, and, on the other hand, that the transhistorical is

---

[4] *ibid.*, p. 79.

not a world beside this world, but is its eternal unity and totality without the ambiguities of temporal existence. In this sense the eschatological symbols of salvation, redemption, and regeneration must be understood. They point to fragmentary and anticipatory realities in time and space, and, at the same time, to the transtemporal meaning of these realities. This method of dealing with eschatology protects against an immanentist utopian interpretation of history. Salvation, including redemption and regeneration, consequently must be considered as the saving power in time and space and, at the same time, as the transcendent union of the fragmentary elements of salvation beyond time and space. Healing, for instance, has, from this point of view, an immanent as well as a transcendent meaning; and so all the other symbols of salvation. In this way history as well as eschatology can be taken seriously.

III

The words *Sōtēr* in Greek, *salvator* in Latin, *Heiland* in German are derived from *saos, salvus, heil,* the latter contained in the English "healing." *Sōtēria,* salvation, is basically "healing." Asclepius, the God of medicine, appears very early amongst the *"theoi-sōtēres,"* the saviour-gods, and reappears even more significantly in the later Hermetic mysteries of salvation. In the apocalypse of Baruch it is said about the new eon that "health shall descend and sickness shall be removed" (p. 73). Jesus is, especially in Mark, to a large extent the healer. In his answer to John the Baptist he points to his healing power as the proof that the new eon has appeared. While men like Empedocles and Paracelsus were priests and physicians at the same time and were praised as saviours for this reason, in our period the connection between salvation and health is almost forgotten.

It seems that we are on the way to rediscover some of these implications of the idea of salvation. The connection of guilt, mental disease, and bodily sickness as we find it in the evangelical reports (cf. Matt. 12 and Mark 2) is today acknowledged by the beginning cooperation of pastoral counseling, analytic psycho-therapy and medicine. The English translation of *"sekōken se"* (Matt. 9, 22) is: "made thee whole," indicating that sickness is disruption, disintegration, falling asunder, while *sōtēria,* salvation, is the reëstablishment of unity, integration, wholeness. Recent Gestalt-psychology and Gestalt-medicine have introduced the concept of wholeness as the ultimate therapeutic principle. It includes not only a balanced state of the body and a centered state of the mind, but also the unity of these two sides of human nature.

Religiously speaking we must say that healing power in the sense of "making whole" is saving power and has cosmic significance. It is the fragmentary anticipation of the "New Being" (see below) in a special section of life. This is the religious glory of medicine.

IV

Not only were the healers of the body and mind called *sōtēres* but also the healers of the body politic — those who create and preserve its wholeness through strength, laws, and order. The Greek *diadochs* and the Roman rulers were called saviours, the Ptolemeans even *theoi-sōtēres* (god-saviours). About Augustus it is said (Priene inscription): "Providence has filled this man for the salvation of the people with such gifts that he is sent as saviour. He shall bring to an end all struggle." The old Jewish Messiah is an example of this saviour-king idea. He too is called "sōtēr." He conquers the enemies who destroy the political existence of Israel and he establishes peace and justice within the nation. The saviour is a predominantly social figure in all periods of Israelitic and Jewish eschatology. He remains a social figure in the apocalyptic visions where he conquers the demonic forces; he is the judge and the universal king of peace, excluding all warlike attitudes and transforming the swords into plows. Even when the social realm is transcended, social symbols are used for the cosmic order. Isis is called saviour because she brought order to men *and* to stars, and Zoroaster calls himself the "healer of life" which has been brought into disorder by the demonic devas.

The social implication of the idea of salvation has been strongly, though without final success, suppressed by the churches. The idea of salvation has been spiritualized and individualized by them. Chiliasm has been interpreted away, most significantly by Augustine. Lutheranism, not Luther himself, has emphasized almost exclusively individual salvation. The earth will be destroyed, not transformed, in the end-catastrophe (differently some Calvinists). Against the conservative-individualistic understanding of salvation in the churches, sectarian movements have preserved the social element of the idea of salvation. (Note the development from Joachim de Fiore to modern Religious Socialism.) Today it is obvious that the spiritual life of the individual is largely determined by the influences coming early from his family and his social surroundings generally and the economic situation especially. Salvation in a purely spiritual sense is revealed as an ideology which contradicts not only the prophetic and apocalyptic promise of cosmic salvation but also Jesus' blessing of the poor and hungry—not because they shall remain so, but because they shall become satisfied in the new order of things.

V

Healing the body and the social-economic order presupposes the healing of disintegrated nature generally. Salvation includes the peace in nature and the peace between man and nature, wherein the former is dependent often on the latter. There is much material in many religions about the peace in nature, its destruction, and its reestablishment. The peace between the animals in Isaiah 11:6 is well known. It is corroborated by Hosea 2:18, where God declares that "In that day" he will make "a covenant with the beasts of the field." "Covenant" in this and other contexts is the sociomorphic concept of natural law, of the eternal order of nature. This order is broken, in nature as well as in man, and now God breaks it on his side, bringing chaos over nature and history. The consequence is that (Isaiah 24:4) the earth mourns and fadeth away, heaven and earth perish and the world falls asunder. (In the same way, with very similar words, the Indian *Mahabharata* describes the Kaliyuga, the period of complete sinfulness.) Salvation comes from divine saviours who reestablish the "everlasting covenant," the original harmony, the peace in nature and with nature. The wild nature of animals is overcome by a shepherd-king, Orpheus, Poimandres, David, Jesus. In many legends the intimate relation between saints and animals is described. They understand their language and preach to them, for, as Clement says (*Strom.* V, 13) the animals are not excluded from the knowledge of God. The animals who are tamed by the divine shepherd-saviour are often interpreted as the nations who fight with one another and against the divine kingdom. Often they are interpreted as the "animal in us," the wild desires in us which are tamed by the saving power. In both cases the vital basis of human existence is acknowledged, the animal nature of individuals and of nations. Only in a cosmic transformation of animal nature can the peace of the soul and the social peace be expected. The myth of the animal peace is more realistic than a utopianism which expects a human peace without a peace in nature, although nature is *in* man as well as outside of man. The salvation of man and the salvation of nature are interdependent, although with reference to both, in fall and in salvation, the turning power is in man.

This is clearly expressed in two myths which point to the relation between man and nature. The first is the myth of the man from above, the *theos-anthrōpos*, the son of man, who is invisible in the period of disruption, who is born as a child with the new eon, in which he becomes manifest, and reestablishes the universal peace. Related to this is the idea of man as the microcosmos who stands in the center of the cosmic forces, uniting them within himself and called to unite them in the whole of nature by knowledge and control of the cosmic forces. The long, partly dark, partly open history of these ideas runs from its Persian-apocalyptic beginnings through Paul and Irenaeus to Nicolaus Cusanus, and from him in two streams, the one from Boehme to Schelling and the romantic philosophy of nature, the other from the mathematical sciences to the industrial control of nature. On both ways man is considered to be the destroyer as well as the fulfiller of nature. In Nicolaus Cusanus this is expressed, according to the god-man idea, in christological terms; later it is understood in general humanistic terms. Nature shall become adapted to man; this is its salvation, as the second group says. (Marx has emphasized that there is no nature at all except "nature for man," or humanly formed nature.) But obviously the control of man over nature is also destructive for nature in many respects. Man brings not only cultivation (the garden as symbol and reality) but also devastation upon nature (the slaughterhouse, the mechanization of animals, etc.). Therefore, we have the romantic-vitalistic opposition against this way and the demand to rediscover the reality of nature in itself and to heal nature and man by a new immediacy of their relation. Theology should go into this discussion the solution of which has innumerable ethical consequences. Christian theology should interpret the meaning of salvation in nature.

VI

A universal cosmic power which is conquered by the saviour-god is Death. Death is a half-personalized reality. He became controller of nature and men when the paradise was lost in the fall. Of course, everything which comes from dust has to return to dust (Gen. 3). But in the original perfection, in the garden of the gods, fruits of immortality (and other foods of the gods) gave actual (though not ontological) immortality. In the situation of salvation this actual immortality is regained by means of the sacramental food by those who receive it in the right way (Ignatius: *pharmakon athanasias*). But in the period between fall and salvation every creature (except some heroic figures who were transferred into the divine sphere) is subject to the power of death (also personified as the demonic "Thanatos," "Hades"). The opposite of Death is Eternal Life, which is equally an objective power, practically identical with the coming eon or the rule of God. The cosmic objectivity of the Eternal Life is expressed in the verbs with which it is connected. It is inherited, we go into it, we take it in possession, or, as II Enoch 65:10, says: "Every perishable will vanish and there will *be* the Eternal Life." This obviously is not the ontological immortality of the soul. Resurrection is the way in which those who have died before the beginning of the new eon can participate in the Eternal Life. It is not a spiritualization of this idea when in the Fourth Gospel the Eternal life is present and future at the same time. This is merely a consequence of the paradox of all Christian eschatology, the unity of the "already" and the "not yet." Eternal death is in its genuine meaning a merely negative concept, namely, the exclusion from the eon in which the Eternal Life alone is real and death is eradicated. A state of eternal condemnation in an affirmative, ontological sense is not only a contradiction in terms, but a defeat of Eternal Life by Death who retains the power to split the creation endlessly. This is the reason for the doctrine of the "*apokatastasis pantōn*," whose danger on the other hand is the mechanization of creaturely freedom and the weakening of ultimate responsibility.

VII

Salvation is the embracing concept, special elements of which are emphasized in the symbols of redemption and regeneration. Redemption emphasizes the fight against the destructive forces which control this eon and the price which must be paid to overcome them. Death has already appeared as such a power. It belongs to the demonic realm, from which redemption is needed. The character of this realm is determined by the evil principle, which is embodied in figures like Ahriman, Satan, the Anti-Christ. It is a cosmic reality and appears as the negative power in history, man, and nature. In history it appears in the great empires, their idolatrous tyrants and their false prophets and Messiahs. In the individual man it appears as a suprapersonal power by which the person is possessed and split and which makes him say and do things with which he cannot identify himself. In nature it produces all the evils. Its rule is especially manifest at the end of this eon, when the world has become old, deprived of its vital forces and open to all forms of idolatry, sin, crime, hate, and self-destruction. The New Testament is so full of these ideas that quotations are unnecessary. Only two facts may be mentioned. The main criterion for the presence of the Kingdom of God is for Jesus his power over the demons and Satan (Matt. 12:28; John 12:31). And Paul describes the victory of the redeemer over the demonic forces in his most triumphant words (Rom. 8). Man cannot liberate himself from these forces. They must be conquered objectively; then he can participate in the fruits of the redemption subjectively.

The need for an objective and universal redemption preceding human acting and striving has become visible to our period mainly through two groups of experience: Socio-analysis and psycho-analysis. The classical representatives of this development are Marx and Freud. Both influenced the first half of the twentieth century so deeply and have been supported by actual history so fully that it was possible for Religious Socialism to reinterpret the concept of the demonic for a generation which had seen in it only the expression of primitive superstitions. It became more and more impossible to overlook the structures of evil in our individual and social existence—structures which cannot be broken by those who are in their bondage but which can be broken by structures of grace, by redemption.

The cosmic significance of redemption appears on a still deeper level if we look at the figures of the redeemers. In his famous *The Origin of the Israelitic-Jewish Eschatology*, Hugo Gressman has interpreted the original meaning of the Ebed-Jahweh passages as ritual hymns referring to the death and resurrection of a redeemer-god. He compares the Ebed with Adonis, Thammuz, Balder, and similar figures—an explanation according to which the use of Isa. 53, etc., for the interpretation of the death and resurrection of Jesus as the Christ would be basically (archetypally) justified. There is, in any case, a widely acknowledged principle in the religious consciousness of mankind which says that the redeemer-god must participate in the evils from which he liberates so that the redeemed can participate in him. This transfers the process of redemption into the depth of the divine itself. It carries the infinite tension between the finite and the infinite into the "Ground of Being," thus making it universal and valid for the status of Being as such. The end of redemption is the "New Being," cosmically, in nature, man, and history. This is the meaning of regeneration.

An additional remark may complete this consideration. In Deutero-Isaiah the redeeming qualities of the Ebed are partially attributed to Israel. Here the idea arises of a social group whose suffering is redemptive for other groups. In the early church and in sectarian movements similar ideas emerged. The last great example is Marx's doctrine of the redemptive quality of the suffering of the proletariat for social history.

VIII

Palingenesia, regeneration, is first of all an eschatological concept and describes the renovation of the world. "In the regeneration" the son of man will sit on his throne (Matt. 19:28). In Mark and Luke the same is expressed by "in the coming eon." In Acts 3:21, it is identified with "the times of the restitution of everything." Baptism brings regeneration because it brings participation in the death and resurrection of Christ and consequently in the "New Creature." Only lately was the word used for ethical-religious renovation in the personal sense. Here we find — as in all other concepts — the preceding of the objective and universal event followed by personal participation. Perhaps we should call it "the pattern of participation," though not in the ontological sense of Plato.

The feeling of the trans-subjective meaning of regeneration is still alive in the self interpretation of the Renaissance. "Renascimento" is the regeneration of a period, a culture out of the sources of its being. It is a social-religious concept, and not a historical-philological one, as revival of the classics.

The regeneration occurs when the old eon has come to an end and the new eon is born. But before this happens a chaos comparable to the chaos before the first creation will grasp the cosmos, nature, and man. Then, after the universal judgment, the new creation will appear similar to the first one before the fall, but liberated from the demonic threat of sin and death.

In all these symbols it is obvious that regeneration is the appearance of a new creation, of a "new heaven and a new earth." In Christ this "New Being" is already real according to the paradoxical pattern of the Christian eschatology.

The term "New Being," used for a long time by me in my systematic lectures, has received an overwhelming confirmation through this study of the original meaning of the concepts salvation, redemption, and regeneration.

The task is to show how the individual, according to the "pattern of participation," is grasped by the power of the New Being, how he is able to accept the message of it in spite of the paradox of its eschatology, and above all, in spite of the experience of guilt and of continuous sinfulness — this task transcends the limits of this paper. But I am convinced that if the objective and universal side of salvation is understood, it will be possible to develop the subjective side, while the reverse is impossible.

Modern philosophy gives two points of contact for the cosmic idea of salvation and regeneration: The one is the insight provided predominantly by Kant, that "world" is not a big thing or sum of things outside ourselves, but that world is correlated to a Self whose world it is. This idea creates a strong connection between the events in man and cosmos. Our world changes when we are changing and we are not alone dependent in this relation.

And finally, it seems as if modern physics has removed the mechanical determinism from the roots of all physical occurrences, thus creating an openness for the new, the lack of which was a main reason for the estrangement between man and nature and a main impediment to the idea of a cosmic regeneration. ❖

EXISTENTIALISM AND RELIGIOUS SOCIALISM

I

The question how the Religious Socialist movement is related to existential philosophy is meaningful only if Existentialism is taken in the large sense of the word. Today, after the French existentialists have made the movement fashionable and widely discussed, a philosopher like Sartre has become its typical representative. Certainly one is still aware of the fact that Sartre is a pupil of Heidegger, that beside Heidegger stands Jaspers, that both of them are dependent on Kierkegaard, and that beyond this Jaspers is strongly influenced by depth psychology and Heidegger by Nietzsche and Bergson. But one is almost completely unaware of the analogy between Kierkegaard's and Marx's attack on Hegel and of the terminological similarity of their descriptions of the human situation. One is further unaware of the significance of the second period of Romanticism, represented e.g., by the later Schelling and many others, for the development of existential thinking.

These facts establish a much larger concept of Existentialism than the one used at the present time.[*] It is *one* line of thought which runs from the catastrophe of Hegel's system (about 1840) to our day. It has been asked whether this large concept of Existentialism does not embrace too

---

[*] Cf. my article "Existential Philosophy" in the *Journal of the History of Ideas*, January, 1944.

much, consequently losing a significant meaning. To this we answer that not "everything" is called Existentialism, as some critics of the larger concept claim, but the word is applied to the philosophy of a number of people who launched a passionate protest against the prevailing ideas of the nineteenth and early twentieth centuries. The philosophers of the schools went quite different ways. Neo-Kantianism and neo-Hegelianism on the one side, positivism and naturalism on the other side determined the philosophical and theological scene. Existential philosophy is a revolt against "everything," namely, the traditional forms of idealistic and realistic thinking.

Religious Socialism has formulated ideas which express the same revolt. Therefore the question of the relation of the two is not only justified, but it can lead to important insights into the character both of Existentialism and of Religious Socialism.

II

The first point of agreement between Existentialism and Religious Socialism is their interpretation of human existence. The term existence points to a conflict between what man essentially is (and therefore ought to be) and what he actually is. While for Hegel, and for his predecessors and followers as well, man's existence is the necessary and adequate expression of his essence, the existentialist opposition tries to show that existence is the contradiction and disruption of what man essentially is. In Sartre's phrase that man's essence is his existence the anti-Hegelian pole is reached. Here man's essence is reduced to undetermined freedom. No norm, no criterion is left, except the dictum that man is whatever he decides to make himself.

The situation of existence is analyzed by all existential philosophers in terms which can be brought under the heading of finitude and estrangement. "Man is finite" is in existential philosophy not a simple statement; it is a challenge of all forms of idealism in which an identity between the infinite and the finite is presupposed, as e.g., in Hegel. In the existentialist view the finite is divorced from the infinite. The inner awareness of our finitude is anxiety, not the fear of something concrete against which we could fight with courage, but the continuous conscious or unconscious presence of the annihilating power of the threat of non-being. Any attempt to overcome this situation will be frustrated. The finite being will be ruined if he tries to become infinite in being or thinking. Man is subject to want and desire, to suffering and passion. He has objects outside himself and he himself is an object to others. Against the idealistic assertion of the identity between subject and object, between thinking and being, Existentialism shows their separation in existence. Here Sartre's analysis is most valuable. He shows how every man, against his passionate resistance, becomes an object for every other man in every encounter. Existence is the continuous loss of freedom within a continuous struggle for freedom. Existence means being made an object amongst objects, a thing amongst things; it means being estranged from true humanity and trying to resist this destiny desperately and vainly.

At this point the line of Existentialism which comes from Kierkegaard over Heidegger to Sartre reveals its profound relationship with the line which comes from Marx and which has been taken up by Religious Socialism. Marx describes the situation of "becoming an object" in terms of estrangement through the economic and social situation of industrial society. Man becomes a facility, a wave, a quantity of working-power. He becomes dehumanized, divorced and estranged from his true humanity. Socialism is the revolt against this structure of capitalist society. In socialism man's essential being, though distorted and almost lost, revolts against the causes of this loss. The causes are structural, implied in the system itself, and therefore independent of the good or bad will of any social group. Socialism is the fight of man for his creative freedom against the forces of industrial society which transform him into a thing.

It is by far the greatest tragedy of our century that this fight has produced a political system in which man's creative freedom is even more lost than in the economic system over which it has triumphed. Religious Socialism tried to prevent this development of the socialist idea, not only in communism but also in socialism. It tried to stress the existential elements in the thought of the early Marx over against the materialistic *and* idealistic elements in the later Marx and in most of his secular followers. Religious Socialism fully accepted Marx's existential analysis of the human situation, but it rejected those remnants of "bourgeois" thinking in Marx which make man either materialistically a thing amongst things (economic determinism) or idealistically a subject with infinite freedom (political utopianism). Existentialism and Religious Socialism agree that man is neither the first nor will ever be the second, but that he is "finite freedom" falling into and fighting against estrangement from his true being.

III

The human situation, as seen in existential philosophy, implies the finitude and self-estrangement of human thought. The existential philosopher knows that he is bound to the existential situation in his thought as much as in his life. Truth is not something which can be found through detached observation. Both the idealist and the naturalist are challenged by Existentialism because they try to escape the destiny of being finite with respect to truth. The naturalist, of course, emphasizes the approximative character of all knowledge, the possibility of error, and the necessity of continual verification. He seems to be fully aware of the finitude of human thought. But he is not. He does not see that the method of experimental verification can be applied only to a rather abstract level of knowledge, but not to the level of truth that matters for our very existence. If the latter is sought, theoretical detachment must be replaced by existential participation. The passionate subjectivity of which Kierkegaard speaks is the right attitude towards existential truth.

This means also a rejection of the idealistic attempt to escape finitude in thought. Idealism assumes that it is possible to look over the whole of truth from a point where the finite and the infinite are identical. The idealist does not deny that the finitude of the philosopher may produce errors and limited understanding. But like the naturalist he considers this a removable weakness, removable not by a detached-calculating empiricism but by an intuitive-rational penetration into the structure of being. If we compare the two attitudes we can say that the naturalist has more insight into man's existential finitude, in life as well as in thought, while the idealist has a deeper understanding of the need of an existential participation in the truth that concerns us ultimately. But neither of them is fully aware of the consequences of the existential element in his thought.

The concept of the "existential thinker" which is central for all forms of existential philosophy appears in Marx in connection with his doctrine of ideology. According to this analytically and critically powerful doctrine the self-interpretation of human groups, religious as well as secular, is bound to their "being."[*] Their sociological state determines their thinking; they produce interpretations of existence which are capable of supporting their will to power and of preserving their actual power. Ideologies express the particular passions and interests of particular social groups. Truth, therefore, can be found only by a group

[*] Cf. Karl Mannheim's sociology of knowledge in *Ideology and Utopia*.

which is not particular but universal, which represents all groups, the whole of society. This group is, according to Marx, the proletariat, or at least a vanguard of the proletariat (including some non-proletarians who have broken away from their own sociological state).

Religious Socialism accepted the doctrine of ideology, but in contrast to political socialism and communism, it used the critical power of the concept also against itself. It anticipated the rise of a new bureaucratic, authoritarian, and even totalitarian ideology in proletarian socialism. Because they were radically suspicious of ideology in all human groups, including their own, Religious Socialists were less disappointed by the development of the modern revolutionary movements than were the secular adherents who saw ideological distortion only in others and the true ideology only in themselves. Religious Socialism, although realizing in unity with prophetic religion the relation of truth to an extreme boundary situation, cannot identify the general human boundary situation with the extreme position of the proletariat, nor the universal truth with the proletarian truth. It does not deny that in a special situation the proletariat and its interpreters are most significant for existential truth, but it adds that ultimately it is the community of the "New Being," the spiritual (not the empirical) Church, which represents universal truth on an existential basis. This opens the possibility that Religious Socialism might dismiss itself in the name of its determining principle.

IV

There are other points at which comparison between Existentialism and Religious Socialism could be fruitful, e.g., their attitude to time and history. The centrality of time and especially of the future mode in most existentialists, the demand for an existential or concerned interpretation of history, the emphasis on action and on an active participation in history, all this is present in Religious Socialism as well as in most existential philosophers. It is a protest against the reduction of time to the dimension of space, and of history to a collection of facts without existential meaning. It is a part of the common fight against a world in which creative subjectivity is transformed into mechanical objectivity, in which men have been made into things within a world of mere things.

Every judgment about the existentialist movement must see it in the framework of late industrial society. Religious Socialism, looking at this framework, finds itself to a large degree within it — on one of its wings, fighting a desperate battle which might well be lost as all former fights against the dehumanizing nature of our social and cultural system have been in vain. But in this fight truths have been rediscovered, truths about the human situation which cannot be lost even if the revolt of Existentialism in all its forms should be frustrated. ❖

THE PRESENT THEOLOGICAL SITUATION IN THE LIGHT OF THE CONTINENTAL EUROPEAN DEVELOPMENT

I

An American churchman and theologian, returning last fall from a visit to Germany, described the situation of Continental Protestantism in the following statement: Neo-Protestantism is dead in Europe. All groups, whether Lutheran, Reformed, or Barthian, consider the last 200 years of Protestant theology essentially erroneous. The year 1933 finished the period of theological liberalism stemming from Schleiermacher, Ritschl, and Troeltsch.

This statement agrees with my own observations in Germany during the summer of 1948 and with the contents of correspondence since then. It agrees with the impressions of many observers, both inside and outside the European Churches, some of whom are detached, some friendly, others hostile. It corresponds with the contents of the creeds which arose during the Church struggle, and with their official pronouncements. Finally, it agrees with the logic of history in the first half of this century.

II

First, let us look more closely at the development before and during the great struggle of the Continental Churches against Nazism. When the twentieth century began, Harnack's *Das Wesen des Christentums* dominated the theological scene. It was based, firstly, on the thesis, explained in his monumental *History of Dogma*, that dogma in its original sense is a creation of the Greek mind and has come to an end, in principle, in the Reformation, actually, in Pietism and the Enlightenment. It was based, secondly, on almost one hundred and fifty years of historical analysis and criticism of Biblical literature, the results of which Harnack formulated in a classical way. It was based, thirdly, on the theology of the Ritschlian school, which had tried, with the help of Kantian concepts, to mediate between the theological tradition and modern naturalism and historicism.

In spite of strong orthodox reactions, neo-Protestantism seemed to have overcome the split between Christianity and the modern mind which plagued the Western world since the protest of the Enlightenment against the traditional theology of all Christian confessions. Dogma was understood as the Hellenization of Christianity and was deprived, in this way, of its sacred, oppressive power. Theology found a new foundation at the very source of Christianity, namely, the man Jesus of Nazareth. Biblical criticism rediscovered this source under the different strata of early tradition, particularly in Paul's dialectics and the mysticism of the Fourth Gospel. Ritschlian theology discredited metaphysics and theological speculation, and established the ideal of a religious-ethical personality in accord with the nobler ideals of bourgeois society and which was supposed to agree with the mind of Jesus of Nazareth. The success of Harnack's *Das Wesen des Christentums* and of the neo-Protestant theology as a whole was guaranteed whenever a synthesis of Christianity and the modern bourgeois world view was an historical necessity, as, for instance, in this country. And the substance of the neo-Protestant attitude was not changed when it was transferred to America, although the social implications of the Ritschlian theology received a much stronger emphasis here than in Germany.

Shortly after Harnack reached the acme of his success, the earthquake which brought about the present European situation started. Three eruptive volcanoes had, of course, already appeared in the nineteenth century; Marx threatened the social ground of the bourgeois neo-Protestant synthesis; Nietzsche, its moral ground; and Kierkegaard, its religious ground. Towards the turn of the century the signs of the coming catastrophe increased. The "underground" individual and collective life became visible in great works of Russian and French literature, in the discovery of Freud and his school, and in the philosophy of life. All this threatened the bourgeois neo-Protestant ideals, the religious-moral personality, and the progressive organization of society. The expressionist painters became the prophets of the imminent breakup of the smooth, harmonious surface of modern existence by breaking the organic-idealistic form into pieces.

Theology, following Biblical criticism, reached a stage in which the Ritschlian synthesis between traditional faith and historical research was destroyed. Albert Schweitzer, at the end of his dramatic book, *The Quest of the Historical Jesus*, put the alternative which is considered to be the result of Biblical criticism, in the following words: "Either consistent scepticism or consistent eschatology." This meant that the mind of Jesus is either completely unknown to us or completely strange to us. No Christian theology can be built on either side of this alternative. And Schweitzer, whom many consider the greatest Christian personality of our time, did not even make an attempt.

At the same time, the problem of the history of religions entered the field. As a result the weak fences of demarcation which the Ritschlians had drawn between the Bible and Church—history on the one side, and the surrounding religions and cultures on the other side, were demolished.

Troeltsch, most sensitive to all these new motives, drew the consequences. He saw the religious a priori in every man and actual revelation everywhere. Lacking Harnack's concept of the "essence of Christianity" and Hegel's idea of an "absolute religion," he undercut the claim of Christianity to uniqueness, ultimacy, and finality. It became relative to Western civilization, an element in the future synthesis which is called "Europeanism." Christianity is relative to the racial and economic basis of European history; the Reformation belongs to the Middle Ages.

Neo-Protestantism started with the Enlightenment and is a radical break with the previous Christian tradition of seventeen hundred years. The synthesis pronounced by Harnack was renounced by Troeltsch. When Harnack spoke in 1923, three years[5] before his own death, at Troeltsch's funeral, the first earthquake of the world in which both men belonged had already happened. They died in an atmosphere strange to that in which they had lived for the most of their lives. And it seems that in Europe neo-Protestantism died with them. It had received its death blow in the hell of the trenches of the First World War and in the following social and political catastrophes. A new intellectual and spiritual climate prevailed in the middle and towards the end of the twenties. The volcano whose symbolic name is Marx had flooded Russia, the volcano whose symbolic name was Nietzsche was flooding Italy and Germany, and the volcano whose symbolic name is Kierkegaard was pouring into the Protestant Churches of the Continent. I speak of symbolic names because each of these movements is infinitely more complex than the name of reference indicates.

This is also true of the theology of crisis. Besides the influence of Kierkegaard, the following forces were effective

[5] ed: (It was actually seven years. He died in 1930. This is a *faux pas* on Tillich's part.)

in its growth: the conservative Lutheran resistance against liberal theology which increased with the increasing radicalism of the latter; Biblical Realism, often allied with pietistic traditions; the so-called Luther-Renaissance, a rediscovery of the profounder aspects of the Reformation's religious-socialist ideas about the relation of God to the world as a whole instead of to the religious-ethical personality alone. All these became powerful through Barth's *Commentary on Romans*, which was neither a commentary nor a system, but a prophetic call addressed to religion and culture, to acknowledge the divinity of the divine, and to dissolve the neo-Protestant synthesis between God's and man's creativity.

The significance of this call became particularly evident when the activity of the so-called German Christians resulted in something which was more a merging of Christianity into German nationalism than a new synthesis. With the disintegration of neo-Protestantism in its liberal-humanistic form, it had become increasingly nationalistic. The lack of vitality, symbolism, sacramental power, community, and authority in the neo-Protestant Churches opened the way for the new vitality, the new symbols and quasi-sacramental activities, the blood communion of nation and race, the authority of the leaders as the divine voice. The classical theological justification of the transition was given by the only first-rate theologian of the German Christians, Professor Emmanuel Hirsch, of Göttingen.

As the motto of one of his books he used the following words: "In the present age of history the destiny of Christianity is no longer dependent on the destiny of the Churches." These are the words of Richard Rothe, the pupil of Hegel and Schleiermacher. According to him, Christianity must express itself through national culture. Theology and philosophy, Christian ethics and national order, Church community and national community must become identical. What Rothe prophesied became possible through Hitler. The increasing estrangement between the Church and the people, which had not been bridged by all the honest attempts of bourgeois neo-Protestantism, can be overcome by the great rebirth, the bodily, psychic and spiritual *renascimento* of the German nation. This message of the German Christians was a temptation even for serious and highly learned people.

It was Barth's pronouncement of the *diastasis*[6] which gave the German Church the power to resist this temptation. And it was the declaration of the end of neo-Protestantism which also helped the non-German Churches to lead the resistance of their countries. No other movement achieved this, not even any of those which prepared the victory of the neo-orthodox theology. Biblicist pietism revealed a surprising inclination towards nationalism. Conservative Lutheranism followed the lead of political conservatism, resisting only when the original alliance between conservatism and Nazism broke down; then it combined political reactionary motives with religious and ecclesiastical ones within its resistance. The theologians who represented the rediscovery of Luther lost their leader, Professor Hirsch, to the German Christians and remained undecided for a long time. The Religious Socialists were in a very ambiguous situation. Except for a few apostates, they easily resisted the German Christian temptation and many of their small number were expelled, imprisoned, or killed. But they could not pronounce the word of *diastasis*, which, in the decisive moment, was the saving word. They had made an attempt at correlation, different from both the neo-Protestant bourgeois synthesis and the merging of Christianity into nationalism. Although I am identified with a special type of this movement and believe that its basic ideas are still valid,

[6] *Diastasis* is a Greek word meaning "a difference of opinion, disagreement" and is used by Tillich as the break-up of an earlier theological synthesis. —Editor.

I cannot deny that it encountered quite an ambiguous situation, when the Nazis came to power. As socialists, whether they belonged to a party or not, they were automatically persecuted and could no longer express themselves publicly. And even if they had been able, they could not have done so convincingly, because the German Christians could answer and did answer, that there is no difference from the ultimate point of view, whether one decides for religious naturalism or for religious socialism. They could even use—and they did use—some of the main categories of Religious Socialism, as for instance the idea of the *kairos*, the fulfillment of time or the providential time; they asserted that the appearance of Hitler was the *kairos*, directly for the German nation, indirectly for all nations. This ambiguity of the external and internal situation silenced the voice of the Religious Socialists. The message of the uncompromising *diastasis* alone was adequate to the historical moment. This fact determines the present theological situation in Continental Europe. And those who won the fight of resistance are now in power, and not only with that right of the victor but also with much historical justification.

III

If we look at Protestant theology as a whole, which I think we must do—especially in the period of the ecumenical conferences—the European situation posits a very serious problem for all Protestant theology. To ignore the Continental development and work for a genuine British theology, an American theology, or a theology of the younger Churches is impossible. It is a betrayal of the will to truth if theology *intends* to be Swedish, Swiss, or American; moreover it is the symptom of an inclination towards a synthesis between Christianity and nationalism, a synthesis which inescapably leads to the death of Christianity within it. Obviously, we belong to a nation, a continent, and a period. When we look at our theology as observers, we may discover that it has a distinctly national color; this contributes much to the richness of Protestant theology. But it does not contribute anything if it is *intended*, for the will to truth is thereby sacrificed. The transcontinental conversation of Protestant theology must continue.

I want to direct attention to four most urgent problems which are implied in the problem of *diastasis* versus synthesis. First, correlation and independence; second, myth and message; third, criticism and authority; fourth, ethics and the end. Here there is no solution but an attempt to show them in the light of the European victory of *diastasis* over synthesis.

The first question is, does *diastasis* mean that there is no correlation between human existence as experienced and expressed in life and culture and in the *kerygma*? Barth answers "No!" In his writing he has explicitly attacked the concept of correlation. Correlation can mean interdependence but does this not establish a partial dependence of revelation on human possibilities, for instance, on the creative possibilities of the German nation including its classical philosophy; or of the Greek culture including its tragedy, the Platonists and the Stoics; or of the Roman law and its eclectic rationalism; or of the American democracy and its pragmatic empiricism? And is it not true that on the mission field correlation would mean a partial dependence of the Christian message on Hindu metaphysics and Confucian ethics?

But if we deny any correlation and emphasize the absolute independence of the message from anything human, then the question arises, how can the message be received and expressed? To this question the theology of *diastasis* has no answer. This fact, however, cannot induce us to return to the answer given by the different forms of the neo-Protestant synthesis. Must we then turn to the classical Roman-Catholic tradition and correlate a substructure of natural theology with a superstructure of revealed theology? This cannot be done, for if man is able to reach God by reasoning, even in an incomplete way, the relation to God is partly in man's hand, just as in Roman-Catholic belief, man can partly determine his relation to God by moral endeavor. The Reformation clearly rejected the latter but not the former part of this assertion. So substructure and superstructure merged in later Protestant theology and the neo-Protestant synthesis was ready.

The problem of correlation cannot be solved by another attempt to build a natural theology. Human existence does not involve answers to the question of man's relation to God; it involves the questions implicit in the very structure of human existence — in the structure of finite being with its anxiety and its courage, in the structure of estranged existence with its despair and self-destruction, in the structure of its ambiguous character of life with its creativity and tragedy the question of God is implied. But the answer, if it appears, appears in revelation. What we formerly called natural theology, the philosophy of religion should be transformed into an analysis of the questions implied in the structure of human existence and existence generally. And Protestant theology, avoiding an impossible *diastasis* as well as a premature synthesis, should develop the correlation between questions and the answer of the kerygma.

IV

The second problem brought into the foreground by the Continental European situation is the problem of myth. It is most passionately discussed and has already led to two formal accusations of heresy against the outstanding representative of historical criticism in Germany, Rudolf Bultmann; and this, in spite of the fact that theologically he is strongly influenced by Barth. The question is, are there mythical elements in the New Testament? Is Bultmann right when he sees as mythological every report in which a supernatural realm breaks into history in a miraculous way? He carries this through with respect to the life of Jesus as well as to the eschatological expectations, to Jesus' resurrection as well as to most of his miracles. It belongs to the intricacies of the Continental situation that Hirsch, the leader of the German Christians, here agrees completely with Bultmann, the leader of the left-wing confessing Church, though Hirsch denounced Bultmann's attitude as inconsistent and dishonest. Bultmann is neither inconsistent nor dishonest; his is the attempt of a great scholar and a passionate theologian to combine theological *diastasis* with scientific integrity.

Is this possible? Neo-Protestantism of the type of Harnack was not worried by such a difficulty. It believed in a definite result of historical criticism, a picture of Jesus of Nazareth on which theology could be built. But no such result was forthcoming and whatever emerged in this way was by no means the basis for the creedal statements with which the confessing Church defeated the German Christians. In each of their many pronouncements, those elements of the Gospel records, which Bultmann calls mythical, play by far the greatest rôle. And all the Continental Europeans who have suffered in the Church struggle are extremely sensitive at this point. It is a betrayal of Christ, I was told in a ministers' conference when I defended Biblical criticism. Similar experiences are told by everybody who has met European theologians, and, often worse, laymen. Is it possible to maintain both scientific integrity which cannot admit a priori limits with respect to its results and the power of the Christian *kerygma* which transcends anything science can show?

A myth is a whole set of symbols expressing man's relation to that which concerns him ultimately, the ground and meaning of his existence. Myth is more than a primitive world-view — with which Bultmann wrongly equates it; it is the necessary and adequate expression of revelation. In this I agree with Barth, who for some questionable terminological reasons calls it "Sage" (saga). But the question is, how can we preserve the truth and the power of the myth while recognizing its mythological character, its quality of being non-historical in the empirical sense? The answer, I think, must be that the Church from its beginning through the present participates in a reality which is different from any other reality and which, therefore, can be called the New Being. The perfect and final manifestation of this reality and, therefore, the foundation of the Church and continuous power in the Church, is that historical event which in symbolic-mythological terms is described as the appearance of the Christ. Such an interpretation breaks down the neo-Protestant synthesis while preserving what is the pride of Protestant theology, scientific honesty, as applied to its own sources.

V

The third problem which the situation of Continental Protestantism places before us is that of authority. By which authority could one resist Nazi authority and be justified in demanding martyrdom? This was the question of the fighting Church. And the answer was first the Bible, and second, the Church, or in one phrase, the Church under the authority of the Biblical message. In remembrance of this experience, a severe Biblicism arose, and with it the request that the Church authorities protect the Biblical message against theological, philosophical, and political distortions. And the Biblical message was identified with the battle creeds of the confessing Church.

For centuries Protestantism was identified with the freedom of conscience, that is, with the freedom of pronouncing what the religious conscience demands. Heresy trials happened but were looked upon as Catholic distortions. However, the development of neo-Protestantism indicated that autonomy inescapably becomes secular, producing an empty space into which heteronomies enter.

This is the essence of the spiritual history of the twentieth century. But is the alternative to autonomy, heteronomy? No European theologian would admit that it is; but most of them act as though it is. No complaint is more frequent in present-day Germany than that the authorities of the confessing Church, who are the authorities of the whole German Church, use their power in a heteronomous way. But how can it be avoided after all that has happened? Shall neo-Protestant radicals, shall German Christians, shall Religious Communists become ministers? The fight against the German Christians was fought on doctrinal terms, centering in the authority of the Old and the New Testament as the norm of the life of the Church. This experience cannot easily be forgotten. But must it not lead to a new Fundamentalism? Every Continental theologian is deeply moved by this question, and some important conversions to Roman Catholicism have taken place because of the seeming inability of Protestantism to give an answer. All over Europe the spiritual influence of the Catholic Church is tremendous. Here the demand for authority is fulfilled in a way with which Protestantism can never compete. Does this mean the end of the Protestant era, at least in Europe? Or will Protestantism continue in terms of American denominationalism, in a natural balance kept from extremes by common sense, supported by social conventions, strengthened by Biblical-evangelistic and humanist-democratic elements? But if this is still possible in America, is it possible anywhere else since the dissolution of the neo-Protestant synthesis and the threefold authoritarian pressure of Roman Catholicism, Communism, and neo-Fascism in Europe and Asia? But besides these pragmatic considerations, what has theology to say? In one of the finest Catholic groups in Germany, I spoke about the union of Catholic substance with the Protestant principle; Catholic substance meaning the tradition in which the New Being has embodied and expressed itself before, in, and after its final manifestation in Jesus as the Christ; Protestant principle meaning the critical power of the prophetic and rational spirit, preventing the tradition from becoming demonic and distorted. The idea was accepted by the Catholic group, but under the condition that the prophetic and rational spirit be subjected to the papal authority. Here the discussion ended. Protestantism must risk, or it ceases to be what it is. But risk means possible failure. The Protestant principle may be forced into the underground of different authoritarian systems, one of which may be an Evangelical Fundamentalism with infallible syndical or Episcopal authorities. But before this happens, we should strive for a fuller reception of the richness, spiritual profundity, and subtility of the Catholic substance without weakening the critical power of the Protestant spirit. It is a hope, not a certitude, that this is still possible in the present situation.

VI

The fourth problem one notices in the European scene is the attitude towards the "end," the eschatological feeling and its many consequences for dogmatic and ethical theology. The end is taken realistically, in a way hard to describe. It is not a primitive calculation of the year of the end or a fantastic description of the final catastrophe; it is not even an identification of the end with the possible extinction of life on earth by atomic death. It is a vivid relating of everything present to the end. The end is taken temporally. It is a temporal event which ends time. Sometimes the end of time is interpreted as the end of historical time. More often the end of time is interpreted in Biblical symbolism as the end of all time. In the latter case a cosmic catastrophe is anticipated. In both cases a geocentric point of view is re-established. The planet in which history has occurred and in which the Logos has become flesh is the center of the universe. The literal interpretation of the Biblical symbols entails a return to pre-Renaissance geocentrism, though not in astronomical terms.

The realistic expectation of the end is the strongest expression of the principle of *diastasis*. It devaluates the all cultural activity, and accentuates the importance of present personal decision and salvation of the individual. This of course, agrees with the mood of people who have lost the hope for any kind of fulfillment in history. But it seems cynical to ask these people, who in the midst of their lives are already, psychologically and economically, and perhaps tomorrow physically, the battle ground between East and West, to believe in any form in the saving power of history. This is not the minority mood of a special group, but it is the predominant attitude toward all history, certainly in the New Testament, and almost of the progress of Church history to the neo-Protestant bourgeois synthesis. It is also the attitude of the ancient nations, including Israel. For, whenever they, even in their best periods, looked towards a period of fulfillment, they attributed it to a transcendent act of God or of divine being. They never derived the fulfillment of history from history. The *diastasis* between history and the Kingdom of God is more natural for the great majority of all human beings within and without Christianity than a man of nineteenth century Europe or twentieth century America can probably imagine. In any case, the problem is again put before us as urgently as possible by the religious and theological situation on the European continent.

Perhaps we can say that every individual or social act in which the power of the New Being is effective has an immediate bearing on the end in the double sense of finish and fulfillment. Nothing good in history is lost even if history should end tomorrow. And the belief in historical providence means that there is no situation in which healing power is absent from history. Faith in the presence of the New Being here and now in history, as judgment and demand, must replace the utopian expectation that the Old Being heals itself through history, or that the New Being becomes the last stage of an historical development.

The problem of diastasis is not an accidental problem caused by the European situation. It was prepared long ago by the development of neo-Protestantism itself and therefore it is a problem of all Protestantism, here and abroad, in East and West, and it may involve a much more radical re-orientation of theology than any of us are aware today.❖

A REINTERPRETATION OF THE
DOCTRINE OF THE INCARNATION

I

The doctrine of the Incarnation concerns an event which *has* happened, and is independent of any interpretation of it. The doctrine presupposes the event and tries to interpret it. The event is the prius of the interpretation, just as nature is the prius of natural science. This excludes the view that the idea of the Incarnation is a product of our religious experience, or of a present interpretation of our existence, something that could be discovered by a thorough analysis of our human situation or of the structure of our world. Neither is Incarnation a universal concept, a truth of reason as the Enlightenment understood it, nor is it an idea describing essential human nature as classical German philosophy interpreted it. On the other hand, it is an event with all the characteristics of an "event in time and space": namely, occurring "but once," unrepeatable, possible only in a special situation, and in a special, incomparable individual form, a subject of report and not of analysis or deduction.

On the other hand, the Incarnation is an event of universal significance, concerning the whole of being, and transforming the conditions of existence generally. Therefore it must be interpreted in universal categories. Without such an interpretation it would be a stumbling-block, strange to our mind and alien to our spirit, and therefore without actual concern for us. Perhaps it would be a combination of words with a numinous sound, to be used in liturgies together with music, lights, and incense; but not something entering the centre of consciousness, uniting with it and creating a basis for thinking and acting. In many cases the praise of the "simple" Christian message, in contrast to a theological interpretation, proves to be only the praise of an outworn and popularized form of theological interpretation of fifty years ago. Theology should not be intimidated by this kind of attack upon its strict and difficult systematic task. It should remember, however, that theological interpretation does not create its subject but must be created by it.

There can be no doubt that the doctrine of the Incarnation needs a reinterpretation. I must confess that, in America, I have realized for the first time the importance of the concept of Incarnation, especially for the theology and liturgy of the Protestant Episcopal Church. But in spite of the religious and theological emphasis laid upon it, I find it difficult to find a clear and thorough interpretation of its meaning.

I became increasingly suspicious, on the other hand, that many people employed the concept of Incarnation in a mythological and superstitious manner: it implies for them the transmutation or metamorphosis of *a* divine being into *a* human being, a polytheistic myth which we find in all paganism, and incompatible with the fundamental truth of prophetic revelation. The God who creates, sustains and transcends all beings, is not himself *a* being, not even the highest. He cannot become the subject of a transmutation or a metamorphosis, and he does not possess the logical structure of a thing with qualities which could be transformed. The mythology of divine transmutation usually has a feeling for this, and establishes something above the different forms in which the divine beings exist; it establishes a really divine, above those human and divine beings which are transformed into each other. The gods who are transmuted are below something absolute, the eternal fate or the eternal one or the eternal Brahma. It follows from this that the transmuted gods have only a relative divinity, that they are half-gods, heroes or demons, as was the logos-god of Arius. When the Christian Church rejected Arianism, it rejected at the same time the conception of the Incarnation as the transmutation of *a* divine being into *a* human being.

But, we may ask, are there not indications that the biblical writers, Paul and John, describe the significance of the historical Jesus in terms of a semi-mythological character? I believe that this cannot be denied. The pre-existent spiritual being (in Phil. 2: 5–11) who resigns his divine form and power, and takes the form of a servant, and is raised by God on high to receive a name which is above every name — this being who makes a moral decision in his pre-existent state — is certainly not God himself, but a divine being. The decision "not to snatch at equality with God but to empty himself" occurs in a supra-historical, mythological sphere; and the same is true of his elevation to the dignity of "Lord." The distinction of the three stages is mythical, using the three modes of time for the destiny of a divine being. Again, in John we read that the "Logos was with God." His function was the mediation of creation. He then entered the world which existed through him, but which did not recognize him and receive him when he came. Here the mythological element is reduced to a great extent by the categories Logos, Life and Light, symbolizing the divine self-expression through creation and within the created world; but it has not disappeared entirely. The "Logos became flesh and tabernacled among us." The divine being, who, like God, is spiritual, becomes flesh, but without ceasing to be the Logos: being in the flesh is merely a transitory stage, as it were dwelling in a tent. "I came out from the Father, and am come into the world: again, I leave the world, and go unto the Father" (John 16:28). Here, obviously, the idea of manifestation is decisive, and not that of transformation: "the only begotten Son, which is in the bosom of the Father, he hath declared him" (John 1:18).

The divine being of which John speaks is a divine principle in which the mythological implications of pre-existence have been overcome to such an extent that the later Logos doctrine could develop from it. It represents a definite step beyond Paul. But in Paul himself there is an element of particular importance for my own task of reinterpreting the doctrine of the Incarnation. If it is true, as Dibelius and others maintain, that the old idea of the Original Man or Man from Above lies in the background of the Christological hymn in Philippians 2, this would have a direct bearing on the doctrine of the Incarnation. But however cautiously we may judge about the idea of the Original Man in Judaism, and its influence on the idea of the "Son of Man coming on the clouds of heaven with power and great glory," and the fusion of this with the Messianic idea, we cannot overlook such Pauline passages as 1 Corinthians 15 in which he writes: "The first man Adam became a living soul. The last Adam became a life-giving spirit. Howbeit that is not first which is spiritual, but that which is natural; then that which is spiritual. The first man is of the earth, earthy: the second man is of heaven. As is the earthy, such are they also that are earthy: and as is the heavenly, such are they also that are heavenly. As we have borne the image of the earthy, we shall also bear the image of the heavenly" (vs. 45–49). Here the stages are as follows: There is first the heavenly man who before his coming is spiritual and immortal; then the physical man, Adam, who is subject to death and brought death into the world, is followed by the heavenly man who overcomes death. The emphasis which Paul lays on the sequence of these stages in a polemic form indicates that he struggles for the historical manifestation of the Man from Above after Adam's fall, an idea which did not exist and could not exist in the pagan form of the myth of the "Original Man."

It follows from this that the biblical interpretation of the Incarnation does not imply that God as such becomes a man, but that a divine being, either the heavenly man, or the pre-existent Christ, or the divine Logos, appears in the shape of a physical man or of a man in the flesh. The statement is not that God becomes man, but that a divine being with human characteristics, the spiritual or heavenly man, or a moral being who chooses self-humiliation, or the creative reason and word, appears in time and space, and is subject to the law of the flesh and of sin, namely, human existence. The paradox of the Incarnation is not that God becomes man, but that a divine being who represents God and is able to reveal him in his fullness, manifests himself in a form of existence which is in radical contradiction to his divine, spiritual and heavenly form. It is not the unity of the infinite and the finite which constitutes the paradox of the Incarnation, but the manifestation of the original, heavenly man as existential man, or of the universal creative reason as individual created reason, or of the spiritual pre-existent Christ as the empirical and historical Christ. The mythological element in the biblical doctrine of the Incarnation enabled it to be understood as the self-manifestation of God in existence through a divine half-being, half-principle which belongs to God and nevertheless shows some essentially human characteristics. The subject of the Incarnation is the original God-manhood, or the spiritual God-man, or the heavenly man, or the creative reason in which man as the image of God participates and which, therefore, is able to enlighten him. There is, in a "mythological" sense, an original "pre-existent" relation between God and man. Finiteness and infinity are, however, correlated concepts: their unity is not paradoxical but, if I may use the abused term, dialectical, the one side necessarily driving towards the other in mutual interdependence. There is no idea of God in which this correlation is not implied. It appears usually as the tension between an anthropomorphic and an unconditioned element in the idea of God, in which he is conceived as the highest being, symbolized in semi-human characteristics, and at the same time as above any picture of being, even above the Highest of being and value. All such conceptions are dialectical but not paradoxical, and belong to every notion of the living God. But the idea of the Incarnation has another character. It is not dialectical. It is not demanded as the immanent side of a tension with the divine transcendence. It was the mistake of Hegel and the German classical philosophy to confuse the dialectical relation of finiteness and infinity with the paradoxical doctrine of the Incarnation. In the first case, with respect to the conception of God, they were right, while Barth and his followers are wrong in denying the dialectical interdependence of finiteness and infinity. But in the second case, with respect to the Incarnation, the Barthians are right in stressing its paradoxical character, while German classical philosophy and its theological followers are wrong.

The insight that the paradox of the Incarnation must be distinguished from the dialectical relation of finiteness and infinity liberates Christology from the impasse into which it was thrown by the doctrine of the two natures in Christ, the divine and the human. The necessity of explaining the full humanity of Christ in terms of Kenosis, as Christ emptying himself of the infinite divine power which he possesses potentially, or as Christ hiding this power which he possesses actually, is a Christology of absurdities and shows that the very starting-point was wrong. It was falsified in the moment in which the mythological element in the biblical praise of Christ's transcendent origin was eliminated for the sake of a more rational interpretation in terms of the Logos doctrine. It was, on the other hand, impossible to avoid this attempt because the mythological elements proved to be dangerous when they were received on originally pagan soil, and the monotheistic safeguards of the Old Testament became ineffective.

The prologue of the Fourth Gospel is the first step towards such a rationalization in the attempt to defend the absolute character of Christ against pagan estimates of his relative significance. In later development, the more the *homoousios* of God and Christ was emphasized (necessarily, against the hero-cult of Arianism) the more the problem of the paradox of the Incarnation became confused with the problem of the dialectical relation of finiteness and infinity. In this, classical Greek theology foreshadowed classical German philosophy. They were both unable to understand that the Incarnation is the paradox of essential Godmanhood, manifesting itself within and under the conditions of human existence which contradicts original Godmanhood. It is probable that both forms of "classicism" were unable to see the problem in this way because the distance between essence and existence (between what man is in his essential, spiritual and heavenly nature and what he is in his existential, material and earthly nature) was not realized as the main problem of theology in general and of Christology in particular. Instead of this, the metaphysical problem of the relation between the finite and the infinite predominated in the doctrine of the Incarnation against the soteriological problem of essential Godmanhood appearing in existence. Athanasius is an exception, however, but he pays the price of a very unsatisfactory solution from the point of view of metaphysics.

These biblical and historical considerations suggest the possibility of a new starting-point which is free from the inescapable absurdities of the attempt to explain the Incarnation in terms of a higher chemistry between finiteness and infinity, and at the same time free from the mistake of Hegelianisn which empties the paradox of the Incarnation by reducing it to a dialectical necessity.

II

The Incarnation is the manifestation of original and essential Godmanhood within and under the conditions of existence. In making this statement, may I emphasize once more that it is in line with biblical thought, while the proposition that God became man, or became flesh, is definitely not biblical. The transcendent Son of Man, the heavenly man, the spiritual man, the Logos became an immanent Son of Man, an earthly man, an historical man, flesh.

We must begin from this point, and translate the mythological, liturgical and numinous form of these statements into a rational and theological form.

In order to do this, it is necessary to deal with some of the concepts used in the general proposition. The first of these concepts is that of *existence* or *existential being*, and I propose to use the definitions which I have formulated in a course of lectures on *Existence and the Christ,* and which run as follows: "First, existence means being, in distinction from non-being; secondly, existence means being in time and space, in distinction from essential being. Thirdly, there is the indication of an antagonism between existence and essence, and the fact of this antagonism is the problem implied in existence." In certain contemporary philosophical developments, especially under the influence of Sören Kierkegaard, the term existence has received a special colour. It implies more than the statement that something belongs to the context of the conditions of time, space, causality and the categories of finiteness. It means that no description of our essential being can grasp our real situation which is characterized precisely by the fact that it contradicts our essential being. The attempt of idealism in Germany, as well as of positivism in England and France, to give a picture of being in terms of essential necessity, misses the point of Existentialism: namely, the power of being, and especially the power of human being, to break through the limitations of its essential character. Idealism has given a picture of man in which human existence, and existence in general, are the necessary realization of what man and his world are essentially: the difference is one of development and not of quality. Positivism has given a picture of man in which human existence, and existence in general, are what they are of necessity, without any distance from an essential character of man and his world. Positivism does not acknowledge any difference between essential and existential being, not even in the restrained form adopted by idealism. Thus positivism has no criterion for actual human existence, while idealism has such a criterion in the concept of man's essential nature. But it does not perceive the depth of the contrast between essence and existence. Christianity, on the other hand, has a complete concept of man's essential nature, as well as of his existence and of the radical contrast between them. This is the reason why it is impossible to develop the doctrine of the Incarnation, and with it the Christian doctrines in general, either in idealistic or in positivistic terms, or in terms of the innumerable combinations between them. No doctrine of the Incarnation is possible without a clear understanding of man's freedom to contradict his essential nature, and of man's fate to stand under the servitude of this contradiction. But on the basis of such an understanding, and with the help of the philosophical categories derived from it, a new interpretation of the doctrine of the Incarnation can be formulated. The Incarnation is the manifestation of essential Godmanhood within existence, and under the conditions of existence, in which it does not lose its essential character. The description of this paradox and its consequences for the transformation of existence is the task of the doctrine of the Incarnation.

It must start with an explanation of essential being in terms of essential Godmanhood. Such an explanation can be given only in fragmentary and negative manner, because we do not know what man and his world are originally and essentially. We have no complete picture of such a world, but only partial insights, commands and judgments, which stand over against our existential situation. Conscience bears witness to another order of things, and our longing for a state beyond the tragedy of existence creates a past or future paradise, a retrospective or prospective Utopia. We know that the disrupted and antagonistic elements of existence belong essentially to a unity, a unity between the self and the world, including even the strange and remote sections of our world, such as the inorganic realm. It is a unity, moreover, of our separated and lonely individuality with the universality and community to which we belong: a unity, above all, of our finiteness with our infinity, of our transitoriness with our eternity, of our contingency with our creativity, of our melancholy with our courage, of our situation at the periphery like all beings with our situation at the centre above all beings. We know that this unity is what we are essentially. We know that even in the existential destruction of this unity, its remaining power maintains existence. We know this because it appears to us as law and command, as judgment and threat, and as promise and expectation. But it never appears as being, as New Being overcoming the contrast between essential and existential being, overcoming law and threat and mere expectation, except in the Incarnation: more precisely, the Incarnation is its manifestation as New Being over against essence and existence.

It is New Being over against essence, because it has actual reality; it is a fact, while essential being as such is merely potential and not actual. The description of the gap between essence and existence must not suggest that essential man or essential being has existed at some time in the past or somewhere in the world, since it is potential and not actual. In the moment in which it becomes actual, which is not a moment in time, the existential situation is given. The transition from essence to existence, in whatever mythical terms it may be symbolized, is the transition from potentiality to actuality. The Fall of man, in Christian and non-Christian mythology, is the presupposition of existence: there is no existence before existence, and no actual reality before the Fall. We must not confuse the temporal symbols of the myth with the ontological relation of essence and existence. Our empirical world is the only existing world; but it is precisely this empirical existing world which includes within itself the strange contradiction between what it is actually and what it is essentially. The empirical, existing world has a tragic character because its very existence implies the contradictions by which it is driven to self-destruction and death. But tragic necessity is the opposite of natural necessity. It is connected with guilt, and consequently with freedom. Without freedom there can be no possible distinction between essential and existential being; and neither idealism nor positivism are able to explain the mysterious combination of freedom and necessity in the tragic character of existence. It is only the distinction between essence and existence which enables us to do this, and this alone would justify the use of these categories in theology.

The New Being created by the Incarnation is above essential being because it is actual and not merely potential; and at the same time, it is above existential being because it brings essential being or essential Godmanhood into existence.

The identification of essential being with essential Godmanhood requires some further explanation. To essential man belongs the unity of his finiteness with his infinity, and it is precisely this unity which I call Godmanhood, because it is an expression of the dialectical interdependence of finiteness and infinity. Man is the only being who possesses a genuine finiteness because he is the only being who possesses a potential infinity; for finiteness has meaning only in correlation with infinity, and *vice versa*. This does not imply, however, any combination between finiteness and infinity, since dialectical interdependence is precisely the opposite of combination. Barth is correct in stressing the statement that God is in heaven and that we are on earth, that God is the creator and that we are creatures; but he is at fault in simply putting these two statements beside one another, without inquiring into the dialectical relation between them. The thought of Barth is not dialectical in the proper sense, and he shares this defect with the liberal theology which he attacks. If, however, dialectical terms are not employed in describing the relation between God, man and the world, the way is open to the error of Barthian supernaturalism or liberal naturalism. On the other hand, it must be understood that heaven is heaven only in relation to earth, and that the creator is creator only in relation to the creature. Thus God cannot be conceived as the creator in any accidental sense, since divinity and creativity cannot be separated. If this is understood, the biblical idea of the eternal Son of Man, of the heavenly man, of the spiritual Christ, of the eternal word or reason, and our equation between essential being and essential Godmanhood, loses its surprising character. It simply indicates that divine self-objectification and essential manhood belong together, because man is essentially the divine image, and anthropomorphism contains an indestructible element of truth.

It follows that essential Godmanhood can manifest itself within existence only in a human being and as a personal life. The question raised by the scholastics whether or not the Incarnation could have taken place in any other being besides man is strictly irrelevant. Essential Godmanhood can become manifest only in an existential man, and not in a half-god or in an animal. This is the humanistic element in the doctrine of the Incarnation. It is essential humanity, and therefore essential Godmanhood which appears as New Being, above essence and existence. A false Christology, which does not take account of the idea of essential Godmanhood, necessarily leads to a barbaric and dehumanized form of Christianity, which issues in fanaticism and conceives the God of the Incarnation as an arbitrary tyrant.

The New Being, created by the Incarnation, is above existential being, because it overcomes the cleavage between finiteness and infinity which characterizes existence, along with the other disruptions of the unity of man's essential being. The victory of the New Being over existence within, and under the structural forms of existence, is the paradox of the Incarnation. I must now indicate its real significance and characteristics in the light of these general considerations.

III

The Christian message declares that Jesus is the Christ, and as such is the place in which essential being has manifested itself in existence in the Incarnation. Essential Godmanhood has become historical Godmanhood in the man Jesus who is believed to be the Christ. The paradox of the Incarnation is the picture of Jesus as the Christ, the picture of essential Godmanhood appearing in existence and under its conditions, but without losing its essential character, and thus creating a new reality in existence which has the power to transform it.

The New Being, manifest in the picture of Jesus as the Christ, represents the essential unity between finiteness and infinity, or the undisrupted unity between man and God. It represents the essential unity between individuality and universality, or the undestroyed community of love and knowledge. It represents the essential unity between contingency and creativity, or the unhampered transition from anxiety to courage and from mortality to eternity. All this is embodied and represented in the picture of Jesus as the Christ.

It is not wise to attempt to express the character of the New Being in Christ in negative and static terms such as "lack of sin" or "lack of error." The real content of the picture is the actual maintenance of unity in all the aspects mentioned above. There is no element of despair or separation in the picture, no suggestion of the revolt of the finite against its unity with the infinite, which is the fundamental characteristic of existence, no element of concupiscence in the form of a will to power or a will to pleasure which would separate him from the unity with his world and with himself, splitting his individuality from his universality. The subordination of the finite to the infinite, and the desire to the love, is maintained in every respect.

This is the picture of the New Being which is given to us, and there is no point in attempting to go beyond it, and to ask for a photographic picture in addition to the religious picture, in the interest of theological inquiry. The photographic picture has never existed, either for Jesus himself or for his apostles. The original picture, which existed from the beginning, was of a numinous and interpreted character, and it was this which proved to have the power to conquer existence. Whatever scientific research may try, and must try to discover, the New Being incarnated in Jesus Christ manifests itself in the religious picture which was at all times the basis of the Christian message. The Incarnation is the manifestation of essential Godmanhood in the picture of Jesus as the Christ. The Incarnation is an historical event, and occurs only once in time and space. The photographic implications of the event are, from the beginning, reduced to unimportance by its interpretation as the appearance of the Christ or as the Incarnation. The event is unknown in any photographic sense, but the religious picture resulting from it has proved to be the power of transforming existence. This is our primary requirement: and in saying this, I may express the hope that one false view is excluded by everything I have tried to say: namely, the mistake of supposing that the picture of the New Being in Jesus as the Christ is the creation of existential thought or experience. If this were the case, it would be as distorted, tragic and sinful as existence is itself, and would not be able to overcome existence. The religious picture of the New Being in Jesus is a result of a new being: it represents the victory over existence which has taken place, and thus created the picture.

There remains something to be said about the concept of the New Being in contrast to essential and existential being, since it has a number of important functions in the doctrine of the Incarnation. In the first place, it offers a new approach to the interpretation of Jesus as the Christ, since it implies that Jesus is the Christ in the totality of his being, and not merely in particular expressions of it. Neither his words as such, nor his internal and external actions as such, nor his sufferings as such, make him the Christ, but the New Being of which they are the expressions. His words alone would qualify him as prophet or teacher, his deeds alone would qualify him as saint or moral example, his sufferings alone would qualify him as martyr or religious genius; but in all these ways of interpreting him he is not understood as the New Being or as the Christ. Secondly, the term New Being indicates the reality of the transformation of existence. It has realistic implications which overcome the idea that Christ is a new law, a more refined command, or a new interpretation of life, which leaves life unchanged. The New Being is a reality which neither a true philosophical theory nor an authentic religious experience can create. It is an event, although it would not be an event if there were no people who could have received it as such. Therefore the term New Being excludes idealistic as well as subjectivistic elements which have distorted the doctrine of the Incarnation in one way or the other. Thirdly, the term New Being indicates the reality of the Incarnation from the point of view of those who participate in it above the contrast between essence and existence. This refers to individual life as well as to history, since being in Christ means being a new creature, and being a Christian involves participation in the New Being who has appeared in history. This participation is possible only by receiving the New Being, and not by trying to produce it, because any attempt to produce it accentuates the contradictory and tragic elements of existence. The term New Being is therefore of particular importance for the interpretation of the Church as the realm in which existence is overcome before any religious activity begins. It is not religious activity which creates the Church, since such activity strengthens the power of existence and consequently prevents the coming of the Church if it is done with the purpose of creating the Church. The Church is the historical embodiment of the New Being created by the Incarnation. The very term New Being therefore excludes any doctrine of the Church which conceives if to be brought into existence by religious decisions. The New Being is the prius of the Church just as it is the prius of Christian experience.

Fourthly, the term New Being has an eschatological implication. The Incarnation is an eschatological event in the sense of an event in which history has received its meaning, and therefore, in principle, its end. Thus the New Being which overcomes both essential and existential being might be called teleological or eschatological being in which fulfilment is given in principle because it is orientated towards the end. If the Incarnation is the appearance of the New Being it constitutes the centre of history, and therefore includes both its meaning and its consummation. What we are essentially has appeared in existence, thereby overcoming existence and creating the New Reality, which is not merely *something* new within existence, but *the* New overcoming existence as a whole. This eschatological aspect of the Incarnation, which is expressed in the term New Being, is correlated with the concept of the beginning of history. The New Being appears first as command and expectation, when the question about it is asked, when man understands his existential situation in which the contradiction and tragedy are manifest as the longing for salvation from it. But this appearance as command and promise is merely of a preparatory character and not the actual salvation itself. The saving appearance is the Incarnation, and nothing before and nothing after it, since the New Being is or is not.

This brings my interpretation to a close. Many problems have not been touched upon. This is the tragic fate of the systematic theologian: he must say everything in order to say anything completely. I have deliberately omitted many of the traditional terms in which Christian theology is usually expounded. It seems to me that any attempt to reinterpret a Christian doctrine must begin with concepts which do not belong to its traditional form; because otherwise it becomes mere repetition and not reinterpretation. The concepts used in this article seem to be useful for the purpose of reinterpretation, and nothing else is required of them. They are simply tools; just as the Greek terms used by the early Church were tools; and if they prove useless, they can be discarded. The reality remains which they try to reinterpret: the New Being in Christ, the appearance of essential Godmanhood in existence, the Incarnation. ❖

THE RECOVERY OF THE PROPHETIC TRADITION IN THE REFORMATION

✳✳✳✳✳✳✳✳✳✳✳✳✳✳✳✳✳✳✳✳✳✳✳✳✳✳✳✳✳✳✳✳✳✳✳✳
LECTURE 1:
THE DIVINITY OF THE DIVINE

✳✳✳✳✳✳✳✳✳✳✳✳✳✳✳✳✳✳✳✳✳✳✳✳✳✳✳✳✳✳✳✳✳✳✳✳

INTRODUCTION

The title of these three lectures, "The Recovery of the Prophetic Tradition in the Reformation," presupposes that this prophetic tradition has been lost. One of the tragic events in the history of the Christian Church is that it actually has been lost to a great extent, namely, to that extent in which the official Church was predominant.

We have in the Book of Revelation two symbols for the end — end in the sense of "finish" and at the same time of "the aim of history." The one is the eschatology which says the last things will come *after* history, in something beyond time and space, in the fulfilled Kingdom of God. At the same time, we have in the same book the idea of a rule of Christ, symbolized as "a thousand years," which will be *in* history. The conflict of these two ideas (Is the aim of history *above* history, or is it *in* history?) has moved our Church history and has permanently produced the problem of the prophetic element in the history of the Church.

There were attempts which emphasized the solution that there is a thousand years reign of Christ in history, and we are expecting it—it must come, and perhaps it is coming immediately. There were movements of this kind— Montanism and others. But it was Augustine who gave the classical solution: that these thousand years have already arrived; they are here and now, in the Church and its control by the hierarchy. That meant that this period is the final period in history, and that revolutionary and prophetic criticism is no longer possible or necessary; everything essential is established, and it is established in the hierarchy of the Church. By this solution, Augustine himself, who had so much prophetic spirit in his personality, largely excluded the prophetic spirit from the official Church. If history is fulfilled, then no radical prophetic criticism is any longer needed.

But movements came up again and again which reacted against this. We usually call them "sectarian." A sect is not characterized by the fact that it has a special idea on which it lives and through which it separates itself from the Church; but a sect is a revolutionary movement which sets against the Church a point of view in which the Church has become conservative and fixed.

The man who more than anyone else influenced the sectarian movements during the Middle Ages and up to modern times is the monk Joachim di Fiore, who put forward against Augustine's idea that the last stage of history has already come, the idea that this last stage is still to come. It was usually called the third stage. And this is the great question between Church and sectarian radicalism: has the third stage already arrived, or can we still expect this third stage?

The Franciscan Order (or at least the radicals in the Order) was willing to fight for Joachim's idea against Augustine's. Through this great fight of the so-called "Franciscan Spirituals" against the official Church, many sectarian impulses came into the Middle Ages; many of the Medieval sects are dependent on this. They were revived in the Reformation, and their influence was great on the American churches and on the radical movements for social justice. (This is the bridge which I wanted to indicate to you from my lectures to those of Dr. Stanley later on.)

There is a kind of general rhythm between church and sect, between priest and prophet; and this is so not only in religion but also in politics. If a revolutionary movement becomes victorious, then it loses its character of a sect and becomes a church, with a hierarchy, with authority, and with suppression.

The Reformation can be understood as an attempt to avoid both the priestly and the sectarian type; and that is why so many attacks have been leveled against it, both at the time of its origin and today, from the ecclesiastical side as well as the sectarian side. The Reformation is comparatively unknown in this country, because we have in this country on the one hand several types of the ecclesiastical religion—the priestly religion—and on the other hand we have the large churches which have grown out of the sectarian type.

So what I shall try to do in these three lectures is to give you neither the spirit of Protestantism (as I did last year) nor the shortcomings and impossibilities of Protestantism. Instead, I want to give you an analysis of this attempt of the Reformation to unite the prophetic with the priestly spirit, to react against the Roman Church in the power of the prophetic spirit, and then to build a church in the power of those priestly elements without which propheticism cannot live—and therefore the reaction also against the sectarian movements.

THE IDEA OF GOD

CALVIN'S BATTLE AGAINST IDOLATRY

The first point I want to speak of is the idea of God, and especially Calvin's fight against idolatry. Propheticism is first of all attack against the distortions of the priestly religion, and the heart of every theological distortion is always the idea of God. Theology is the "logos of God"; therefore whenever theology is distorted, it always starts with the idea of God, and that idea is always the center.

Calvin was in this respect the most sensitive of the Reformers. One can almost say that he had a kind of pathological anxiety lest he relapse into polytheism. This anxiety has expressed itself several times in history, in early Judaism, in Islam, and in Protestantism. It is an interesting object not only of theological study, but also of the history of art, since one of the by-products of this kind of prophetic attack is the destruction of images, an anti-artistic attitude known as iconoclasm. This is true of Judaism, of Islam, and of Protestantism.

The ideas of Calvin in his fight against idolatry are extremely interesting and of the greatest consequence for the life of unnumbered millions of human beings throughout history and even in the present. Calvin distinguishes the essence of God, as he is in himself, from his relation to us. His essence is unapproachable; it is the deity of the divine. It is (Calvin used the word long before our modern theologians did) *numinous*; it is mysterious; and it never ceases to be mystery even in revelation. Calvin says, "His essence is indeed incomprehensible, so that his majesty is not to be perceived by the human senses." "*Numen*," as the Latin text says, escapes all human means of understanding.

This God is a *numinous* character; the ground — or more exactly, the abyss — of the divinity.

This God is transcendent in such a radical way, for Calvin, that every visible incorporation must be denied; Calvin says that we may not dare to form any carnal conceptions of God. These "carnal conceptions" are the polytheistic distortions; but they are also the pictures and symbols of God in Christianity. Where there are such symbols in the Bible (and Calvin could not deny that there are), they indicate their symbolic character by making manifest the presence of God and at the same time the incomprehensibility of God.

Then Calvin says something about the true symbols which is very modern theology: as true symbols they point beyond themselves. All signs which God gave in order to testify to his presence are significations of his incomprehensible essence. Therefore, Calvin says, these symbols have to be momentary, evanescent, self-negating; they express the presence of the numinous — the divine — not only by what they are, but even more by what they are not. The truth of a symbol is that it drives the mind beyond itself; the best contemplation of the divine being is when the mind is transported beyond itself.

All this leads to an utterly sharp distinction between the true God and the idols. No theologian has profounder and broader discussions of the meaning of idolatry than Calvin. In this fight against the false religion, the central motif of Calvinism becomes visible. It is not his interest in the "history of religion" [*Religionsgeschichte*, i.e., non-Biblical religion] — in fact, he condemns this history as a whole; it is not only his anti-Catholic aggression; but it is his insight that *every* religion in its very essence has the idolatrous element.

Calvin has nothing of the tolerance of the Renaissance philosophers who take the pagan divinities into their own thinking. He has no appreciation of what he calls "the sacramental idolatry" which Luther could not get rid of entirely. He fights against the pictures in the churches because they may be misused as idols; hence the emptiness, the soberness of the Calvinistic churches. This is dictated by the unconscious fear of and the conscious attack against idolatry.

It is obvious that on this basis Calvin must demand the sharpest possible break between religion and revelation. He says every religion is essentially idolatrous, because man tries to make God a picture of himself; man wants to be the creator of his God. There is no one who does not try to grasp God according to his capacity, and to shape such a God as he can understand on his own level. This temerity is innate in us, and appears at the moment we come into existence.

Calvin's classical formulation, which every man who today speaks of rationalization in psychology, of ideology in politics, can take as his own expression, is: "The mind of man is a perpetual factory of idols. Human creativity drives in the direction of the creation of God, and therefore religious creativity is something which must be radically denied." The majesty of God against the idols can hardly be expressed in a more radical way.

LUTHER'S "LAW OF CONTRAST"

Now I come to the other side of this: Luther's idea of the "hidden God." This idea, which was not manifested primarily in attack, but in expression and description, was carried through in Luther as something I can call "the law of the paradox" or "the law of the contrast": if God is beyond all human possibilities, then his acting must transcend everything human—all human expectations.

This law of contrast is described by Luther again and again. "The paradoxical character, the experience of God, is experience through absolute contrast," he says. "God's activity in the world is completely contrary to our expectations. It is hidden, or spiritual; it is the absolute opposite of what we think. Things which are hidden before God are clear to the world, and things which are hidden to the world are clear to God. What are the virtues of God? They are weakness, passion, cross, persecution—these are the weapons of God. The experience of the absolute distance between God and man is the determining factor; the power of man is emptied by the cross, which in its weakness represents the divine power. Foolishness is the right understanding; not knowing where to go is knowing where to go.

"The paradoxical character of the divine acting has the consequence that everything which comes from God is persecuted in the world. Whoever has not escaped the praise of men, nor has suffered in his work blame, challenge and persecution, has not yet reached the perfect justice," he says. "Consequently God drives men into even heavier sins in order to be recognized by him, out of the contrary. His will is first of all to destroy everything which we are ourselves, so that his own Being can replace ours."

The law of contrast dominates even the idea of prayer. Luther says that we pray for something, and God brings us into more damnation; and under this storm he hides his own salvation. God must be understood, therefore, in mental darkness, in openness and emptiness.

The fulfillment of the law of contrast is the cross of Christ. Here he has conquered death by life and created a new life. Therefore in him the law of contrast has become more manifest than anywhere else. We see the humility only if God helps us to discover in him the divine. And what is true of Christ is true of the Church: the true Church is hidden in all periods of history; its manifestation is only a manifestation of the flesh; according to the spirit the Church is hidden. Therefore the witnesses of God in our Church history are those who are persecuted by the official Church.

The law of contrast is true even of love and wrath. God is love essentially, but his love is hidden under his wrath. His love is his *proper* work, his wrath is his *strange* work; but he uses his wrath permanently in order to actualize his love.

This is Luther's doctrine of the law of contrast, and this doctrine is behind all the paradoxes of Protestant thinking. You find it everywhere—in Kierkegaard, in Barth, and in Protestant theology wherever you look.

THE DRIVING POWER IN ALL BEING

How is this related to the problem of God and the world? Here again, both Reformers have an idea of God which is so overwhelmingly powerful that it is hard to mediate its meaning today even to theological students. Both of them have the idea of an activity of God which is all in all; and this is expressed most dynamically in Luther.

First of all Luther denies that God is something like an object besides other objects—a thing, a person. God is the driving power of being in everything that is. He is the ground and the power of being. So Luther says, "Nothing is so small but God is even smaller; nothing is so large but God is even larger. He is an ineffable Being, above and outside everything we can name or imagine. Who knows what that which is called 'God' is? It transcends body, spirit, everything we can say, hear or think.

"From this it follows that God is nearer to all his creatures than they are to themselves. He has found the way for his own divine essence to be completely in all creatures, and in man especially, in a deeper and more internal and more present manner than the creature is to itself. So that he embraces all things and is within them; and at the same time he is nowhere, he cannot be comprehended by anyone."

The essential presence of God is not that of a static or a physical substance; but it is dynamic and personal. We can say, in modern terms, that in these formulas Luther overcomes the cleavage between the pantheistic and theistic elements—indeed, he has said that himself. God is at the same time in every piece of sand totally, and nevertheless in all and above all and out of all creatures.

The non-objective character of the divine is expressed in his voluntaristic quality. Luther says (this is a genuinely Lutheran term), "God is heroic and without rule. God is he for whose will there is no reason or cause, for he does not will something because it is good, but conversely, it is good because he wills it."

Behind all this is the doctrine of God's absolute power. (Luther took this from certain scholastic theologians.) God's absolute power is differentiated from his ordered power. The absolute power means that nothing is safe; it makes for an absolute positivism. Everything given is given because it is given—there is no reason why it is given.

In these concepts of the Reformers lies one of the main roots of modern positivism; the voluntaristic interpretation of God has given rise to the interpretation of God as the incalculable ground of being. The world process itself is his ordered power, his power in which he has conceded to give some rules; but these rules are not absolutely safe—neither the moral nor the ecclesiastical rules. God has given them; but this idea of the absolute power is like a threat behind them, like an abyss in which they may be swallowed in every moment. We do not know exactly what the will of God ultimately is.

GOD'S OMNIPOTENCE

From this follows a great concept of omnipotence, of God's almightiness, in which the ridiculous and absurd concepts which prevail in popular thinking are completely overcome. For Luther, almightiness is God's continuous, irresistible activity, which Luther describes in the following words:

"I call omnipotence of God not that power by which he does not make many things he could make—this is a childish concept; but the actual power by which powerfully he makes everything in everything. Therefore prescience and omnipotence are one and the same thing; God acts in everything and through everything."

From this Luther gives an interpretation of nature and history. He says: "Therefore the creatures are, so to speak, the masks of God. All creatures are God's masks and veils. God makes them work and help him to create many things. Therefore all natural orders and institutions are filled with the divine presence, and so is the historical process. The great men are also the masks of God, as Hannibal and Alexander. The Goths and the Vandals and the Turks"—and today we would say the Nazis—"are driven by him to attack and to destroy; and in this sense he speaks to us through them. They are God's word, although they destroy.

"The heroes especially, who break through the ordinary rules of life, are armed by God. He calls them and forces them on, but only when their hour has come, at their *kairos*. Without this 'right hour' nobody—no hero, no nation—can do anything; but if this right hour has come, no one can resist it. But although God acts in everything in history, history is at the same time the struggle between God and Satan and their purposes." And Luther mediates these ideas by saying that God acts substantially even in Satan—and rightly so, because how could Satan have being without God if God is the power of being in everything?

The consequence of this is that the doctrine of creation and the doctrine of preservation are not distinguished. God is creative in every moment in everything. Modern creationism (the doctrine of the process which is creative in every moment, as we have it in *Evolution Créatrice* by

Bergson, or in the process philosophy of Whitehead) is an expression of, and is historically dependent on, these ideas of Luther.

THE DOCTRINE OF PREDESTINATION

(Now I come back to Calvin.) It is always the same point I want to make in this lecture: the divinity of the Divine, the ultimacy of the Ultimate, the unconditional character of the Unconditioned. That is the point where the Reformation starts. Calvin's doctrine of Providence is very prophetic, insofar as he foresees something which came much later, namely, the deistic idea of God. This is the idea of a God who sits beside the world and lets it go its way; a God who allows the world to be ruled, controlled, measured, and transformed by men, and who doesn't interfere — who lets them do what they want to do. He is, as in later centuries was done even more decidedly, put by the side — on the edge — of reality, where he sits and looks at the world, which *we* have in our hands.

It is interesting that Calvin, in a period in which only the very beginnings of modern industrial society were visible, foresaw the development of this industrial society, and fought against it. For such a God, who sits beside the world, is something which he can stand as little as Luther could. Against this he says that all that science explains in terms of causality are only secondary causes, but the real cause in all this is God. This leads finally to the famous doctrine of predestination.

This doctrine is so much misunderstood that I think we should look at it from the point of view I want to make here: that of the unconditional character of the Unconditional, of the majesty of God. The reason for this doctrine is the desire to have a guarantee of one's own salvation. In Paul, in Augustine, in Luther, in Calvin — in all of these men it was this motive which brought them to this doctrine. If my salvation is dependent on myself, then I am never certain that I am saved, because I know that everything I do is distorted and imperfect. Therefore it must be dependent on something else; and that is the reason which has produced this doctrine.

Calvin's doctrine of predestination was originally not what it became later, especially in later Calvinism—a description of people who sit on their chairs and watch how God governs the world. This is the non-existential interpretation of this doctrine, this is the transformation which has made this doctrine an impossibility, and I would say even a daemonic blasphemy. Originally it was an immediate expression of the desire for the absolute certainty of one's own salvation.

It is interesting that this doctrine of predestination appears again and again in those men whom we evaluate as the highest expression of the religious power in mankind: in the great prophets of Israel, in Jesus, in Paul, in Aquinas, in Augustine, in Luther, in Calvin, in the Jansenists; while on the opposite side, which protests against the doctrine of predestination, the sharpness of this doctrine is dropped—in Pharisaism, in early Greek Christianity, in Origen, in Pelagius, in Gregory the Pope, in the Franciscans, in the Nominalists, in the Humanists, in the Arminians, in the Socinians—and, of course, in modern deists and rationalists and in "liberal Christianity."

We say the first are the high points of religion. Are we justified in saying this? Is the doctrine of predestination, which is a doctrine of God and not of man, an expression of the right idea of God in his relationship to man?

Two Sources of the Doctrine

First let us look at the context in which this doctrine appears. It has two sources. The one source is the question that we all ask: "Why are people excluded from a full human development?" The psychologically or otherwise crippled; the disinherited in economic as well as other respects, or, in a more directly Christian sense, those who have never met Christianity in reality or psychologically, even if they live in a Christian country—what about them? What is the reason for this unequal state of things?

These are questions which are asked by everyone. I cannot imagine that anybody can really suppress these questions; and I agree with Calvin when he says that you cannot suppress natural questions in the name of false modesty. And of course you cannot suppress them in the name of moral Pharisaism by saying that all these people are worse, and we are better; we few people who have the right Calvinistic belief are the good people, and the billions and billions of mankind in all countries who have never been contacted by this true doctrine are worse. Who would dare to say such a thing!

But there is another question which is behind the doctrine of predestination, namely, the question of personal salvation. Calvin says about this: "The doctrine of predestination is the guarantee of the certainty of salvation because it makes us independent of the oscillations of our own being." This was the same idea by which Paul, Augustine, and Luther lived. They discuss in themselves the alternative: either I am partly saved by my own good actions, including faith, and then I can never come to certainty of my salvation (as the Catholics never shall come); or I am saved only by the grace of God. And then the special and concrete character of this grace must be visible in the election which elects me, especially.

THE ABSOLUTE WILL OF GOD

These are the alternatives, and out of them the doctrine has come; and from there we must understand it. Now let me give you a definition: "Predestination," Calvin says, "we call the eternal decree of God by which he has determined in himself what he would have every individual of mankind become. For men are not all created with a similar destiny, but eternal life is foreordained for some and eternal damnation for others. Every man, therefore, being created for one or the other of these ends, we say is predestinated either to life or to death.

"On what basis can we say such a thing? On no other than because it is the will of God—the absolute will of God, which is determined by nothing. God saves whom he will of his mere good pleasure. His judgment is incomprehensible. An accusation of God for this reason is rejected. We teach nothing but which experience has proved: that God has always been at liberty to bestow his grace on whom he chooses. God favors his elect because he will, and has mercy because he will. If therefore we can assign no reason why he grants mercy to his people, but because such is his pleasure, neither shall we find any other cause but his will for the reprobation of others. The irrational will of God is the only cause of election and reprobation; it is a doctrine of the groundless will of God, taught since Duns Scotus. There is no rational criterion of election and reprobation."

The reason why Calvin emphasizes this side so much he expresses when he says, "For if it [he means the divine will] has any cause, then there must be something antecedent on which it depends. This it is impious to suppose, for the will of God is the highest rule of justice, so that what he wills must be considered just, for this very reason: because he wills it. The search for something beyond his will makes his will dependent."

Again, you see, this is a doctrine about God and our relationship to him, and from there we must understand the Reformation. It is the absoluteness of the Absolute which is expressed in most radical terms in Calvin's fight against idolatry; in this expression of the omni-activity of God in Luther and Calvin; in this idea of God as acting heroically and without rule; and in this doctrine of predestination, which Calvin himself calls "the horrible decree," but which nevertheless he accepts.

THE TENSION IN PROPHETICISM

What is happening in all this? We feel somehow grasped by the power of this idea of God, which is so infinitely beyond what we hear said today about God in sermons and textbooks and in almost every religious utterance. We simply don't know any more what the power of God was except when we undergo the impact of these words, of which I have intentionally quoted many to you.

But on the other hand, what about the feeling that this cannot be the whole religious truth? It is the feeling that the unconditional element, which is so powerfully expressed by the Reformers — so prophetically, in the radical sense of the word — needs to be embodied somewhere; otherwise it could not be expressed. The conditional cannot be extinguished, otherwise God's glory *in* the finite world would itself be extinguished.

Therefore we, as well as the Reformers, all feel that it is necessary to preserve such realities as freedom (which makes for responsibility), the message of forgiveness (which must be received by people who have faith), the moral judgments and differences between good and evil, the institutions in which all this is expressed, and the doctrines which describe it. All these things are finite, and they stand in a tremendous tension in prophetic religion with the prophetic message. (That is what I tried to explain last time when I was here for two lectures about the spirit and the reality of Protestantism.)

THE ORTHODOX RESOLUTION

This comes out again in the Reformation and in what followed. Once more God became enclosed in institutions and doctrines—in Calvinism more in institutions, in Lutheranism more in doctrines. The orthodox period started. What does the orthodox period mean? It means that the prophetic witness about the divinity of the Divine, which we have heard in all its implications, suddenly becomes a matter of disposition and organization. We have it. There it is. And now the same thing which was used for the tremendous attack on the embodiment of God in the institutions of the Roman Church becomes embodied in the institutions of the Protestant Churches.

THE PIETIST AND DEIST RESOLUTIONS

Furthermore, God, in order to be expressed in these terms, must be a matter of experience; and so the pietists in Europe and the evangelists in this country emphasized the religious experience—God embodied in the religious experience. But the religious experience was hardly to be distinguished from the general human experience, from the light of reason in man; and so God became embodied in "enlightenment" in the "period of Enlightenment."

This was the victory of the deist God against which the Reformers had fought with all their passion, religious and otherwise. In our society God has become either a reality on the boundary line, and we are very eager to prevent any interference in our productive life; or he has become a being beside other beings. And if he has become a being beside other beings, then he has ceased to be God; and the atheistic answer of modern Existentialism is the only deserved answer to this kind of preaching of God.

Therefore the Reformation doctrine of God is not a doctrine beside other doctrines; but it is the expression of the prophetic principle in its very heart, which is always the doctrine of God — the God who is heroic and present in everything and driving everything, the good and the evil. This God is something we can hardly endure. He is a God who contradicts too much our desire for our own creativity. We all have the instinct to put God again at the edge of reality, at the boundary line, or to make him a being beside others whom we can manipulate more or less in secular or religious terms. The end of this God came when Nietzsche wrote the famous sentence (I think the most important of all his sentences), "God is dead!" This was the end of this development of God — this God *is* dead; and it is good that somebody had the courage of despair to declare that he is dead.

A NEW REFORMATION?

Now the question is, is there a possibility of rediscovering this God of the Reformation? There are signs, symptoms, which seem to point to a rediscovery of the hidden God, the God who acts paradoxically or by contrast, the God who is the ground of being itself, the power of being in everything that is. And this is decisive.

If this God can be rediscovered, then we will have something like a new Reformation, but which looks absolutely different from the other Reformation. We cannot apply these great and powerful words of Luther and Calvin directly to our situation; but we can interpret them — what it really was that drove these people. And I think that what should drive us today, too, is the search for the God who is beyond what we usually call "God," the God who is a ground below all the special beings, including a God who is a special being.

If we could understand again what the prophetic witness of the Reformation meant, it would not be a fight with ecclesiasticism so much as a fight with the well-balanced secularism of today, which also has religious elements in it; which calls itself theistic, but which has no idea of what God once meant in New Testament times and meant again for people in the period of the Reformation.

****

LECTURE 2:
THE HUMAN PREDICAMENT

****

The subject of these lectures, "The Recovery of the Prophetic Tradition in the Reformation," was discussed a week ago in connection with the idea of God. At that time I said that wherever prophetic attack was leveled against society or Church, it was in the name of God and in connection with the distortion of the idea of God either in secularism or in the Church.

OUR SEPARATION AND OUR SERVITUDE

THE CORRELATION OF GOD AND MAN

But whenever an idea of God is enunciated, it is always in correlation with an interpretation of man, and *vice versa*. You could talk about God without talking of man only if God were an object beside others, but that is exactly what all prophetic religion denies. You cannot talk about him except in the situation of correlation with him.

This was strongly expressed by Calvin in the introduction to his great dogmatic work (in some ways the greatest Protestantism has ever produced), *The Institutes*, in which he says that the content of all wisdom consists of two parts: the knowledge of God and the knowledge of oneself. But this knowledge of oneself also is not a theoretical doctrine of man; it is not a doctrine of man in which we can speak about man in a detached way — in a way in which man becomes one object beside others, in terms of ordinary psychology or sociology. When the Reformers — and all prophets — speak of man, when they speak of human misery, the correlation between the knowledge of God and knowledge of man is the correlation between the divine majesty and the human misery. It is neither a theoretical doctrine of God nor a theoretical doctrine of man; but it is the double experience — divine majesty and human misery.

Calvin says, "The miserable ruin into which we have plunged by the defection of the first man compels us to raise our eyes towards heaven, not only as hungry and famished to seek thence fulfillment of our wants, but as in fear to learn humility." In other words, he says we seek God not only in the desire to be fulfilled, to overcome the desire of our finitude; but on the contrary, our relationship to God includes fear and humility. The idea of God in Calvin, and in all prophetic tradition, is not the correlate of our desires, but the object of our humility. God is not derived from us, because he stands against us. This is a criticism of all attempts by psychologists and sociologists to attribute the idea of God to human desires.

THE RUIN OF THE SELF

The converse is also described by Calvin when he describes the human situation. He says: "In the light of this idea of God we are able to look at ourselves." Nobody—not even Luther—has expressed the human situation with more sharpness, more radicalism, and more pessimism than Calvin. Nothing is left of the Renaissance idea of "the creative man." He says: "If we compare God with ourselves, he must be our judge. Men want to avoid the judgment, and we can do so only if we look solely at the world; for as long as our views are bounded by the earth, perfectly content with our own righteousness, wisdom, and strength, we fondly flatter ourselves and fancy we are little less than demigods. But if we elevate our minds to God, what we thought virtue in ourselves, under the pretext of righteousness, will soon be known as the greatest iniquity. What strangely deceived us under the title of wisdom will be despised as extreme folly; and more, what was the appearance of strength will be proved to be most wretched impotence."

The appearance of the divine means the ruin of our self-consciousness. This ruin of our self-consciousness is what all the Reformers proclaimed. The most shining becomes the most sordid in the view of the divine purity. We cannot endure this, because from our natural proneness to hypocrisy any vain appearance of righteousness abundantly contents us instead of the reality. Man (this is the contention of the Reformers, and in this they are all alike) is unrealistic because he cannot stand his own reality. Man continually produces idols (as we heard last week), or, as we say today, ideologies, or rationalizations. He cannot stand his own reality; he has to look away.

(An interesting situation in the light of the history of realism in the modern world is that, in contrast to idealism, realism largely comes from the Reformers' stand against all wrong ideologies. It is not by chance that the neo-Reformation theology of today, as represented by Karl Barth and others, uses the term "realism" and fights against idealism much more than against materialism or atheism.) To the Reformers, the real enemy is idealism, for they felt that man is by nature idealistic about himself, producing ideologies and therefore idols.

Now we must ask, why is man in such a state? It certainly cannot be his original state, because his original state is created goodness. But man has become, as Calvin says, "a sad ruin." He cannot boast about his essential perfection, as the Renaissance man does; for, Calvin asks, what is that original condition from which we are fallen? It is the dignity of man which we have lost. And Calvin said that during exactly the same years in which we have the great hymns about the dignity of man by the Renaissance philosophers.

This depravity embraces all parts and functions of man. Calvin says: "We cannot escape this world of misery which is in man by saying that it refers to our flesh alone, and not to our soul or spirit." Against the Catholic doctrine of the negation of the flesh, Calvin speaks of the totality of the distortion. He says that what the human spirit thinks and acts is mere vanity, that it is distorted and confused, that the human heart is an abyss of horrible confusion. Then he says the following words, which horrify you as they horrify me, but which nevertheless have conquered a large part of the world:

"Let us hold this, then, as an undoubted truth, which no opposition can shake: that the mind of man is so completely alienated from the righteousness of God that it conceives desires and undertakes everything that is impious, perverse, base, impure, and flagitious; that man's heart is so thoroughly infected by the poison of sin that it cannot produce anything but that which is corrupt; and that if at any time men do anything apparently good, yet the mind always remains involved in hypocrisy and fallacious obliquity and the heart enslaved by the inward perverseness."

These words certainly mean the end of the dignity of man, the end of the idea of the creative man, the end of human nature as the center of nature and as the saving power in and above nature.

LUTHER'S CONCEPT OF SIN

But into the deepest roots of the Reformation doctrine of man we are led again by Luther, for here the religious point of view has been made in the most decisive and the clearest way. The first question Luther asks is, "How can we know sin?" Here he shows, as always, his profound psychoanalytical view of man; he has a real analytic knowledge (if "analysis" means going into deeper levels). He says: "One cannot know sin directly, because in order to know the negative we must know the positive. And the positive is the communion with God by his justifying act and our receiving faith." Therefore the real sin is the refusal of the gift of God, or, as Luther calls it, unbelief. He says, "Unbelief is the sin altogether."

This word, "Unbelief is the sin altogether," is one of the most revolutionary words which have ever been said, if we understand it rightly. It does not mean that we are sinful if we don't believe in unbelievable things, but it means that separation from God is sin, in the singular and not in the plural; that there is only one sin, namely, unbelief, in the sense of separation from God; and that therefore sin is not a special moral failure, but that there are ultimately no "sins" but only this one sin, namely, separation. That is what he calls unbelief.

So we can say, nothing justifies except faith, and nothing makes sinful except unbelief. The main right is faith, and the main wrong is unbelief. Therefore the word "sin" includes what we are living and doing, apart from faith.

This definition of sin excludes the quantitative and relative distinctions between mortal and venial sins, between heavy and light sins. These distinctions are made from the point of view of morals, from the point of view of the natural law, but they do not mean anything with God. Each and every thing that separates us from God is of equal weight; it has the same qualitative character. Therefore our life as a whole, our nature and our substance, are corrupted; our whole being, not only one part, is determined by sin.

Luther teaches that all those special acts we do which we call "sins" are the fruits of a radical and hidden power of sin. He calls this by the traditional term of original or radical or principal sin, the source of all the others. It was called at that time "*concupiscentia*"; perhaps today what Freud has called "libido" comes nearest to it. It is the direction of the will of man towards himself, and it is an always acting and driving force. It is never without our will because man, according to Luther, is essentially will. Never to be overcome by ourselves, it is a tyrant in us, although it does not come from our created nature.

THE UNITY OF SOUL AND BODY

And this concerns our whole nature. "The whole man," Luther says, "is spirit and flesh." Man does not consist of two parts; every cell of our body is spirit, and every thought of our mind is flesh. "Flesh" does not refer to a special part of us, but describes the turning away from God, while "spirit" describes the turning towards God. In this sense Luther can even speak of two total men: the man who is totally, including his mind and spirit (which is more or less his cultural life), flesh—that means, subdued to the structures of evil; and then the other man, who is, including his body and his soul and his mind, totally spirit, and who therefore turns toward God. What Luther fights against is a dualistic anthropology (in technical words)—a doctrine of man in which man is built up in different parts.

For Luther there is no rational position above our existential situation of unbelief and concupiscence; to turn away from God is to turn to the world and to the self. This refers to the will as well as to knowledge; we are not free to turn to God and to know him. "Our natural powers with respect to God are completely corrupt," he says. With respect to God, no neutral acts are possible; even at their best, they are evil since the standard for human perfection is not obedience to moral laws, but obedience to the one Law — namely, the full and voluntary love towards God.

"Even he who has received his grace is not free from the power of this corruption, which can be overcome only in a gradual process and which demands life-repentance and penitence. Even the Christian cannot say of himself that he loves God with a full love so that he does what God does voluntarily, as his own will, in freedom and with joy." And this is the criterion: "Enforced obedience is not fulfillment of the divine law; only voluntary acceptance of the divine will is fulfillment of the divine law." This is the ultimate criterion. Any enforced obedience to the law is not based on faith (which is defined as "communion with God"), and therefore it is an expression of our sin, and nothing else.

I would say that this is a trans-moral, ecstatic idea of sin. I know of no one, except perhaps Paul, in whom is so completely expressed, and so powerfully, the idea that sin is not a moralistic concept, not a concept with respect to the Law, but a religious concept—namely, the lack of communion with the source of our being. Therefore, according to Luther, sin goes into the realm of nature; and although he expresses this in half-mythological terms, I would say that he is much more modern in this respect than any of the idealistic philosophers between his day and ours. He says: "I believe that the natural senses also are corrupted, and that the body is distorted in senses, blood, and nerves." According to him, Adam had another sense-intuition before the fall; and the nature of man, as Luther finds him physiologically and psychologically, is as it is not through necessity of creation or through natural law, but through corruption of the original law of nature and creation.

This unity of soul and body with respect to sin is one of the most important concepts in the Reformation which we should recover. It destroys the "moralism of consciousness" as our recent psychological development in the last fifty years has destroyed the psychology of consciousness by the rediscovery of the unconscious. In the same way, for Luther, it is always the whole man which is in sin or in salvation.

THE UNIVERSALITY OF SIN

Since the living substance is perverted, all men, through their origin from the living substance of the human species, are sinful, according to Luther. Here another very modern idea is expressed in religious and partly legendary and mythological terms, namely, the idea that sin and salvation are not matters of the isolated individual, but that we are all bound together. This concept, whatever the psychological term for it may be (as, for example, "collective unconscious"), is much nearer to the Reformation theology than any philosophy, psychology, or ethics of consciousness.

Luther says (following Augustine in this): "Mankind is a *'massa peccatrix'*" — a mass which is sinful, a sinful whole. This is so not because of the sexual act — this act as such is not sinful, although it too is corrupted as are all human acts — but because it is the human nature in every man which is corrupted. In this sense sin is universal. It is a divine decree, but a decree which we accept willingly — through our will. Luther says about this most difficult problem: "I am generated in vice, and did not assent. But now the vices are made my own, since now I know that I act against the Law. Now sin is my sin, approved by my will, and accepted by my consent."

This means that Luther sees that the two elements, in all of these considerations, must be the universal structure of human existence on the one hand, and responsible freedom on the other hand. This is the reality in which we are living; and if a rationalist says this is contradictory, then I would simply ask him to read the Greek tragedians. He would find that these people knew exactly the same situation: the curse on the one hand, the responsibility on the other hand; and both united in a way which cannot be described in terms of our ordinary language.

THE DIVINE ATTACK

But Luther goes beyond this. He has his own mythology — taken from the tradition, of course, but strengthened and expressed in a much more powerful way. He takes his symbols from the idea of a satanic kingdom on the one hand, and the wrath of God on the other hand. In this idea (beside all the superstitious elements which were in Protestantism as much as in Catholicism at that time), Satan is the dynamic and structural unity of evil.

This doctrine of Satan should not be rejected on the basis that such a being does not exist — that is not a matter even for discussion — but it should be interpreted in terms of structures of evil, of which we have all had a great deal of experience since the year 1914, if not before. These structures of evil — these daemonic and satanic structures — are what is behind these ideas. They are not mythological imaginings, although their form is mythological imagination; and their meaning is something quite different. Luther knows about the super-individual power which creates the individual movements which do not come from the individual, which are strange to it, and which try to destroy it.

But this diabolical destruction (and here again the genius speaks) is on the other hand the wrath of God, namely, the power of God which leads us to self-destruction. Therefore it often happens that in Luther's words the daemonic and the divine attack are not distinguished. God attacks, but he attacks through his wrath, and the tool of his wrath is the devil. This is one and the same act. Sometimes it seems as if the dark will of God—his wrath—and the diabolical will are identical; the devil is the organ of the wrath of God, and sometimes the wrath of God itself.

Much has been made of these ideas by Lutheran mysticism and Lutheran philosophy of life. When today we look back at the development of philosophy over the last three or four hundred years, then we must say that this one line of thought (which today occurs in this country partly as process-philosophy and partly as pragmatism, and on the Continent partly as the "philosophy of life" and partly as Existentialism) can historically and systematically be traced back to these ideas of Luther, through men like Jakob Boehme, Schelling, Schopenhauer, Nietzsche, Bergson, and so on. The line of thought here is one. This line of thought (I cannot go into this, unfortunately) is Luther's vision of the life-processes, in which God is always present. But often—or always, somehow—he is present in them in terms of wrath, or in the daemonic way.

THE DOCTRINE OF HUMAN SERVITUDE

But of course I cannot leave it here; for whenever Luther speaks thus, he adds something else. He says: "All this is only the *strange* way in which God acts; the purpose of all this acting is the kingdom of love. Therefore the real meaning of these negative forces is the realization of love. But who can know this? Only those who look through the external side." You remember that I said a week ago that everything is a mask of God, and we must look through it. The mask of God is this acting (as I have just described it), but behind this is the loving will of God. But God needs this kind of acting. He leaves sin to self-destruction, and by this he shakes up those who are lazy and those who are self-complacent. Satan is the servant of the divine love because he shakes those who rest in themselves.

All this leads to the doctrine of human servitude, which has become one of the principal marks of Protestant thinking. Here again we are in the prophetic tradition. Everywhere in the prophetic tradition we have this idea of human servitude. The divine act begins everything and fulfills everything; and cooperation with God on the same level is impossible. Since modern liberal theology, especially in this country, was a theological cooperation between God and man, the neo-Reformation theology came as a shock — a tremendous "therapeutic shock," and as such extremely wholesome.

The question of freedom (again let me make this clear, although I think I have already done so) is *not* that of psychological freedom. Man is always man, and he is distinguished from nature through his freedom. Neither Augustine nor any of the Reformers had any doubts about this point. But the freedom of which they are talking is the freedom of turning to God — and there is no freedom there. Luther says, "It is good so." Let us hear him:

"As to myself, I openly confess that I should not wish free will to be granted me whereby I might endeavor something towards my own salvation [that is, free will *only* in the sense that he might endeavor to do something towards his own salvation], because, even though there were no dangers, no conflicts, no devils, I should be compelled to labor under a continual uncertainty; nor would my conscience ever come to a settled certainty however much it sought to do so in order to satisfy God — as I myself learned, to my bitter cost, through so many years of my own experience."

Here Luther explains why prophetic tradition always speaks of "the servitude of the human will." It is because, if we are dependent on ourselves, we can never be certain of our own salvation. But on the other hand, Luther makes it very clear that this does not mean philosophical determinism. He says:

"But by necessity I do not mean compulsion. That is, a man void of the Spirit of God does not do evil against his will as by violence, but he does it spontaneously and with a ready willingness. And this willingness and desire to do evil he cannot abandon, restrain, or change by his own power. Ask experients whose inclinations are fixed upon any one thing how hardened against all persuasion they are.

"But on the other hand, when God works in us, the will is changed by the Spirit of God so that it desires and asks not from compulsion, but responsively from pure willingness, inclination, and accord. All this we do willingly and readily, according to the nature of will; for if it were forced, it would no longer be will since compulsion is unwillingness.

"Thus the human will is, as it were, a beast between the two. If God sits thereon, it wills and goes where God wills; if Satan sits thereon, it wills and goes as Satan wills. Nor is it in the power of its own will to choose for which rider it will run; but the riders themselves contend which shall have and hold it."

This is a vision of the divine-daemonic struggle in the soul of every human being. Instead of the individual separated from every other individual, morally autonomous, making decisions for good and evil, these are two absolutely different images of the human situation. The one is the prophetic tradition; the other is, ultimately, moralistic humanism, even if it is expressed in terms of theology.

THE NEW REALITY

This ends our consideration of the negative side of the human predicament. As is to be expected, this is the most emphasized side in the Reformation theology, against the Catholic attempt to make everything less serious. Nevertheless, man's predicament is not described only in terms of separation and servitude. Theology—both Reformation theology and prophetic theology—is also the description of *the new reality*. But this description always has an element of expectation, of eschatology, of looking at that which is not yet and will come.

It is in terms of this "not yet" that we must understand the positive description of man. The Reformers did not say, "Here we have the holy man, the saint, the new reality; we can grasp it; there it is." They said, "There it is; but it is as though it not yet were, and its fulfillment is a matter of expectation." This eschatological element in the doctrine of man is also something which belongs to all prophetic tradition, from beginning to end.

Faith is the Gift of Grace

Of course, if the situation is as I have described it in the words of the Reformers, there is only one way out—and it is concentrated in the term "grace." Grace produces one thing: faith; and not vice versa. One of the greatest perversions of

Protestant preaching was that people were told, "You must believe, and then you will have grace." This is the exact opposite of what every Reformer always said: namely, that faith is the first and basic gift of the divine grace. Faith simply means the acceptance of the gift of God—the reunion with God. This is what precedes everything else; and only if this happens, and in the act itself in which it happens, is faith possible.

So we have two distortions here; and if these evenings give you nothing else than the removal from theological thinking of these two distortions, then I am happy! The one is the concept of faith, which does *not* mean believing in unbelievable things, but which means being grasped by the divine reality and reunited with it. The second is that neither faith nor any other thing we do precedes grace, but grace (namely, the presence of God) precedes everything else. These are the two things the Reformers say; and it is a real sign of the tragic situation of mankind that they have been so greatly distorted into their exact opposites. The prophetic tradition derives everything from God.

The idea of faith in Luther embraces the whole subjective side of religion, the whole relationship of God and man. It is reception of the God who gives himself, who makes himself present, who makes himself small in Christ, who forgives sins (and however the formula may run). It is always *receiving* or *accepting*. It has nothing to do, for Luther, with the *"fides acquisita"* — the willingness to believe in opinions about God on the basis of a general Christian tradition. It does not mean *"fides historica,"* or the acknowledgement of historical fact ("at some time something happened"). "It is," Luther says, "the gift of God which obtains for us the grace of God, expunges the sin, and makes us saved and certain, not by our work but by Christ's work."

Faith in the religious sense is the work of the divine Spirit, which again means the presence of God. It is a dynamic motion of the soul, receiving that which is unconditional and ultimate, uniting itself with God and his will. Consequently, the inhibitions against faith are not of a theoretical character but are based in the self-relatedness of man and his resulting unwillingness to receive the divine community because this would deny human self-love.

Again and again Luther emphasizes the receptive character of faith, doing nothing, only receiving. The Law demands acting; faith demands receiving. In faith all the goods of eternal life are received: the forgiveness of sins which gives us a quiet conscience, and the power of love which "re-turns" our spiritual vitality towards God and man. Therefore faith is a living and restless thing; the true living faith can by no means be lazy.

The Paradoxical Character of Faith

Since faith has to do with God's actions, it has a paradoxical character, for God's acts are paradoxes for human reason—they contradict human expectations. This is true first of Christ, becoming "my Christ" in faith. Luther says, "As you believe about him, so you have him. Faith makes a unit of Christ and man, so that each has what the other has. Christ and myself must creep into each other, so that I am in Christ and Christ is in me." This simply means the venturing character of faith.

This paradoxical character is even more evident when Christ crucified is considered. It is faith in spite of appearance: "He who believes in Christ must recognize wealth under poverty, honor under blame, joy under sadness, life under death. Because of these paradoxes, the believer from the point of view of nature is crazy and a fool, for he believes in the Cross of Christ, in which every human possibility is negated." Therefore this is the final form of faith, in which no human experience or reason is left. Nevertheless we feel it is true.

Faith is a real transformation into dynamic actuality; and in psychological terms Luther says: "Faith makes the person, and the person makes the works — not works the person. Therefore works are natural consequences, but they have no saving power. Where there is the right faith, there follows action; and the greater the faith, the more action. The right faith is a strong, powerful, active thing. Nothing is impossible to it; it does not rest and stop. It is like original sin, the inner forming power of the soul."

All this means the reversing of morality and religion. Luther identifies the moral Law with death, devil, and sin, in hundreds of works. For Luther the Law is most threatening because it sets our own being, from which we are separated, against us. It condemns us. In Luther's description, there is nothing more rasping than uneasy conscience and despair. He anticipates all modern Existentialism, including Pascal and Kierkegaard, when he describes the conscience as the anxiety which might be produced by the rustling of a dry leaf on a tree, or when he describes his own periods of despair, which never ceased till his death. He called them "*Anfechtung*," meaning daemonic attacks in which every meaning was lost. And he describes how out of these experiences arises enmity against God, the will to escape him, and even hate of him.

Profound psychological problems are involved here. Fortunately, I cannot go into them! I might, however, make one comment about them. Some psychoanalysts might say, "This is the bad thing about Protestantism and about a man like Luther, that it sets up such absolute categories that there is no escape other than in terms of acceptance of forgiveness." If I rightly understand Karen Horney's last book, this is just what she says: that this ideal which Protestantism has is so high that it necessarily crushes man's conscience, casting him into despair and resulting in neurosis.

On the other hand, if we follow the wisdom of the Catholic Church, against which all these things were said, then we have differentiations — gradations — of duties and of obligations. If everybody is to do according to his ability in his special status or in his special psychological and sociological conditions, then the absolute ideal is lost. And here I think we have a fundamental problem before us. Catholicism and modern psychology are in a kind of alliance against the absolute categories of the Protestant prophetic message; and the question of how to solve this problem is a very hard question — perhaps one of the most central of our day.

The Lutheran and Calvinist Views of Human Existence

Let me conclude with the two views of the existence of man if he participates in the new being — the new reality — which, although always in the future, is yet in some way paradoxically present.

Luther's view of human existence in the Christian realm is a vision of rising in the courage to face Law and death and devil and everything negative — all forms of non-being, including death as well as sin — in the absolute courage of being accepted by God. It is participation in that which transcends these negativities in all respects. Then there is also the downfall again into a situation of ultimate despair. Luther describes his experience of this as being so much worse than every conception of hell could be that hell cannot hurt anybody who has experienced such attacks. In these experiences Luther's self-consciousness, so to speak, goes up and down, and the line upwards is almost invisible.

In Calvin we have a quite different attitude. It is that of one who, with the same foundation as Luther, understands the new life as the steady ascent, without terrible agitations, without Luther's oscillating, erratic, up-and-down line. The Calvinist life is a self-controlled, self-educating, self-perfecting way nearer to the form of the divine.

These two conceptions have influenced the destiny of the world to a great extent. Out of the Lutheran doctrine of man have arisen the depths of philosophical insight and the daemonic power of the attacks against God and reason. On the other hand, out of the Calvinistic form there has arisen this hard, Puritan, self-controlled existence which today needs so much psychoanalytic help because in it the dynamic forces of life are suppressed.

Luther's idea of love and the Christian life is repentance and ecstatic love; Calvin's idea of life is self-surrender and self-control, and action on the basis of this in the service of the Kingdom of God. Both have behind themselves the same negative doctrine about human existence; both agree that only the presence of the divine can give the courage to overcome this. But then they go separate ways and create two types of life, which have moved the world in the twentieth century in a way which they themselves would never have expected, and which we ourselves are slowly trying to understand.

****

LECTURE 3:
THE NEW COMMUNITY

****

This third lecture under the general title, "The Recovery of the Prophetic Tradition in the Reformation," deals with "The New Community." This is the point in which the

Reformation (and perhaps every prophetic movement, every rediscovery of the prophetic spirit) is in the greatest difficulty. The question is, in what sense can the prophetic message create a living community? This question is *the* question of Protestantism.

The problems connected with this question are manifold, and most perplexing both to the Reformers as well as to us. In some ways these questions express the "sore spot" of the whole history of Protestantism. Therefore, instead of somewhat ecstatic statements about the divinity of the Divine (which we heard in our first lecture) and gloomy statements about the nature of man (as in our second lecture), tonight we shall hear about the wrestling of the prophetic spirit with the problem of embodiment, of becoming an historical reality.

There are four main problems to which I want to direct your attention. The first can be called "Spirit and Authority," in particular the problem of Biblical authority. The second is "Faith and Organization"; it is the problem of the relationship of the personal faith, which receives the prophetic message, to an ecclesiastical organization. The third is the problem of "The Prophetic Word and Priestly Symbolism": how can that which comes as the Word of God against the priestly reality become again a priestly reality itself? And the fourth problem (of which we have spoken, and which is so powerfully expressed by the Reformers, especially in the doctrine of God) is "The Ultimate Concern and the Life of Society."

THE REFORMERS' UNDERSTANDING OF THE CHURCH

There are the four problems, and they are all rooted in the fact that, without exception, the Reformers had a definition and interpretation of the Church which we can only call "spiritual." (This is true of all the Reformers, in spite of the great differences which we shall see later on.) Let me, as I did on the other evenings, give you directly the words of the Reformers.

For Luther, the Church is an assembly of all those on earth who believe in Christ, an assembly of the hearts in one faith — the Communion of the Saints. The unity of these men is neither Rome, nor the Pope, nor ritual activities, nor ecclesiastical orders; it is Christ. Christ gives meaning, vitality, and will to the congregations. Not the will of the individual members, but the objective gift of Christ, makes the Church. So Luther can also call it "the assembly of the faithful, a Christian sacred-people, the congregation of the regenerated and holy. It is holy because Christ is its head, and the Holy Spirit works in it. It is hidden in spirit, or invisible [that is, an object of faith, and not of grasping or touching]. As a spiritual reality it is hidden as Christ is hidden, and God is hidden, and the human heart is hidden."

Here you see immediately the full spiritual character of this idea of the Church. We find it also in Zwingli, the Swiss Reformer (whom I name for the first time, because he is important for the problems connected with our subject tonight). Zwingli says: "The Church is the Communion of the Saints, that is, of all those who are faithful." The invisible Church, for him (and this was a very important and effective idea), "is the body of those who are elected by God, in all times, within and outside the historical Church. This body is invisible. It is created by the Spirit. It needs no guide and no vehicle. Therefore the visible Church should never try to distinguish those who are real Christians and those who are not, because the real Christians are in an invisible community through all ages."

This becomes sharply formulated by Calvin: "The basic sense of the word 'Church' is the Church as the invisible community of all elected. Thus it includes not only the saints resident on earth at any one time, but all the elect who have lived from the beginning of the world." Election and visible

Church do not coincide at all, for there is a spiritual acting of God apart from the preaching and the sacraments. Of course, preaching and sacraments are the regular modes, but the other ways are open, too, for God. So Calvin says:

"When the apostle makes hearing the source of faith, he only describes the ordinary economy and dispensation of the Law, which God generally observes in the calling of his people; but he does not prescribe an unvarying rule for God, precluding his employment of any other method. For God has certainly called many by giving true knowledge of himself in an internal manner, through the illumination of the Spirit without the intervention of any preaching." This means that although God is not bound to the ordinary way of actualizing his purpose—the way of preaching and the sacraments—he normally uses this way. But he is above his own way, and he can grasp everybody internally whenever he wants.

Obviously, this spiritual concept of the Church devaluates the empirical Church; so Calvin says: "The Church in this sense is an emergency creation, an adaptation of God to our finiteness; it is not the historical reality of the new being. It is conditioned by purposes, not by being. The real being of the Church is the hidden body of those who are elected; and the purpose of the visible Church is only to create faith and to find people who are predestined or elected."

The basis of the spiritual Church, as I have described it in these words of the Reformers, is the message of Christ, or (however it may be expressed) of justification by faith— secondarily the sacraments also, but first of all the message. The Reformers believed that wherever the message of Christ is given, it cannot remain ineffective; that is, that where it is present, there are Christians. This is an ecstatic confidence in the spiritual power of the Word without any organization, without anything except the message.

Spirit and Authority

But even so, the question was, where can one find the Word? And the answer was, "In the Bible." The tradition is distorted, the Church has fallen into heresy, and the pope is the anti-Christ; so the only place where the word of God can be found, said the Reformers, is the Bible. Then arose the great problems of the authority of the Bible: Why the Bible? If the Bible, in what sense? And second, if the Bible, how to interpret it spiritually? And what about the tradition which has given us the Bible?

Luther's "Testimony of the Holy Spirit"

Let us now look, in the light of these questions, first at Luther's doctrine of the Bible. There was a doctrine of the Bible in the Middle Ages and in the Renaissance—a doctrine of the Bible as the Divine Law against the Church Law, in the later theologians of the Middle Ages, the so-called Nominalists. There was a doctrine of the Church in the Humanists of the Renaissance, going back to the sources; and one of the real sources is the Bible. Later Catholicism had a doctrine of the authority of the Bible, in both secular and theological terms; and often the Reformers did nothing but repeat that kind of Biblicism.

But Luther goes beyond this. He brings the doctrine of the Scripture into unity with his new interpretation of religion as a personal relation to God. He says: "The Spirit who has created it testifies to its truth in our hearts, and only through this witness of him who has created the Bible are we able to believe it. Everyone will be certain about the Gospel who has in himself the testimony of the Holy Spirit, which is

239

the Gospel. The believer becomes certain; the unbeliever remains uncertain."

What is the object of this "testimony of the Holy Spirit"? It is the Word of God within the Bible, the message of the Gospel and its articles. This message existed before the Bible, according to Luther, in the preaching of the apostles, and the writing of the Bible is an emergency act. Therefore only the religious content, not the writing itself, is important. It is this message which is the object of the experience of the Reformers. Thus must the famous words be understood, "that the criterion of apostolic truth in the Scripture, and the standard of the value of the different writings, is whether and in what manner they deal with Christ and his work. This is the only criterion."

This criterion is fulfilled especially, according to Luther, by the Fourth Gospel, by Paul's epistles, and by 1 Peter. And on this basis Luther makes very courageous statements: for instance, that Judas and Pilate would be apostolic if they gave the message of Christ, and Paul and John not, if they did not. Or that everybody today who had the Spirit as powerfully as the prophets and the apostles could create new Decalogues, and another New Testament. "Only because this is not the case, we must drink from their fountain." These words are the extreme anti-legalistic, anti-Nominalistic, and anti-Humanistic interpretation of the Biblical authority.

From this point of view, Luther could make strong criticism of the Biblical books. It means nothing to him whether the "five books of Moses" are by Moses or not— Luther knows that the texts of the prophets are in disorder, and that the later ones are dependent on the earlier ones. He knows that their concrete prophecies often proved to be errors; that the Book of Esther and the Apocalypse of John do not belong to the real Scripture; "the Fourth Gospel excels the Synoptics in value and power; James' Epistle has no evangelical character whatsoever."

This was all extremely bold and extremely spirited, and therefore it could not stand. No church, as an educational and political institution, can avoid an element of legalism; and Protestantism used the Bible legalistically. That was the way in which Luther's spiritual freedom was lost; but it was not entirely lost. I believe that Protestantism in our period of history was able to receive the critical movement of historical research of the Biblical books because Luther's prophetic spirit had undercut the legalistic Biblicism of the later Middle Ages — the legalistic Biblicism which after him found a most terrible expression in his own churches. Luther himself was far above the Lutheran churches; and the very fact that Protestantism was able to stand something which as far as I know no other religion ever was able to stand — namely, criticism of its holy books in terms of historical honesty — that we owe to Luther's courageous statements about the authority of the Bible.

Calvin's "Document of Truth"

When we come to Calvin, the problem becomes immediately actual. Here already the second generation speaks; and here the completely legal mind — in spite of its tremendous religious and moral power — expresses the authority of the Bible in forms which are quite different from Luther at his best. If we make this comparison, we cannot conceal that Luther was by no means always at his best, by no means always at the top of this spiritual freedom he had when making the statements I have quoted. Calvin says: "At length, that the truth might remain in the Word, in a continual course of instruction to all ages, God determined that the same oracles which he had deposited with the patriarchs should be committed to public records. With this design the Law was promulgated, to which the prophets were afterwards annexed as interpreters." Look at these terms! "Deposited," "public records," "law," "promulgated," "annexed," "interpreters" —every word of this sentence betrays legalistic thinking.

Therefore, according to Calvin, the Bible must be obeyed: "Hence originates all true wisdom, when we embrace with reverence the testimony which God has been pleased thereon to deliver concerning himself. For obedience is the source, not only of an absolutely perfect and complete faith, but of all right knowledge of God. The obedience to the document of truth presupposes that the document is written, and the heavenly doctrine cannot be lost or corrupted. So the Scripture, collecting in our minds the otherwise confused notions of Deity, dispels the darkness and gives us a clear view of the true God. This, then, is the singular favor, that in the instruction of the Church God not only uses new teachers, but even opens his sacred mouth." God is a teacher, through the Bible; so we have both sides: a teacher who preserves us from weakness in the doctrine about him, and the authority to which we must be obedient. In other words, we have intellect and will, instead of the immediacy of the religious experience.

This comes out in the fact that that which Calvin emphasizes is *written*. Calvin says: "For if we consider the mutability of the human mind, it will be easy to perceive the necessity of the heavenly doctrine being thus committed to writing, that it might not be lost in oblivion, but used by all those to whom God determined to make his instructions effectual." In the same sense, Calvin speaks of the "peculiar school of the children of God."

The way in which this has been done becomes clear when we see what Calvin means by "the testimony of the divine Spirit": "For as God alone is a sufficient witness of himself in his own Word, so also the Word will never again be believed in the hearts of men until it be confirmed by the internal testimony of the Spirit, which convinces us that they [the prophets] faithfully deliver the oracles which were divinely entrusted to them."

This means that the testimony does not witness that Christ is my Savior, but it witnesses that the Biblical words as a whole are faithfully delivered divine oracles. "They who have been inwardly taught by the Spirit feel an entire acquiescence in the Scripture, and that it is self-authenticated [carrying with it its own evidence]. Though it elicits our reverence by its internal majesty, it never seriously affects us until it is confirmed by the Spirit in our hearts. Therefore, being illumined by him, we now believe the divine original of the Scripture."

This is enough to show how the same term, "testimony of the divine Spirit," means two quite different things. In the one case it means the immediate conviction that the message of God is for me; in the other case it means the conviction that the Bible is the original and authenticated statement of God. This is also expressed in the way in which Calvin describes the divine origin of the Bible. He speaks of "the dictation of the Holy Spirit"; he speaks of the dictation of the Spirit of Christ; he speaks of the apostles as "the pen of the Holy Spirit." He thrusts aside Luther's criticism of the Biblical books; he says they cannot be refuted on the basis of internal characteristics.

Thus Protestantism established "the law-book of truth." In the history of Protestantism, Calvin conquered Luther completely with respect to the establishment of the Bible as the written authority. So in what sense can the Bible now be the authority in the Church? The answer is that the Bible interprets itself; everybody who reads it knows its meaning. (This again is a non-legalistic, spiritual confidence in the power of the prophetic Word; and it is interesting that this spiritual idea worked: there is no doubt that a common Protestant spirit exists. If you come from outside the Protestant world, then you see, in spite of the 270 denominations in this country, that Protestantism is a reality which has a common spirit and a common character.)

No relationship to the tradition could be established by the Reformers; by their criticism they had cut the connection with the past, except for the Bible. A theory, later described by Kierkegaard as "becoming contemporaneous with the Bible" (I call it, in a less friendly way, "the jumping theory" of Protestantism—namely, jumping over 2000 years from today to the period in which the Bible was written), developed. The tradition was not recognized. Of course it was effective, but it was not envisaged; and the real relationship between Bible and tradition, between the Christian present and the past of the Bible, was not given. Everything between was considered to be human.

(As an interesting sidelight to this, Karl Barth has called the discipline of Church history "the auxiliary science in theology." This means that it reminds us that a few human things have happened in the meantime, but that this has no fundamental significance whatever. It is not a theological discipline; it is only an auxiliary discipline. This is the consequence of cutting off the tradition.)

What you see here is the following thing: you see the great, prophetic, spiritual start with respect to the Bible in Luther. Then you see the impossibility of maintaining this, even in Lutheranism—and by no means in Calvinism—and the resulting settling down to a new authority which, by the way it was formulated (as "dictation of the divine Spirit"), became more suppressive than anything in Catholicism.

Faith and Organization

Now I come to the second problem, that of faith and organization. The spiritual Church which I have described had no definite organization. But here, according to their different evaluation of the Law, there is a great difference between Luther and Calvin. For Luther, of course, no organization of the visible Church had any divine authority. Even the vocation of the minister is a matter of expediency — and so is everything else. We have already spoken about the general priesthood of every believer: every believer can be a minister if he has the abilities and is called by a congregation; and if the call ends, he loses his function and is what he was before — a layman, even in the technical sense.

Calvin, again, was more removed from this absolutely spiritual idea of the organization. He introduced offices of the Church and descriptions of the Church which show a different spirit. For Calvin, the Church is constituted by divine Law. It is characterized by three marks and four offices. The three marks of the Church are doctrine, sacraments, and discipline. Doctrine and sacraments are the marks of the Church for Luther, too, and for all Protestants; but discipline is something peculiar to Calvinism.

Here we see the same thing: the spiritual freedom of Luther's beginning becomes embodied in an organized form in which discipline makes the existence of the congregation historically possible. Calvin says: "As some have such a hatred of discipline as to abhor the very name, they should attend to the following consideration: as the saving doctrine of Christ is the soul of the Church, so discipline forms the ligaments which connect the members together and keep each in its proper place."

There are also four offices of the Church, which are demanded by the Bible. Calvin says: "There are four orders of offices established by Our Lord for the government of his Church: first the pastors or ministers, then the doctors, then the presbyters, and fourthly the deacons." (The fact that it is these only and not others does not concern us here.) The reason for these four offices is no sociological or historical reason; it is divine Law. So again an element of canonic Law, of divine Law, comes into Protestantism to enable it to maintain itself as an organized power.

This second point (I could say much more about it, but I don't want to!) had infinite consequences. While the Lutheran churches in Europe, which had no organization of themselves, became very soon departments of the State administration, the Calvinistic congregations, in which the Spirit was modified by the Law—the spiritual ecstasy by the daily hard work of discipline—not only produced the most powerful forms of historical Protestantism, but for this very reason saved Protestantism historically in the struggles against the Counter-Reformation. It is very interesting to see this situation—to see that in order to actualize itself in time and space, the prophetic spirit had to be transformed into the spirit of the Law.

The Prophetic Word and Priestly Symbolism

Now I come to the third point: the prophetic word and priestly symbolism. Luther knows ultimately only one thing in religion: the Word of forgiveness. Everything else is secondary. Wherever this Word of forgiveness is spoken and heard, there God is present. Therefore special services on Sundays or other occasions are not necessary in principle; they are merely adaptations to the poor people who cannot read and who have no other way of hearing the message.

For Calvin, however, it is a matter of discipline to participate in the services. This means that the *inner* necessity to participate in the church services is gone. Two forms of expediency have replaced it. The Catholic must go to the Mass; presence at it is a matter of salvation. The Protestant must participate either because that is the only way of hearing the Word, or because it is a matter of discipline. Thus the reason for the church services, for the cult, is not situated in the center of Christianity. This is, of course, one of the reasons why so many Protestant churches, during the centuries, were empty; there was no *religious* demand behind the coming to church.

This also had consequences for the relationship of Word and Sacrament. If the Word is everything, the Sacrament is only a visual confirmation which you might or might not have. Luther tried to save what could be saved by emphasizing the mystical presence of the Body of Christ in the Sacrament of the Lord's Supper. Zwingli dissolved it (in a Humanistic way) into an occasion for remembering the death of Christ. Calvin mediated between them. But, because of the absolute emphasis on the prophetic Word, on the message of God and forgiveness, of judgment and promise, all of them lost any ultimate necessity for the Sacrament. Therefore the sacraments were very largely dying within Protestantism. They were maintained only by that great power which we call custom — ecclesiastical custom, the memories of our own childhood. But systematically it was hard to give a theological reason for the Sacrament.

But if everything is based on the Word, then the consciousness which hears the Word is overburdened. Therefore today we have a reaction against the intellectualization of the Word in Protestantism. We are trying again to discover a way for symbols, for revealing symbols — symbols which reveal immediately, which open up something of God and something of the soul at the same time, so that they can meet. But such symbols — how can we find them? Can we find them if they are not really believed? And how can the Protestant spirit — the prophetic spirit — believe in the necessity of symbols? That is another fundamental question of Protestantism.

THE ULTIMATE CONCERN AND THE LIFE OF SOCIETY

LUTHER'S DOCTRINE OF THE STATE

Now my last point: the ultimate concern and the life of society. Luther's doctrine of the State is one of the things from the point of view of which all Protestantism, especially all Lutheranism, is condemned. I was told by somebody who had had a very good education that he knows only one thing about Luther, namely, that Luther was against the Peasant's Revolution! This is certainly not the beginning of the Reformation; and it shows how completely un-understood and distorted the picture of the Reformers has become because of the infinite difficulty of relating the ultimate concern — the ultimate message of the divine as divine — to the daily-life problems of our social and political existence.

Luther tried to renew the original radicalism of early Christianity, in which no relation whatsoever to the State was envisaged. He renewed the ethics of love, of suffering, of humility: he interpreted the Ten Commandments in the sense that the Second Table must be understood in the light of the First, namely, as love of God. This, however, he said, was possible only in paradise; it is man's essential nature, but not what man is in existence today. For here, today, in our period in history, in time and space, we need all those things which are against love — power, and property, and force. They are unavoidable.

But how can this contradiction be overcome? In Catholicism, the solution was that some people represent the spiritual idea completely — the monks and, partly, the clergy; and on the other hand, other people — namely, the laymen — represent the needs of this world completely. Such a division of functions and meaning does not exist in Protestantism. As we saw in our two preceding lectures, the demand of God, the judgment and the promise, go absolutely to everybody in the same way. Everybody is under the absolute demand; but at the same time everybody is in a special office in our sinful existence. There, in this office, in this function, in this profession, or whatever it is, man must love and suffer, as Christian. And yet he must command and punish, as citizen.

This means that Protestantism has moved the whole problem of the two moralities which we have in the medieval Church into the depths of the individual personality. Nobody can escape this situation. Nor can we follow the sectarian attitude, which negates every positive law, every participation in the State. We must do both things.

Luther's solution is that the one is the *proper* work of love and the other is the *strange* work of love. The proper work of love is self-surrender and suffering; the strange work of love is power and punishing, taking up arms and so forth. But now, he says, this strange work of love seems to be anti-love; nevertheless it too is in the service of love, for there could be no love if there were no order, power, and life of the State. That is Luther's solution. I think it is an astonishingly profound solution, this idea of God's "proper work" and God's "strange work." It is the only way I can see in which the absolute dualism between the two realms—the realm of love and the realm of power—can be overcome in the depths of the individual.

It is understandable that on this basis Luther was very radical in his demands for the use of the sword. Someone has said that Luther glorified power for the sake of power; but that is not true. He acknowledged the necessity of power under the conditions of sin, and he combined with this a deep resignation and a hidden hope for salvation from the whole power game with its resulting war and destruction.

Furthermore, Luther replaces the element of rational criticism by a strong historical positivism: the existing powers are right, even when they are evil, because they are brought about by the Providence of God. Revolution against them is not allowed, for it is the negation of the principle of order and is self-contradictory. Even in paradise (the symbol for what we are essentially) there were degrees of power and authority; and in the state of sin, authority needs force. Luther despised the masses; he felt that wise men are very rare — as rare as real Christians. The people must be forced. Educational optimism is far from everything he believed.

Someone has said that this was the way in which Lutheran Protestantism in particular became the soil for Nazism. This is, of course, infinitely primitive and unhistorical; but there is one little point of truth in this statement: namely, that on this basis it was possible that the German nation, educated for hundreds of years by Lutheran ethics of positivism, of subordination to the given authorities, was not able to resist. Resistance had for them the character of revolution, and revolution was condemned from the very beginning as a revolt against the divine Providence.

ZWINGLI'S VIEW

All this is quite different in Zwingli and Calvin. Zwingli developed most of the decisive ideas of the theocratic, territorial Church. The State must be based on the Word of God; the Commandments are the highest sources of the civil law. Therefore the government must be Christian amongst Christians, and it must guarantee the preaching of the pure doctrine. In Zurich the Reformation was introduced on the basis of the decrees of Christ: the best State is that in which the divine Word is most controlling; therefore a government which contradicts these decrees must be dismissed with God. This is the word of revolution, "dismissed with God." And this is valid not only for a special country; but every country is responsible for all Christian countries. So Zwingli tried to create (what later on Cromwell did so successfully) international alliances for the establishment of Christian nations. Zwingli himself met his death in the war resulting from this theology, while the same idea in Cromwell saved world Protestantism and has created the spirit behind two crusades of the Anglo-Saxon countries for Christian and humanistic politics, and is just on the way to produce a third crusade for the same purpose. (Here you see how important for world history the ideas of poor little theologians can be, sometimes long after their death!)

CALVIN'S THEOCRATIC IDEA OF THE STATE

Calvin praises much more than Luther ever did the meaning of the State. He had learned this as a Humanist, not only from the point of view of the repression of sins (in which he agreed with Luther), but also from a positive, rational point of view. He favors an aristocracy as the most ideal form of leadership; and he attacks the sectarian radicals who want to remodel the whole world into a new form without any tribunals or magistrates or civil authorities: "But he who knows how to distinguish between the body and the soul, between this present transitory life and the future eternal life, will find no difficulty in understanding that the spiritual kingdom of Christ and civil government are things very different and remote from each other, since it is Jewish folly to seek and include the kingdom of Christ under the elements of this world." (This is an anticipating condemnation of large sections of American liberal theology and denominational development.)

Now I will give you a quotation in which the difference and at the same time the connection between the Kingdom of God and the State, as well as the relation of both to the doctrine of man, are most clearly expressed by Calvin. This can be considered the charter of the Calvinistic theocracy:

"For that spiritual reign, even now upon earth, commences within us some preludes of the heavenly kingdom, and in this mortal and transitory life affords us some prelibations of immortal and incorruptible blessedness; but this civil government is designed, as long as we live in this world, to cherish and support the external worship of God, to preserve the pure doctrine of religion, to defend the constitution of the Church, to regulate our lives in a manner requisite for the society of men, to form our manners to civil justice, to promote our concord with each other, and to establish general peace and tranquility; all which I confess to be superfluous, if the Kingdom of God, as it now exists in us, extinguishes the present life. But if it is the will of God, that while we are aspiring towards our true country, we be pilgrims on the earth, and if such aids are necessary to our pilgrimage, they who take them from man deprive him of his human nature."

These words speak of the theocratic task of the State to guarantee the true religion. They indicate a pessimistic feeling about the world. Especially important is the formula of the theocratic idea of the State. Theocracy does *not* mean hierocracy (the Roman Church is not a theocracy; it is a hierocracy — the hierarchy rules); theocracy is when God's will rules directly through the laws of the State; and these two concepts should be distinguished. Thus Puritanism was theocratic, while the Roman and Greek Churches are not.

For Calvin, the basis of the magistracy is *both* Tables of the Law; the Old Testament shows this clearly. Then he says: "Christian princes and magistrates ought to be ashamed of their indolence if they do not make religion the object of their most serious care. It is the honor of God they defend by doing so; it is wrong to confine magistrates entirely to the administration of justice among men in disregard of what is much more important, the pure worship of God." On this basis Calvin also solved the problem of revolution in a different way from Luther. First he agrees with Luther: the individual citizens can only suffer. But there are lower magistrates, and they might react against the highest offices, the princes and kings, if the Law of God is at stake.

THE DYNAMIC POLARITY OF PROTESTANTISM

We have seen in these considerations tonight that the more Protestantism becomes actualized the more the prophetic spirit becomes embodied in an organization; and this organization shows anti-prophetic traits—it shows the characteristics of the Law. On the other hand, the more it remains spiritual, the more it leaves a vacuum for other forces which invade our daily life. Therefore Calvinistic Protestantism has the power to resist such intruding forces, but it is subject to the Law. Lutheran Protestantism left a vacuum for other forces, and they invaded it and created the crisis of the twentieth century.

I believe that no formula can solve this problem. The tension between the prophetic principle and its realization is an everlasting problem of religion, for it is rooted in the basic relation of God and man—that God, who infinitely transcends man, becomes manifest to man and appears among men. When men receive him, they inescapably make an idol of him, and produce idols day by day; and the prophetic spirit must rise again and must protest.

Religion stands in this dynamic polarity; and my last word to the problem of Protestantism is that, however poor and weak it may be externally, Protestantism is the strongest inner dynamic power in the history of religion and of Christianity—as long as it is conscious of its function of showing the tension of these two elements, which is another expression of the tension of human existence itself.❖

THE EUROPEAN DISCUSSION
OF THE PROBLEM OF THE
DEMYTHOLOGIZATION OF THE
NEW TESTAMENT

Dr. Davidson, ladies and gentlemen. When I returned from lecturing trips to Germany in 1948, '51 and '52, and was asked, "What's going on in theology there?", I always answered without hesitation, "The discussion about demythologization." I believe this answer will have to be given for a long time to come, and I don't see that this discussion will cease for a long while yet, not only in Europe, but perhaps also in this country.

The meaning of the difficult term "demythologization" is: liberating the New Testament message from the mythological form in which it is cast. The attempt to do so was provoked by one article, first spoken and then published, by Professor Rudolf Bultmann, professor of New Testament in Marburg, Germany. When I myself was professor, in Marburg, in 1924, he was already my colleague, and he has ever since lived and worked in this little, beautiful, but often depressing place, famous for its philosophical tradition (the neo-Kantian school) and for its theological tradition (the main representatives of the Ritschlian school and of theological liberalism generally).

A year ago Professor Bultmann was in this country and lectured in Union Theological Seminary and in many other places, and I had the joy to have him with me for a whole day, in which we could exchange our opinions. These biographical notes have more than mere anecdotic interest. They illuminate the situation out of which Professor Bultmann's article evolved. In the year 1941, when he first delivered it, and 1942 when it was first published, the fight of the confessional church movement against the invasion of the Church by Nazism was still in progress, very intensely and dangerously so. May I repeat what I always say when speaking about these events: Don't call it "Confessional Church," because this gives the impression of being one church beside other churches, as for instance in this country the Episcopalians are a church beside the Presbyterians. Nothing like this was the case in Germany. It was the one great church with Lutheran background and some Reformed influences. But within this church a resistance movement arose against Hitler's attempt to make the Protestant churches a tool for his political purposes. In this fight, the only criterion the churches had which gave them the possibility of rejecting the Nazi invasion and the ideology of the so-called German Christians, was the Biblical message. And on this basis a strong Biblicism developed in emphasis and in dogmatic interpretation. The Bible as the Bible was the only weapon which this German church, and later the churches of the conquered countries, had in their resistance against the totalitarian power of Nazism.

The consequence of this situation was an almost complete break with the tradition in German theology represented, since the turn from the 18th to the 19th century, by the great names of Schleiermacher, Ritschl, Harnack, and Troeltsch. In Marburg there was one representative whom I would especially like to mention here, because of his strong influence in systematic theology, namely Wilhelm Herrmann of Marburg, who was the teacher of not only William Adams Brown, but also of President Coffin, and, through him, of many other members of the faculty of that time. And Herrmann's influence was also the chief influence on

Bultmann when he studied at Marburg. Bultmann often confessed that his ideas were not imaginable without Herrmann's influence.

But this tradition was almost completely broken. I remember when I first came back to Germany in 1948, I was sitting with Professor Bultmann in the only room of his house remaining to him, and we shared the feeling that now we were the last two remnants of the old German theological tradition. It was of course sentimental, and not quite justified, but it was somehow real when we looked at the younger generation, because for them the break was almost total since they had no chance, in the years of the fight and the war, to continue the theological development from Schleiermacher to Troeltsch.

Into this situation Bultmann came with his article. In itself it was not a new question. Those of you who have read Schweitzer's *The Quest of the Historical Jesus* — every student of theology should read this book; it is one of the first theological "musts," and I have very few — know that Bultmann's question is very old, as old as the problem of the historical interpretation of the New Testament itself is. But Bultmann asked this question in the new situation in a new way, and it was this that made him so exciting for the whole European theological world. Bultmann himself was not simply a continuation of the so-called liberal tradition — not even under the influence of Herrmann — but he was, as were all of us, deeply influenced by Barth's commentary on Paul's letter to the Romans. When this appeared early in the twenties, it disturbed and shocked everyone, it was a prophetic call for us. So at that time Bultmann, as well as I myself, supported Barth's fight against the liberal tradition of the past. And we should not forget, either, that Bultmann was one of the leaders — on the left wing, of course — of the confessing church movement. So it was not simply a repetition of the old liberal tradition which is implied in

Bultmann's problem, but it is a reception of its truth in a new way and under new conditions.

The reaction to Bultmann's article was very strong from all sides. There was reaction, mostly angry, from the traditional Lutherans, who never had really lost the tradition of Lutheran Confessionalism. There was embarrassment among the leaders of the confessing church movement, since Bultmann himself belonged to these leaders. There was an angry reaction from the liturgical movement and its leaders, people like Asmussen and others. There were synods consisting often of younger ministers who never had heard about the old liberal tradition and its problems, and who tried to make heresy trials against Bultmann. There were ministers who fanatically wanted to expel him from any position of influence in the church. There were bishops who prohibited the magazine containing Bultmann's article from their parish houses.

All this was a symptom of the fact that this comparatively short article of Bultmann's had hit the central point of the situation, and that something happened which the churches in Europe had not expected. But there it was, and it could not be silenced anymore. When you come to Europe today, it is not as it was before, with Karl Barth in the center of discussion, but it is now Rudolf Bultmann who is in the center.

After this description of the situation, I now want to discuss what Bultmann means by "myth" when he speaks of the "demythologization" of the New Testament. He begins by saying that "the picture of the world in the New Testament is mythical." And in a short preliminary survey he points to the fact of the tripartite world — heaven, earth, hell, — of beings in each of these places: on the upper place God and his angels, in the middle, man; and in the underworld, demons; and on earth, too, not only man but also the fight between the divine and the demonic forces, and the continuous causal effects which the activities of these beings have on nature and on the psychological structure of the human mind. And there is mythological thinking not only in a vertical line, the three "storeys" of the world, but also in a horizontal line: the two aeons, the one in which we live and the one which is to come; the end-catastrophe, a visible catastrophe in time and space; the judgment, which will be an act in terms of a great cosmic trial; and after this, the Kingdom of God will be established. In this frame, according to Bultmann, the history of salvation is going on. One feels in the New Testament message that the end is near, that God has sent His Son. This Son was pre-existent in heaven, and, according to a different tradition, He came into existence through the virgin birth. He has expiated through His blood the sins of the world. He has come to resurrection and ascension. He has destroyed the mythological powers of death. He is sitting in a particular place, at the right hand of God, and will, probably already in this generation, return to the earth for judgment and victory. Those who have the Divine Spirit have the guarantee that they participate in the future victorious establishment of the Kingdom of God, and they can be sure of being united with this Divine Being.

Now this means that most of those ideas which we find in all creeds of the Christian churches are under the judgment of mythology. No wonder that under these circumstances all those who kept to the creeds, directly or indirectly, were deeply worried when a theology made such statements.

The question then, asked by Bultmann, was: "Can the Christian preaching request that the man of our time accept all this in its mythological form?" We all have practical experience with innumerable people whom we valuate highly, but who reject Christianity because of the mythological form in which its message appears. Bultmann points to this fact, and he adds that it isn't only a matter of these people, but there is something very seriously theological implied if we ask everybody to accept the mythological form of this message — which he cannot do if he lives in the picture of the world as we have it. He cannot do it without intellectual asceticism. He then disintegrates faith into a work which he has to perform, namely to overcome his doubts, his living in a modern world view. This is not only "work" in the bad sense of an attempt to do something for God from ourselves, but it is also bad insofar as it is arbitrary. There is no reason to demand of anybody such intellectual asceticism.

But this is unavoidable because the mythological picture is a primitive pre-scientific kind of thinking. As such, nobody can seriously accept it, and therefore the question is, "If the biblical message is tied up with it, what can be done about the biblical message?" He gives special examples which he already had indicated in the beginning, but now carries through more fully. For example he says that none of us is able to use anymore, in any literal sense, the categories "above" and "below." We know, in the world of space in which we are living, that there is no "above" and "below," which means, according to Bultmann, that the idea of the ascent and descent of Christ has lost its actual meaning if taken literally. In the same way, the demons, who were originally astrological powers, are no longer astrological powers, because the stars are demythologized by modern astronomy, and so are the events in the human soul. And what is true of the demons is true of the angels, so that healing power, as caused by divine-demonic powers, is not seriously held by most people, and this refers to the whole of the miracles. It is impossible for us to expect a final catastrophe some time in the year so and so. It is impossible to give up the unity of the self, which is a presupposition of our psychological thinking, for a transcendent causality of a magic character, as it is presupposed in demons and sacraments. We don't believe, he continues, that death is the punishment for sin, but we know that death is a universal natural event. We don't believe any more in the sacrificial mythology of the substitute-death of Jesus for our sins. And with respect to Himself, if the mythological presuppositions were true, He would not have to be afraid of death, knowing that in three days He would return. The resurrection of Christ as a miraculous event in nature is something which we cannot accept. The Gnostic idea of a cosmic event which happens to a God-man coming down to earth and returning to heaven, and our own reception into a sphere of heavenly light, is something which cannot be accepted by us anymore.

Now what can we do with this situation? It is impossible to say that we must leave out a few things and save others. The answer cannot be a partial answer that we try to save this or that mythological element and give up those other mythological elements. That was done during the whole period of historical criticism where theology always tried to save a little bit and give up a little bit again the next time, until nothing remained. He believes that a radical reorientation is necessary, but in such a way that the meaning of the mythological symbols is saved, and the form, namely the mythological form, is given up. In this point, besides a few others, Bultmann deviates from classical liberalism. He wants to preserve the center of the Christological message, but he does not want to preserve it for the price of accepting the mythological expressions which contradict everything which we believe.

Now I come to Bultmann's method of interpretation. Bultmann has what he calls an existential interpretation. This interpretation has two sources. It is in both cases influenced by Soren Kierkegaard. The first influence appears through Karl Barth, in whose fight against old fashioned liberalism he has participated. He has accepted Barth's doctrine of sin — of the separation between God and man, of the self and its existential decision. The concept of decision, especially, is the central concept taken over by Bultmann from Kierkegaard. The other influence, also ultimately stemming from Kierkegaard, is through the philosopher Heidegger, who was for some years our colleague in Marburg, and with whom we had a very strong and continuous exchange of ideas, and Bultmann much longer than I myself. What Bultmann took from Heidegger was the existential analysis of the human situation, and especially that part of the human situation which Heidegger calls *Verfallenheit*, to be translated perhaps by "being delivered to death and estrangement." The myth is an expression of the human situation in man's world. And this is the method of interpreting it, that you must always understand what does a doctrine mean for the interpretation of man's existence in death and estrangement. The myth has not only the character of being primitive science, but also − and much more important and serious for the theological problem− it has the character that the divine, which is experienced as being transcendent, appears within the world under human categories; that we speak of God in terms of spatial transcendence ("above", "beyond"); that we express the qualitative transcendence of God in terms of quantitative spatial transcendence. Decisive for the understanding of the myth in its true meaning is not this objectification, this transformation of the mythological meaning into a description of inner-worldly characteristics; its interpretation is rather the power to interpret existence, which is expressed in them.

But in the moment in which we deal with the thought form of the mythological, in which it appears, we must reject it. Bultmann tries, in his demythologization, to save the *truth* of the myth, not to remove it. And the truth of the myth is its existential meaning *for us*. The existential relation to us is the decisive thing in every religious expression, and only if this relationship is given can we speak of the truth of a myth. He says that the New Testament partly recognizes this situation, and he shows that there is a continuous tendency in the New Testament to demythologize the message. There is, on the other hand, a primitive tendency in the New Testament to take the mythological elements literally. In any case, the task today is to follow the first line which is indicated in the New Testament, and not the second which we also find in it. The New Testament myth, according to Bultmann, is essentially that of Jewish apocalyptic and of the Gnostic myths of salvation. These two elements, the vertical and the horizontal, are always present in New Testament symbolism. They are partly in tension and partly united. They point to the human situation in its despair and its hope. This is the meaning of these different myths of salvation, in existentialist analysis. In this way, apocalyptic eschatology and Gnostic dualism are demythologized and have become something which is existentially understandable for us because every human being knows that this is his situation, if it is explained to him in the right way.

In the same way, the Spirit is not a natural power but the power of the new creature to become grasped in a personal decision. Its fruits are not physical or psychological manifestations; its fruits are, rather, love and faith. This is the demythologization of the Spirit, which as Bultmann points out is already very much visible in Paul's writing on Spirit and love.

The question must be asked: "What about the mythological character of the Christ event?" According to Bultmann, its description in the Bible is one of historical reality and mythological interpretation. The mythological element interprets the significance of the appearance of Jesus. Ideas like that of pre-existence or virgin birth have no other meaning than to interpret His significance. Then he asks: "Is the cross of Christ also mythological?" And the answer is: It is, if it is interpreted as the death of a pre-existent, incarnate Son of God who, being sinless, brought Himself as a sacrifice, thereby producing a cosmic event in which the demonic rulers of the cosmos were overcome. If this is taken literally, he says, the cross *is* mythological. But this, according to Bultmann, is a cosmic symbolization of what the cross means existentially for us, namely that in order to become truly human, in order to be saved from the power of death and estrangement, we must participate in it. It is something which is present, and the myth has only the function to make it clear that it is not the death of a noble man, a tragedy like many other tragedies, but that it is something which is related to us, which concerns us ultimately and radically, and demands our participation in it. This significance cannot be seen in the event as such, but in the message which combines it with the resurrection.

And now we come to the point which is perhaps most important: the problem of the resurrection of Christ. Bultmann emphasizes that Cross and Resurrection are one event. The resurrection is not a miracle which gives witness to Jesus, that he is the Christ. Against this he says we must participate *in* the resurrection, as we do *in* the cross, and both as one act. "Faith in the resurrection is nothing other than faith in the cross as a saving event." In this sense, Bultmann says, "The Easter event, as the resurrection of Christ, is not an historical event. As an historical event we can grasp only the Easter faith of the disciples." "The Christian Easter faith is not interested in the historical question." The *message* of Easter is saving, or, as he calls it, eschatological happening. And the same is true of the Church. The Church is an eschatological concept, according to him, whereby "eschatological" means something which has started but which is not finished, which drives into the future again and again. This, he says, is *not* mythology because it is not supernatural, encroaching into nature, but, rather, an historical happening in time and space. And just this is the paradox of the Easter message, that something which simply happens in time and space, without mythological background, is that which is the saving event. *One shall not rationalize it* in supernatural categories, as we do if the myth is taken literally.

I want now to deal with the main points of criticism as they are given in the discussion. There is the criticism by the New Testament critics, and also by many other critics in all European countries. The questions asked by all these people are very similar. In the conceptual realm, it is the question of the meaning of myth. In the theological realm, it is the meaning of the resurrection of Christ. In the existential realm, it is the meaning of *skandalon*, offense, stumbling block. In the philosophical realm, it is the question of subject and object. In the practical realm, it is the possibility of communication.

The concept of myth has two sides in Bultmann. First its primitive world view, and second the way in which the transcendent reality is drawn into the categories of temporality. And for Bultmann, the one is dependent on the other. His critics say that with respect to the first, he makes modern science the criterion of the Bible insofar as the New Testament expresses itself in terms of the tripartite world view. Can we do this? With respect to the second definition, they say that every speaking about God is symbolic-mythical. Even Bultmann's own speaking of God's acting in history, of God's loving, of God as father, and so on, is symbolic-mythical. Bultmann answers by distinguishing a myth which has supernaturalistic character and is in affinity with the primitive world view, and a myth which has paradoxical character. As an example of this central distinction in Bultmann, we can note an example of the supernaturalistic myth in which the forms of the primitive world view are used: Jesus is a heavenly being who changes His place, His form of existence, and after He has appeared in this changed form, He returns to His former place and resumes His former position. If "symbol" is understood in the other way, in the sense of not supernaturalistic but paradoxical, then the same thing would mean: the man Jesus as a man, unconfirmed by miracles of any kind, is the revelation of God. There are no two places to which he belongs, but there is one and the same place. But there are two qualities, the one is for an empirical approach, the other is for faith. And this other quality is visible only through existential participation.

Now let me give you three footnotes to this myself. First, the supernatural becomes intolerable if biblical authority is given to an obsolete world view. In this respect I would say that the attack of Bultmann must be maintained a hundred per cent, and has always been maintained. Secondly, even the existentialist interpretation — in this I would agree with his critics— needs symbols. God's "acting in history" is a highly symbolic formula, as everybody would realize who thinks about the many categories of time and space implied in such a simple phrase. That means that even existentialist interpretation cannot get away from the use of symbols because every talk about God uses symbols, and in this sense myths which I would call sets of symbols which are related to each other. Thirdly, I would say that demythologization should be: 1) An act in which the symbolic is recognized as symbolic and literalism is undercut. And we must do this very radically in all these points to which Bultmann refers. 2) It should be related, in any special case, to our experience of estrangement and reconciliation. Without this existential relation of the biblical symbols, they should not be used and preached. This is one of the main points to which I will return later. 3) We should not be afraid, if we have done all these things, to use symbols as the only language in which religious truth can be expressed. This is the first point around which the discussion revolves.

The second point, that which produced most concern, centers around the resurrection of Christ. In the discussion I found very few defenders of pre-existence, virgin birth, nature miracles, ascension, final catastrophe, or a supernaturalistic interpretation of Spirit and the sacraments. These were not the points the critics were worried about. I had the feeling that generally speaking they agreed with Bultmann, though they did not always say so. But the focal point was the resurrection. Again, there is not much discussion about the meaning of the objectivity of the fact as such. Barth, to whom I now refer, deals most passionately with this problem in the third volume of his *Dogmatics*. He asks: Can we demythologize the report that this dead man Jesus has returned to life in this world, moving about and speaking and teaching for forty days? — For Bultmann, such a statement is primitive supernaturalism. For Barth this statement is the central message of Bible and Church. Jesus was with the disciples and revealed to them the meaning of His existence. But Barth agrees that this cannot be stated as a historical fact. He prefers to call it a legend or saga. But things which cannot be stated historically, can happen, he insists. They can happen in time and space. In order to accept this, he says, no willful sacrifice of the intellect is needed, no "ascetic" work of dishonesty, but we can accept it with joy, voluntarily. Concerning this criticism, to which I have not found an answer by Bultmann himself, I may put two questions to Barth: What does he mean with the word "real"? Is "real" in time, physical time? What does resurrection mean in physical terms? That the atoms of a body have moved from one place to another and were transformed into something else? Secondly, what is the evidence for the forty days, which he emphasizes again and again? Has he historical evidence for it? Then this evidence is very poor. Or is it guaranteed by faith? But then if you guarantee facts by faith, which facts can you not guarantee by faith, and where is historical criticism?

The next point is the concept of offense. Bultmann believes that he shows the real offense of Christianity by removing the wrong offense. The offense of Christianity is not the offense that we have to discard our world view, our understanding of nature, but it is a religious offense: Namely God in history, under the conditions of sin, estrangement and death. This is the offense, and this is a qualitative offense which is a religious, and not a logical or supernaturalistic, offense. Or in other terms, what he demands is not the logical but the existential paradox.

This seems to me true and a very necessary affirmation. But I ask: Is it possible, without symbols of the paradox, to speak about the paradox powerfully, namely, "God emptying himself," and other such formulas? This leads to one main criticism, namely that the existential interpretation is subjectivistic. Schleiermacher, who is subjectively interpreted in Europe, is still the bugbear for many theological children over there: if you say "Schleiermacher," they run away, not because of what he is, but what he is supposed to be. Bultmann is accused of bringing everything into the experience and decision of the individual. Especially attacked, of course, is that the resurrection is the resurrection belief of the disciples. And not only this, but also the continuous existentialist relation to our own self, the interpretation of the Christian message, as self-understanding of human existence in man's relationship to God, world and himself. This is called subjectivism by many of his critics.

I will say two things in defense and two things in critique of Bultmann. First, he knows that even visions are not necessarily merely subjective, that they have a spiritual reality transcending their merely psychological meaning. Secondly, the existential self-interpretation of the human situation as he gives it is just the opposite of subjectivity. In this sense it is entirely wrong to say that he wants to follow

Schleiermacher in the way in which he is misrepresented, namely subjectivistically.

In criticism: the complete lack of cosmic symbolism as we find it in the Bible and Christian theology. He always has only ethical symbolism. This is connected with a conflict I have had with him ever since I have known him: I am by blood and passion an ontologist; he is by blood and passion an ethicist. And on this point I would say that many of the representatives who criticized him feel that something is lacking, namely the participation of the cosmos, the transition from the ethical to the ontological. My second criticism against him is his contention that what Christ really means for us is that he puts us before a concrete ethical decision. Now this is not what he wants to say. He also wants to say that Christ makes this ethical decision possible. But if he says this and carries it through, he would be driven to concepts of cosmic symbolism which cannot be avoided the moment you speak of grace. He is very much against the concepts of the unconscious and everything this means for sacramental thinking. He does not like symbolism. When I first wrote my article on the demonic, he retorted: "What sort of new category are you bringing in now?" I cannot say that since he has a very strong anti-mystical bias (which is always connected with an anti-philosophical or an anti-ontological bias), he moralizes Christianity —which the neo-Kantians have done since Ritschl, and here he has very strong traces of Ritschlianism.

The practical problem: Can the necessary demythologization be communicated to the congregation? And here we find a tremendous conflict. There are some people who live in the myth as a reality, without even trying to mediate it to their natural world view, which they of course share with everybody, whether or not they are scientists. Some of Bultmann's critics say: "Look at the Catholics; they don't need demythologization! They take all this without difficulty." This is one group. And many

Protestants are the same. The others see the incompatibility of the mythological forms if taken literally with the world view in which they naturally think and live: then they either sacrifice their honesty or throw the whole thing out the window. And often it has been thrown out long ago by their fathers or grandfathers, and they have no idea how a mythological thinking can have any meaning for them. This duality puts the minister before a tremendously difficult alternative. Must he sacrifice the one group for the sake of the other group, who in the Pauline sense are the weak ones from whom the minister must keep hidden his greater knowledge? This is the great question which of course is also put before Bultmann, and before every scientific theology. Here the existential concern of the whole discussion becomes a real concern not only of the minister, but also of everybody who feels obliged to help anybody else in his religious difficulties. And that means that this whole discussion is far removed from being simply an academic discussion. It is a most existential discussion and one which puts each of you before a decision.❖

VICTORY IN DEFEAT:
THE MEANING OF HISTORY
IN THE LIGHT OF CHRISTIAN PROPHETISM

THE NECESSITY OF A
CHRISTIAN INTERPRETATION OF HISTORY

There is no Christian doctrine of history comparable to the Christian doctrines of God, of the Christ, and of the church. In traditional theology the meaning of history has been discussed implicitly in the discussion of revelation, providence, the Kingdom of God, the state, the last things. But it has found little independent and explicit elaboration. Several facts are responsible for this situation. First of all, the limited interest of the New Testament in history as such has prevented the church from a direct wrestling with the problems of an interpretation of history. The feeling that the end is "at hand," the ambiguous attitude to the Roman state and the indifference towards the Greek culture, the tremendous emphasis on personal salvation and the otherworldliness of the early Christians, made the question of the meaning of history irrelevant. It is impossible to derive a Christian interpretation of history directly from the New Testament. This is different in the Old Testament, which points to the meaning of history in its interpretations of the history of the Jewish people and the nations surrounding it. Many elements of a Christian interpretation of history are given in the Old Testament. But one thing is absent in the Jewish prophets as well as in the apostolic and post-apostolic writers: A direct interest in the meaning of history as such. Everything is related to Israel or to the church as the representatives of the Kingdom of God. The nations are elevated and thrown down according to their justice or their hubris, they are used as tools for the protection or for the punishment of the selected nation, they will be conquered and judged in the final manifestation of the Kingdom of God, but they are not themselves bearers of the meaning of history. This is the basic reason for the absence of a doctrine of history in traditional theology.

A second reason is the absence of a positive interpretation of history in Greek and Hellenistic thought. If one dealt with history one did it in terms of a philosophy of nature. The great world-cycles included equally nature and man. Human history was interpreted as a mere expression of human nature and, consequently, as unable to produce anything essentially new. People who were nourished in this tradition had no strong impulse to become interpreters of history, even if they were converted to Christianity.

But there is a third powerful cause of the absence of an interpretation of history in early Christianity: The fear of the church. Whenever a prophetic understanding of the meaning of the Christian message became theologically formulated the church leaders disavowed it. They were afraid that the emphasis on the future which is essential to a prophetic interpretation of history would undermine the emphasis on the present hierarchical system which, as they assumed, represents the last stage, the end of history. The third stage, the last empire, the 1000 years, the reign of Christ, has already come upon us, declares Augustine against all millenarian movements. Christ reigns through the hierarchy and its sacramental graces. Nothing essentially new beyond this situation can be expected. Therefore it was the sectarian movements which, in their protests against the hierarchical church, represented the prophetic spirit and developed a dynamic interpretation of history. Those contemporaneous theologians who try to produce a Christian doctrine of history are directly or indirectly dependent on the sectarianism of the Middle Ages and the Reformation and their secular transformations in modern times. Where such an attempt is rejected ecclesiastical, antisectarian spirit is effective.

The present situation of Christianity and the world makes a Christian interpretation of history imperative. Since the first half of the nineteenth century and definitively into the twentieth, conditions have radically changed. The transcendent hope which characterized the early church, the transcendent unity of church and world in the Middle Ages, the rational unity of modern society in the period of Enlightenment, no longer exist. Man's historical existence is threatened, its rational unity is split, its transcendent unity is gone. The question of history can no longer be avoided by philosophy and theology. It has become a central human concern, whether it is expressed in secular or religious terms. The spirit of prophetism has again moved Christian thought and Christian life — and not only in sectarian groups.

The method in which theology must deal with the problem of our historical existence is analogous to the way in which it has dealt and always should deal with the problems of our existence, namely, developing the questions implied in human existence and establishing the answers in the light of the biblical message.

PROBLEMS OF HISTORICAL EXISTENCE

The word "history" designates both the event and the report about the event, historical happening and historical consciousness, the objective as well as the subjective element. They cannot be separated. Mere happening is not yet history, mere consciousness is empty. Only if event and report meet each other do we have history. History starts where historical consciousness starts and where it expresses itself in historical traditions, sagas, legends, epics, records. The prophetic interpretation of history as we find it in the first book of the Bible contains all these elements. Its long genealogical lists point to the continuity of the historical process as well as to the historical tradition. The stories of Genesis are important not as historical sources but as symbolic expressions of the prophetic interpretation of history.

The subjective-objective character of history points to the human character of historical existence. History is a human affair. Nature has history only insofar as it participates in human history, or insofar as we are willing to call the changes and evolutions in nature historical. In the latter instance, it should be made clear that the statement is made analogously and not properly. The proper concept of history belongs to the human realm.

For history is the place of human freedom. Events are historical insofar as they are partly dependent on human freedom, including man's freedom to contradict and to destroy himself. History is the place where human creativity is at work, transforming and expressing man's world. History is the place where purposes are realized or defeated, where meaning and meaninglessness are experienced. History is the place where power is united with value and value is supported or ruined by power.

Historical events have a uniqueness which is missing in nature. Therefore historical reports are reports about individuals and individual constellations, while natural sciences seek for universal structures and general laws. A natural law is repeated in all its different embodiments, an historical fact is not repeatable. This agrees with the character of historical time. In history time reveals its mystery, namely, that it is not a circle which returns to its beginning but a straight line running ahead towards something. Historical time is irreversible, while in nature a law of repetition is effective — but not absolutely. In nature also unique constellations occur, and the whole process points to a beginning and an end instead of to an endless circular repetition. This is the background of the biblical view that the universe participates in the history of man and that the meaning of the universe and the meaning of history coincide. In nature time is subjected to space and, consequently, the mystery of time is hidden in nature. In history, on the other hand, space is subjected to time so that in history the mystery of time can become manifest while nature remains hidden. This is the background of the ambiguous attitude of the Christian world to nature and of the ambiguous attitude of the ancient world to history. While antiquity did not see the new towards which time runs and which is realized through history, Christianity did not consider the old which determines nature and its self-repeating cycles. The decisive mode of historical time is the future, while the decisive mode of natural time is the past. A theological interpretation of history must be concerned with the character of time in both directions. It must give nature the right place within a fundamentally historical interpretation of existence.

One of the most serious arguments against an historical interpretation of existence is the absence of a united history. It is hard to speak of *the* history while most historical processes remained separated and largely independent of each other. It is just in our period that mankind as such begins to be the subject of history. Up to now history has been carried by groups of nations, continental or cultural units separated from others. And even today, when mankind has become the subject of history, this happens through world wars and leads to a split which separates the masses of both groups radically from each other. Mankind has become the subject of history only in military and diplomatic terms. The Bible is well aware of this situation as the Tower of Babel shows. Nevertheless it envisages the unity of history from the beginning to the end, and above all it envisages a definite beginning and a definite end of history. If we consider the millions of years of the prehistorical development of mankind, and the impossibility of sharing any sharp transition from prehistory to history, if we further look at the probability of a slow extinction of the human race under changing astronomic and climatic conditions, perhaps after many preceding historical catastrophes — if we consider all this, the question of the unity of history, of its beginning and its end, becomes even more puzzling and the biblical vision even more paradoxical.

The first answer which has always been given to the question of the beginning, end, and meaning of history is what we could call the "center of history." The center is not the geometrical middle between beginning and end but is that event in history in which the meaning of history has become manifest to a historical group. In this sense the exit from Egypt was the center of the Jewish history; the establishment of the Republic was the center of the Roman history; the Revolutionary War was the center of the American history. In the same way, but in a more universal perspective, the rise of the bourgeoisie and its rational principles was the center of history for a democratic interpretation of history, and the rise of the proletariat and its egalitarian principles was the center of history for a socialist interpretation of history. Christianity is based on faith in Jesus, the Christ, as the center of all history. With the character of the center the meaning of history is given, and with it the periodisation of the historical process including its beginning and end. The beginning in all these cases is the legendary or historical event in which what appears in the center of history is prepared and anticipated; and the end is the victory of the values embodied in the special historical group over against the resistance of all other groups and their values. When the Roman law has conquered the inhabited world, when democracy or socialism has been introduced into the life of mankind, when the nations have come to adore Jehova on Mount Zion, when the reign of Christ is established on earth — the end of history is at hand. And the beginning, seen in the mirror of the end and in the light of the center, lies in those events of the remote past in which the history-conscious group started its way to power and value. The calling of Abraham and the fall of Adam are the symbolic-legendary expression of the beginning of history for the synagogue as well as for the church. The question then is: Is there a center of history whose claim to be the universal center is justified? Are there events in past and future which can be called symbolically the beginning and the end of all history?

HISTORICAL EXISTENCE
AND THE INTERPRETATION OF HISTORY

History cannot be interpreted from a point above history. There is no such point for man. Man is existentially historical and he cannot escape this situation. Only at the end of history will the meaning of history be fully explicit and only at the end of history will man be beyond history. Therefore every interpreter of history is inclined to see himself near the end of history, either at the start of the age of reason, or at the turning point from the class society to the classless, or at the point in which the evolution of the divine power in history has reached its last stage, or at the moment in which the kingdom of heaven is at hand. In some way history must have taken its decisive step, must have revealed its mystery, before an interpretation of history is possible. But again one must ask: How can the claim that the self-manifestation of history has occurred be justified?

History goes on! In what sense is it possible to say that it has come to an end?

This claim is usually made by an historical group or movement whose self-interpretation includes an interpretation of history as a whole. This is the case in all examples given before. It is clearly the case in the biblical interpretation of history. In every page of the Old Testament the selected nation appears as the world-historical nation. The prophetic interpretation of history is given in terms of the divine judgment over, and the divine promise to, Israel. As members of the "nation of history," the prophets speak of the meaning of history. Historical participation is the key to the interpretation of history. This is not different in its secular forms. The key is always the active participation in the life of the group which is assumed to carry the historical movement and to drive it toward its end. Only he who participates in the struggle of the proletariat is able to understand its mission and to interpret history in the light of this mission. Only he who participates in the crusades for democracy is able to interpret history as the progressive realization of democracy in all mankind. Only he who participates in the struggle of Christianity with the empires of this world is able to give a picture of history in terms of the City of God and the city of the earth. There is no objective place in which one can be released from such a participation. But if there is no "objective" interpretation of history the question is urgent: Which key opens up universal history? Is there a group or a movement, participation in which would open the door to history? Is there an essentially universal group whose self-understanding implies the understanding of all history? Christianity says: This group is the church, that is, the "assembly of God."

All these questions become most urgent when one looks at the tragic character of man's historical existence, at the fact that historical greatness leads almost inescapably to historical destruction. The rise and fall of empires has always inspired attempts to understand the meaning of those events. The integration and disintegration of cultures and systems of value has always produced a profound anxiety about the meaning of historical creativity. The destiny of the masses of men under the impact of never ceasing historical catastrophes has driven innumerable people to despair about history and to attempts to escape history by mystical elevation to a transhistorical divinity. This desire to escape history would become irresistible if there were not a group which unites the power of transcending with the power of transforming history, a group which in this respect is beyond tragedy. Christianity asserts that this group is the "church," the "assembly of God." But no one who makes such an assertion should forget its extremely paradoxical character. And if one did forget it, he could be reminded of it by those naturalistic doctrines which are not hiddenly idealistic — teaching educational and political progress — but by those forms of naturalism which derive the tragic character of history from man's nature, so that no healing can be expected as long as man is man. The cynicism and pessimism which are necessary consequences of such a position have come into the open in the so-called existentialist movements of the last 100 years. What can Christianity answer to the question implied in these expressions of the despair about history? Is not the history of Christianity itself a tragic history and as such a part of the tragedy of human history generally? No easy answer should be given to this question.

THE SYMBOL OF THE "KINGDOM OF GOD" AS THE CHRISTIAN ANSWER TO THE QUESTION OF HISTORY

In the light of the question of the meaning of history, the symbol "Kingdom of God" becomes understandable. It is the answer to the questions implied in historical existence.

The word "kingdom" points to the basic historical force, namely the organized political group, in which power and value are united and, at the same time, stand in an unavoidable tension. The tragedy of history is the tragedy of the organized historical groups. The split within historical humanity is the split between different organized historical groups. The relativity of our historical understanding is conditioned by the relativity in power and value of every special historical group. In the symbol "Kingdom of God" all these negativities are seen to be conquered in an ultimate transformation and fulfillment of history. If God is the organizing power — symbolically speaking, the king — no special group is the bearer of history but a group which is essentially universal and which embraces potentially all human groups and cosmic realms. The historical cleavages are overcome in the unity of the Kingdom of God. The tragedy of greatness has no place where God alone is great. The tension between value and power is removed since the power of God is the highest value. History is one in fact, even if not empirically, because the moving power in all history is the expectation and arrival of the Kingdom of God. Wherever history is real the Kingdom of God is implicitly present as the power and aim of the historical movement.

The symbol "Kingdom of God" has both dynamic and static elements. It works and struggles in history and it is the eternal fulfillment beyond history. In colorful images the Bible describes the battles between the demonic kingdom and the Kingdom of God. Although the final victory of the divine kingdom is guaranteed, the battle is serious and those who participate in it are by no means certain about the outcome. They experience continuous defeats and need the prophetic and apostolic word of assurance and promise. The tragedy of history is presupposed in the biblical message of the kingdom, but the tragic answer is not accepted as the last answer. The Kingdom of God is fighting in history and victorious above history. It is both immanent and transcendent. In its historical appearance it is always ambiguous, soaring between defeat and victory; its ultimate victory is hidden under its ambiguity, an object of courage and hope, but not of evidence. And this will be so long as history lasts. It was the mistake of some modern theologians that they envisaged a state of history in which the tragedy of our historical existence would be removed and the Kingdom of God would be unambiguously manifest in time and space. Recent events have overwhelmingly shown the false utopian character of such an expectation. They have reestablished the biblical view that the final victory of the Kingdom of God is an eschatological vision, transcending all history. The victorious kingdom is not a future period of history, but it is that above history in which history is fulfilled, in which God is "everything in everything" and the demonic kingdom brought to nothing. It is impossible to say much more than this about the transcendent side of the Kingdom of God — except in poetic imagery; and theology certainly should not take these images literally.

CHRIST AS THE CENTER OF HISTORY

But theology can and must say more about the immanent side of the Kingdom of God, about its fight in history. The point in which history has its center is, according to the Christian view, the appearance of Jesus of Nazareth as the Christ who brings the new eon and with it the end of history. In the event which is called Jesus, the Christ, history has revealed its meaning — by anticipation in the Old Testament, by actualization in the New Testament. In Jesus as the Christ the Kingdom of God is present, manifestly defeated as always in history, but hiddenly winning its definite victory. Here the interpretation of history becomes Christology, namely the assertion that Jesus is the Christ, that is, he who brings the kingdom.

Christianity has derived from its Christological creed a periodisation of history in which two main periods are distinguished: that before and that after the appearance (epiphany) of the Christ. The period before his appearance is interpreted as the period of preparation, in all sections of the world, but especially in the selected nation. In it the coming of the Christ, and with him the coming of the kingdom, is prepared. The period of preparation leads to the point in which no further preparation is needed, because the *kairos*, the right moment, has arrived. In this moment the reality of the Kingdom of God appears in a personal life and creates a group with a new historical consciousness, the church. According to the feeling of this group, the end has arrived in principle. Therefore an interpretation of history is possible. Nothing absolutely new can happen any more. The final victory of the kingdom has been won. Actually, of course, the periods before and after this moment overlap. In the midst of Christendom and everywhere outside it there are groups which never have experienced the "center of history," for whom this point is still in the future. It is the function of Christian missions to overcome this situation and to bring all mankind into contact with the center of history. Therefore missions presuppose and spread a Christian interpretation of history. In the missionary enterprise, interior and exterior, the historical consciousness of Christianity finds a practical expression. Missions are dependent on a Christian interpretation of history and conversely. Missions transform the period of preparation into a period of reception. Their success is a continuous witness to Jesus the Christ as the center of history, and to the Christian interpretation of history.

One may ask whether such a doctrine of history is not idealistic and whether there are not quite different forces that determine the course of historical events, especially economic want and political will-to-power. The answer is that these and all the other forces which drive men in their historical activities are the means through which meaning is realized in history, the tools, so to speak, of both the Kingdom of God and the demonic kingdom. In giving this answer one simply says that the struggle of the Kingdom of God in history goes on under historical providence, that is, under the divine activity which drives everything towards its possible fulfillment in spite of continuous defeats. The often used and abused symbol that God is the Lord of history means that the materialistic interpretation of history is right, that the will-to-power interpretation of history is right, that the interpretation of history in terms of contingency is right — each of them balanced by the others and all of them right as far as they go. But through the working of these forces, the ground of all forces — the power of being itself — is at work, hidden, yet manifest in some moments to those who are able to look into the depth of the historical movement. This does not mean that one can ever say that a special good is brought about by a special evil. It was the mistake in Hegel's grandiose philosophy of history that it claimed to understand the logic of the divine providence. This was arrogance of reason. Faith in historical providence is the courage to see meanings in that which seems to be meaningless, victory in that which seems to be defeat, fulfillment in that which seems to be destruction, the Kingdom of God in that which seems to be the demonic kingdom.

The Kingdom of God is the aim of history. History will come to an end when the physical, biological, or psychological conditions of our historical existence disappear. Whether this will happen by physical catastrophes or slow developments in the living substance on earth, whether it will happen by forces from outside or by man's power of self-destruction, the era of human history is limited. But in every moment of this limited period, the Kingdom of God is acting, judging, purifying, and taking into eternity what is created in history. The end of history is not the indefinite moment in time in which historical life on earth is extinguished. But it is the eternal breaking into time and elevating the fruits of the historical process, meanings, values, beings into the transcendent unity and purity of the Kingdom of God. This is the sense in which the eschatological imagery of the Bible must be interpreted. What is imagined as a future event is happening always in history, the fight of the divine and the demonic, the defeat and the ultimate victory of the Kingdom of God.❖

JEWISH INFLUENCES ON CONTEMPORARY CHRISTIAN THEOLOGY

It is an honor and a joy for me to speak, in the frame of this lectureship which is dedicated to Jewish theology, about the relation of Jewish to Protestant thought. I gladly accepted this invitation because for several decades I have been conducting a never ending conversation with some of my Jewish friends about the relation of their brand of Judaism to my brand of Protestantism. And I am certain that this living disputation will not stop as long as we live. For it is much older than we are; it is as old as Christianity and in some respects even older than that. And it cannot cease before the end of history. It is one of those conflicts which is rooted in human existence itself, in the deepest levels of man's nature.

I do not think it was the intention of those who asked me to speak tonight that I mention the influence of some Jewish on some Protestant theologians with respect to special points of historical research or philosophical analysis. What I thought to be my task is an elaboration of those elements in religious thought, in which Judaism is a permanent corrective of Christian, and especially of Protestant theology. What is important is not accidental influence exercised by some scholars on some other scholars of the same field but the essential influence which the existence of Judaism and its theological representatives had and should have on Christianity.

I

Yet neither this larger scope nor the fact that I am not an expert in exegetic and historical theology must prevent me from expressing the gratefulness which my colleagues in Old and New Testament exegesis and in Church history feel about the contributions of Jewish scholars in these realms of research. I want to mention a few of these contributions: On the interpretation of the Old Testament there are two main roads of cooperation which proved to be fertile, the one is Biblical archeology and the other is textual criticism. The excavations in Palestine made by both Jewish and Christian scholars have unearthed documents in stone which often have confirmed Biblical reports whose authenticity from a merely exegetic point of view was questionable. At the same time the intensive analysis of the Biblical and other sources by Jewish scholars helped greatly to establish better texts for many difficult passages. This also worked in a more conservative direction. The direct and unbroken participation in the tradition of Judaism which is the advantage of the Jewish scholars, makes it possible for them to see genuine tradition in places where Protestant research was inclined to reject its authenticity. On the other hand — to show the mutuality of this cooperation — the relative independence of the Christian scholars of the Jewish tradition made it easier for them to see the history of the religion, of which the Old Testament is the witness, in the light of the general history of religion. The result was the distinction of the basic sources of the Pentateuch, and with it the general outline of the development of Old Testament religion — something which has been accepted by all scholars who apply historical methods to their interpretation of sacred books. Let me mention in this connection only the names of professors Ginsberg and Morgenstern. And as one born a German I also want to refer to the translation of the Bible by Martin Buber and Franz Rosenzweig which expresses Hebrew rhythms and Hebrew visions in the

German language and gives a feeling for the original Biblical text to people who are ignorant of Hebrew.

For the exegesis of the New Testament, Jewish theology has naturally contributed to an understanding of the Jewish scene, within which and against which the early Church arose. These studies have become more and more important, and have shown that some New Testament ideas which were assumed to be dependent on Greek influence can be explained more easily in terms of contemporary Judaism. Again, this does not refute the generally accepted assertion that Judaism in the period of the New Testament was deeply influenced by Persian and Hellenistic ideas. But Jewish theology has an even more important function for the interpretation of the New Testament. It can show, so to speak, the Jewish side of the picture, the tragic element in the conflict between Jesus and the Jews. The Church has almost exclusively spoken of the Jewish guilt in the rejection of Jesus as the Messiah. But Protestant theology which is not bound to any tradition of this kind has to take into historical and systematic consideration the tragic side of the events in the apostolic and post-apostolic period. I realized the practical significance of this problem only when several years ago I was asked by an important Jewish group to deliver a paper surveying the attitude of the Christian churches to Judaism. Besides many other things which were discoveries for me, I found that not later than the Fourth Gospel a development started in which Pilate, the Roman proconsul who crucified Jesus, became more and more the innocent victim of Jewish pressure, forced to act against his own will. In one of the later legends he appears as a Christian martyr and in the Ethiopian Church even as "Saint Pilate." In this way the Church justified its religious anti-Judaism which is the soil on which the political Antisemitism of the last 100 years could grow. Of the New Testament scholars who have made the most important contributions to the interpretation of the events in which the

Church is rooted, I want to mention Montefiore and Klausner.

It may be worthwhile to consider at this point the basic religious problem implied in the historical criticism of the Biblical literature. In both Judaism and Christianity, it is the main mark of distinction between the liberal and the orthodox wing of theology. In this respect the theological cleavage does not run between Judaism and Protestantism but between Jewish and Protestant liberalism on the one side and Jewish and Christian orthodoxy on the other side. And it seems that in both Jewish and Protestant theology, movements are effective which try to overcome the obsolete cleavage between old fashioned liberalism and a hardened or fanatical orthodoxy. The cooperation of Protestant and Jewish theologians as such, as indicated in the second part of this article, may become an important factor in this respect.

But before this a third realm must be discussed in which Protestant theology has received and must permanently receive the cooperation of Jewish theologians; Church history. A task they both must perform is the description and interpretation of what has been called Jewish Christianity, meaning Christians who came from the Synagogue. They were an important group in the early decades of the Church and disappeared when the Church had been conquered by Christians who came from Paganism — the so-called pagan Christians. Protestant theology must understand not only the early but also the lasting significance of Jewish Christianity for the preservation of the prophetic spirit within the Christian churches, and it needs help given to it by Jewish theology.

Another historical problem of the Church in which Protestant theology has received and needs help from Jewish research is the relationship of mysticism and Biblical religion. There are Jewish as well as Protestant theologians who believe that there is only the relation of contrast between them. But lately Jewish mysticism has become better known by the work of Jewish scholars, amongst whom I want to mention my friend Gershom Scholem of the University of Jerusalem. It has become clear that the special type of mysticism which the great physician and philosopher of nature Paracelsus and the Protestant mystic Boehme represent, and which had a tremendous influence on the German classical philosophers, the French philosophers of life, and the Russian philosophers of religion — that all this is deeply influenced by the Cabbala and its mystical speculations about life and evil. We have to accept that there is at least *one* line of Protestant thought which could be called Protestant mysticism, in a particular sense. This is a confirmation of the belief of some Protestant theologians — which I emphatically share — that prophetic and mystical religion are not mutually exclusive and that, therefore, Protestant theology must revise its attitude towards mysticism.

This is even more obvious if we look at another type of Jewish mysticism, which is not speculative like that just described, but which is practical, determined by the law, and present in the daily life of most primitive people. I refer to Hasidism as interpreted by Martin Buber. However the historical analysis given by Buber is valuated, he speaks of the realities of an intensive religious life. And it was important for Protestant theology to find that reality can unite what theological abstraction has separated, the mystical experience of the presence of the divine and the acceptance of moral law in the daily life. This is what present-day Protestant theology can learn from the mystical trends of Jewish theology.

Let me mention a last point in which Jewish historical theology has influenced and can influence Protestant theologians — the relation of religion and visual art. Since the excavation of the synagogue in Dura, Jewish theologians have discussed the question of artistic symbols in prophetic religion. Everybody knows that Judaism, Islam and

Protestantism, especially of the Calvinistic type, have in common a tremendous fear of pictorial representations of the divine. Behind this lies the anxiety about a relapse to idolatry, perhaps the repression of a hidden longing for idolatry. The result can be twofold. It can be that the temple in which the divine is present and an object of adoration and contemplation, is transformed into a school for law, as in Judaism, or a school for doctrinal teaching, as predominantly in Protestantism. This takes away the experience of the holy and contributes to the secularization of religion, either in a more moralistic or in a more intellectualistic form. The other way transforms the rejection of pictorial representation of the divine into something positive. It makes the holy felt by creating an empty space whose emptiness, however, is filled with the infinite, just because representations of the finite, of a man and animals and flowers, are excluded. This corresponds with the holy void between God and man, the transcendence of the divine beyond everything human and sub-human. I cannot go here into the question whether, in spite of this basic attitude, visual art can have a function in Judaism and Protestantism beyond the limitations or distortions to which it is subjected today in both of them. But I want to give an example of the collaboration of Jewish and Christian theologians which I have experienced myself. A few years ago Doctor Finkelstein, Chancellor of the Jewish Theological Seminary, invited some theologians and artists who are interested in the relation of religion to art to a discussion group in his seminary. There were representatives of Judaism, Protestantism, Catholicism, Islam and Humanism. We all learned from each other and brought back to our own group the solutions which had been tried in the other groups.

II

All that I have discussed up to now was essentially on a historical level. However, since history is always report and interpretation together, many references to systematic problems have been made. They shall, from now on, be the central focus of our consideration.

I begin with the strongest influence of Jewish on Protestant theology of which I know; the influence of Martin Buber's philosophy of religion, especially his doctrine of the I-Thou correlation between God and man. Through the great Swiss theologians, Barth and Brunner, Buber's basic idea has become a common good of Protestant theology and it is still increasing in significance.

It is a reaction against the tendency of the industrial society in which we are living to transform everything into an object, an "It", as Buber says. Men become things, living beings become mechanisms, thinking in universals replaces the encounter with individuals. Men are made into objects of calculation and management, of research and test, into means instead of ends. The I-Thou relation, the person-to-person encounter is lost. God himself becomes a moral ideal or a philosophical concept or a being whose existence or non-existence can be argued for. But a God who is an object is not God at all. God is encountered before anything else and this encounter has the character of an existential approach to God and against a theoretical one. It is not inadequate to state that Buber, before Kierkegaard became known, introduced the Existentialist point of view into theology. He has made clear again, what theology always should have known, that without an encounter with God in the center and the ground of our personal existence, God is an empty word. This insight was decisive for a reinterpretation of the meaning of revelation in Protestant theology. From an existential point of view it is impossible to equate revelation with information about divine things. The God of the prophets and the Reformers is not an object of information, but he is present in a personal encounter; and such an encounter has revelatory character. One must be in it, in order to experience its revealing power. It is not necessary that everyone receive a new revelation, but everybody must enter the I-Thou correlation between God and man which underlies the great revelatory events of the past. You may be informed about them by religious instruction, by Bible reading, by study. But if this is all, you have information about past revelation, but you don't have revelation. For you, the God for whom the revelation witnesses is still an "It", an object beside other objects of whom you have heard reports, but he is not a Thou for you as an Ego, and he is not an Ego for you as a Thou.

The importance of this insight cannot be overestimated. It liberates religion from the two main forms of an I-It relation between God and man, which have struggled for the last century in Judaism as well as in Protestantism. The so-called orthodox wing and the so-called liberal wing in both religions, are in a permanent danger of objectifying God. Both need the existentialist criticism in which Kierkegaard and Buber join and which underlies much of the latest Protestant theology. Orthodoxy, called in American Protestantism "fundamentalism", considers revelation as a deposit, made by God through prophets and apostles, and now standing within history as an infallible document, legally sealed and proclaimed. God is bound to his words which are printed in a book, in a school, embodied in ritual and sacramental forms. God is in the bondage of his own self-manifestation. There he is to be found and nowhere else. He is a piece of reality. He can be managed in doctrine and cult. This is the point against which the prophetic wrath was directed and against which the existentialist theology of a man like Buber gives us new weapons. And it does not need to fall down on the other side of the edge. It does not need to transform the God of the I-Thou correlation into a moral principle or a logical ideal. This was the permanent danger of the liberal wing of Judaism and Protestantism. God became more and more the symbolic representation for everything which is good in man. He became the ethical principle behind the conventional laws of a bourgeois society which differed very little, whether it had in its background Jewish or Puritan legalism. The religious side of the law disappeared in both groups as unessential, even if it was actually preserved in traditional attendance in synagogue or church. The existentialist approach is like a breaking of the prophetic Spirit into the arid fields of this kind of a moralistic religion which claimed to be intellectually respectable. A way is opened for a religion in which Spiritual power and cognitive honesty are united.

Behind all this stands the God-experience of Judaism, accepted by Christianity when it accepted and defended the Old Testament against pagan trends entering the Church. But Christianity is always in danger of succumbing to such trends. Christian trinitarianism can threaten its own monotheistic foundation. Theologically this is not necessarily so. But popular Christianity is wide open for pagan influences; and often popular religion forces doctrines upon the theologians against which they try to resist. In this situation the power of the Jewish experience of God can become an ally of Christian theology against its own popular and hierarchical distortions. I do not speak of the thin and abstract monotheism of the 19th century theology, of the God who stands apart from it, leaving it mostly alone, breaking into it from time to time, governing it as lawgiver and judge. This is not the God of Biblical religion. But I speak of the God who is the creative ground of everything and in everything, who is always present, always creating and destroying, always experienced as nearer to ourselves than we ourselves are, always unapproachable, holy, fascinating, terrifying, the ground and meaning of everything that is.

This is the living God, dynamic in himself, life as the ground of life, and therefore not so far from the trinitarian God as popular distortions and theological concepts seem to indicate. It is a great experience to feel the permanent awareness of this God in prophetic personalities within present day Judaism. It can awake and has awakened in Protestant theologians a God-consciousness which had a deep influence on their religious life and their theology.

But even this is not the last and most important point of Jewish influence on Protestant theology. The I-Thou relation is not only a relation between God and man, but also between man and man. Judaism has rightly been described as "ethical monotheism." The monotheism of the Old Testament is not a monotheism of number, but of quality; it does not say that one god is better than many. Why should it be? But Jewish monotheism says that the God of Israel is the God of the world, because he is the God of justice. This alone makes him universal. For justice is, by its very nature, universal. The God of ethical monotheism is both the exclusive and the universal God, and he is exclusive because he is universal, because he represents justice even against his own nation.

This ethical element in Judaism conflicts with the sacramental element in all religions, including Christianity and Judaism itself. The contrast must be considered more fully, because only in relation to it can the whole significance of Judaism as a corrective to Christianity be understood. The holy has a double relation to man, a relation of giving presence and commanding transcendence. The former is the basis for the sacramental type of religious experience, the latter is the basis for the ethical type of religious experience. Every living religion is a union of both types, but usually in such a way that one or the other type prevails. If it becomes not only prevalent but exclusive, the religious experience has ceased. It is replaced by magic if the sacramental side becomes exclusive. It is replaced by morals if the ethical side becomes exclusive. In some forms of sacramental Christianity which have relapsed into primitivism, magic practice has removed genuine religious experience, while in some forms of ethical Judaism ethical legalism has removed genuine religious experience. But these extremes are not the theological problem. The permanent problem in all religions is the balance between the sacramental and the ethical element. And it is obvious that in Judaism the balance falls more on the ethical, in Christianity more on the sacramental side. Therefore Judaism is a permanent ethical corrective of sacramental Christianity. And this is the main significance of Judaism for Protestant theology.

Every reality is Sacramental in which the holy is experienced as present. In this sense Judaism had and still has strong sacramental elements: Israel is the religion of the covenant which is given, before anything is demanded. The law is felt first of all as a gift, as an eternal divine reality which has appeared in history. It has sacramental quality before it has commanding quality. This, by the way, is something else that Christian theology has to learn from Jewish theologians. Christian theologians often think about the law solely in terms of the Pauline-Lutheran criticism of legalism. Surely they know that the law does not necessarily imply legalism. But since actually the religions of the law have become legalistic religions, they often forget that for the religious Jew the law is not oppressive but liberating. It is grace, before it is demand.

Looking at the content of the law we find that the sacramental and ritual element takes a large place, and everybody knows about its place in the history of the Jewish religion up to the present day. But since the criticism of the cult by the great prophets, Judaism has never forgotten that the condition of its covenant with God is justice, and that without the obedience to the moral law even the strictest fulfillment of the ritual law is without value. Judaism is the religion of expectation. Although the holy is present, the divine promise is not fulfilled. The messianic age has not yet appeared, the Messiah is still to come. All sacramental activities have an element of anticipation; they are, as Albert Schweitzer has called it, "eschatological sacraments." That which ought to be, the new earth, the rule of God, has not yet come!

In Christianity, the decisive event *has* occurred. The Messiah has appeared in an historical person. The holy is present in its abundance. The coming eon has already started. This changes the balance between the sacramental and the ethical. The sacramental is immensely increased in importance. In the sacramental power of the priest, the rule of the Christ is actual. The last stage of history has come. The Church and its institutions are identical with the Kingdom of God. Here it is, beyond criticism, infallible and unchangeable. The prophetic expectations, the demands for justice, the criticisms of the cult: all this is pushed into the underground. Certainly it came out again and again, most explosively in the Reformation. But the sacramental principle, the presence of the Christ, remained the foundation also of the Protestant churches. In them, it was not hierarchy and cult which represented the presence of the holy, but it was the Bible and the pure doctrine. But the social emphasis, the demand for justice, was even less emphasized. The Roman hierarchy was replaced by the princes or by members of the ruling classes. This alone made a strong prophetic criticism almost impossible. The Protestant churches accepted the cultural and social patterns of the nations in which they were established. They became nationalistic and consecrated a pagan nationalism. Here are the roots of the tension between Judaism and a nationalistic Christianity. Nationalism denies justice and is afraid of the prophetic attack on its consecration of injustice. This explains the weakness of the resistance Protestantism showed against the Nazis and the almost complete lack of criticism of their attempt to eradicate the Jewish people.

Resistance and criticism were broken by the amalgamation of nation and religion. In Germany this general danger of Protestantism was increased by the Lutheran attitude towards the state and its authorities; the belief that even the worst government has divine authority and must be obeyed in all matters which do not concern the Spiritual life of the Church. Protestant theology had to reconsider its social ethics in the light of these events. But it did so only after the Church itself was persecuted by a paganized nationalism. Perhaps the most important part of Jewish influence in this respect was not what the Jewish theologians had to *say* but what Judaism represents by its very existence. It puts before the eyes of the Christian world a tradition in which the balance between the sacramental and the ethical element was always on the side of the ethical. It tells the Christian churches that they need a principle of permanent, prophetic self-criticism within themselves and their nations.

But one may ask: Is it not enough that the Church has the Old Testament? Is this not the document of prophetic self-criticism to be used against the Church as it was once directed against the religious nationalism and paganism of old Israel? But history has shown that this is not so. Self-criticism is good, but we all know that it is so much interwoven with self-justification that its transforming effect is minimal if it is not supported by criticism from the outside. This is not an abstract consideration, but it is an autobiographical experience I had in European and especially German Protestantism of the last decades. I cannot imagine that the religious social movements in which I myself participated could have developed without a continuous direct and indirect influence of the prophetic and critical spirit in contemporary Judaism. In the so-called religious-socialist groups a give and take between Christians and Jews was taking place from their beginning after the first world war. The interpretation of history, created by these groups and given to the Christian churches as an addition to their theological substance, would not have been possible without the Jewish influence. And since these ideas have permeated all Protestant churches, American as well as European, to a considerable extent, one can see here the climax of Jewish influence on Protestant theology. It is the general reawakening of the prophetic spirit in the Protestant churches which is the most important fruit of the contemporary reception of Jewish elements by Protestant theology.

It is not my task, and it would be beyond my power, to show the other side of the picture, the Christian influence on Jewish theology. It certainly does exist. But I am happy if I have succeeded in my short survey in showing that in our period something is going on between Jewish and Christian thought which has not happened since the two religions parted in life, thought and destiny in the first and second centuries. There is a new situation today: Jewish thinking can be received by Protestant theology. And as a Protestant theologian I am glad and grateful for the gifts we have already received.❖

RELIGIOUS SYMBOLS AND OUR
KNOWLEDGE OF GOD

The fact that there is so much discussion about the meaning of symbols going on in this country as well as in Europe is a symptom of something deeper. I believe it is a symptom of two things, something negative and something positive. It is a symptom of the fact that we are in a confusion of language in theology and philosophy and related subjects which has hardly been surpassed in any time in history. Words do not communicate to us anymore what they originally did and what they were invented to communicate. This has something to do with the fact that our present culture has no clearing house such as medieval scholasticism was, and Protestant scholasticism in the 17th century at least tried to be, and philosophers like Kant tried to renew. We have no such clearing house and this is the point in which I am in sympathy with the present day so-called logical positivists or symbolic logicians or logicians generally. They at least try to provide a clearing house. My only criticism is that this clearing house is a very small room, perhaps only a corner of a house, and not a real house. It excludes most of life. But it could become useful if it increased in reach and acceptance of realities beyond the mere logical calculus. The second point which I want to make is that we are in a process in which a very important thing is being rediscovered: namely, that there are levels of reality of great difference, and that these different levels demand different approaches and different languages: that not everything in reality can be grasped by the language which is most adequate for mathematical sciences; the insight into this situation is the most positive side of the fact that the problem of symbols is taken seriously again.

I

I want to proceed in my own presentation with the intention of clearing concepts as far as I am able. And in order to do this I want to make five steps, the first of which is the discussion of "symbols and signs." Symbols are similar to signs in one decisive respect: both symbols and signs point beyond themselves to something else. The typical sign, for instance the red light of the corner of the street, does not point to itself but it points to the necessity of cars stopping. And every symbol points beyond itself to a reality for which it stands. In this, symbols and signs have an essential identity — they point beyond themselves. And this is the reason that the confusion of language with which I started this lecture has also conquered the discussion about symbols for centuries and has produced confusion between signs and symbols. The first step in any clearing up of the meaning of symbols is to distinguish it from the meaning of signs.

The difference which I see as a fundamental difference between them is that signs do not participate in any way in the reality and power of that to which they point. Symbols, although they are not the same as that which they symbolize, participate in its meaning and power. The difference between symbol and sign is the participation in the symbolized reality which characterizes the symbols, and the non-participation in the "pointed-to" reality which characterizes a sign. For example, letters of the alphabet as they are written, an "A" or an "R" do not participate in the sound to which they point; on the other hand, the flag participates in the power of the king or the nation for which it stands and which it symbolizes. There has, therefore, been a fight since the days of William Tell as to how to behave in the presence of a flag. This would be meaningless if the flag did not participate as a symbol in the power of that which it symbolizes. The whole monarchic idea is itself entirely ununderstandable, if you do not understand that the king always is both: on the one hand, a symbol of the power of the group of which he is the king and on the other hand, he who exercised partly (never fully, of course) this power.

But something has happened which is very dangerous for all our attempts to find a clearing house of the concepts of symbols and signs. I have experienced this in three seminars which I have had in Columbia University with my philosophical colleagues there. The mathematician has usurped the term "symbol" for mathematical "sign," and this makes a disentanglement of the confusion almost impossible. The only thing we can do is to distinguish different groups, signs which are called symbols, and genuine symbols. The mathematical signs are signs which are wrongly called symbols. Let me again say something about language. Language is a very good example of the difference between signs and symbols. Words in a language are signs for a meaning which they express. The word "desk" is a sign which points to something quite different — namely, the thing on which my paper is lying here and at which I am looking and which hides me partly from you. This has nothing to do with the word "desk", with these four letters. But there are words in every language which are more than this, and in the moment in which they get connotations which go beyond something to which they point as signs, then they can become symbols; and this is a very important distinction for every speaker. He can speak almost completely in signs, reducing the meaning of his words almost to mathematical signs, and this is the absolute ideal of the logical positivist. The other pole of this is the liturgical or the poetic language where words have a power through centuries, or more than centuries. They have connotations in situations in which they appear so that they cannot be replaced. They have become not only signs pointing to a meaning which is defined, but also symbols standing for a reality in the power of which they participate.

II

Now I come to my second consideration dealing with the functions of symbols. The first function is implied in what I have already said — namely, the representative function. The symbol represents something which is not itself, for which it stands and in the power and meaning of which it participates. This is a basic function of every symbol, and therefore, if that word had not been used in so many other ways, one could perhaps even translate "symbolic" as "representative," but for some reason that is not possible. If the symbols stand for something which they are not, then the question is, "Why do we not have that for which they stand directly? Why do we need symbols at all?" And now I come to something which is perhaps the main function of a symbol — namely, the opening up of levels of reality which otherwise are hidden and cannot be grasped in any other way.

Every symbol opens up a level of reality for which non-symbolic speaking is inadequate. Let me interpret this or explain this in terms of artistic symbols. I resisted for many years the temptation to call works of art symbolic for the simple reason that there is a special artistic style which we call symbolistic and which produces only bad works of art. For this reason I disliked the idea of saying that works of art are symbolic. But in the meantime, the more I tried to enter into the meaning of symbols, the more I was convinced that it was a function of art to open up levels of reality; in poetry, in visual art, and in music, levels of reality are opened up which can be opened up in no other way. Now if this is the function of art, then certainly artistic creations have symbolic character. You can take that which a landscape of Rubens, for instance, mediates to you. You cannot have this experience in any other way than through this painting made by Rubens. This landscape has some heroic character; it has character of balance, of colors, of weights, of values, and so on. All this is very external. What this mediates to you cannot be expressed in any other way than through the painting itself. The same is also true in the relationship of poetry and philosophy. The temptation may often be to confuse the issue by bringing too many philosophical concepts into a poem. Now this is really the problem; one cannot do this. If one uses philosophical language or scientific language, it does not mediate the same thing which is mediated in the use of really poetic language without a mixture of any other language. This example may show what I mean by the phrase "opening up levels of reality." But in order to do this, something else must be opened up — namely, levels of the soul, levels of our interior reality. And they must correspond to the levels in exterior reality which are opened up by a symbol. So every symbol is two-edged. It opens up reality and it opens up the soul. Here I could give the same example — namely, the artistic experience. There are people who are not opened up by music, or who are not opened up by poetry, or more of them (mostly in Protestant America) who are not opened up at all by visual arts. The "opening up" is a two-sided function — namely, reality in deeper levels and the human soul in special levels.

If this is the function of symbols then it is obvious that symbols cannot be replaced by other symbols. Every symbol has a special function which is just *it* and cannot be replaced by more or less adequate symbols. This is different from signs, for signs can always be replaced. If one finds that a green light is not so expedient as perhaps a blue light (this is not true, but could be true), then we simply put on a blue light, and nothing is changed. but a symbolic word (such as the word "God") cannot be replaced. No symbol can be replaced when used in its special function. So one asks rightly, "How do symbols arise, and how do they come to an end?" As different from signs, symbols are born and die. Signs are consciously invented and removed. This is a fundamental difference. "Out of which womb are symbols born?" I would say out of the womb which is usually called today the "group unconscious" or "collective unconscious," or whatever you want to call it — out of a group which acknowledges, in this thing, this word, this flag, or whatever it may be, its own being. It is not invented intentionally; and even if somebody would try to invent a symbol, as sometimes happens, then it becomes a symbol only if the unconscious of a group says "yes" to it. It means that something is opened up by it in the sense which I have just described. Now this implies further that in the moment in which the inner situation of the human group to a symbol has ceased to exist, then the symbol dies. The symbol does not "say" anything any more. In this way, all of the polytheistic gods have died; the situation in which they were born has changed or does not exist any more, and so the symbols died. But these are events which cannot be described in terms of intention and invention.

III

Now I come to my third consideration — namely, the nature of religious symbols. Religious symbols do exactly the same thing as all symbols do — namely, they open up a level of reality, which otherwise is not opened at all, which is hidden. I would call this the depth dimension of reality itself, the dimension of reality which is the ground of every other dimension and every other depth, and which therefore is not one level beside the others but is the fundamental level, the level below all other levels, the level of being itself, or the ultimate power of being. Religious symbols open up the experience of the dimension of this depth in the human soul. If a religious symbol has ceased to have this function, then it dies. And if new symbols are born, they are born out of a changed relationship to the ultimate ground of being, i.e., to the Holy.

The dimension of ultimate reality is the dimension of the Holy. And so we can also say, religious symbols are symbols of the Holy. As such they participate in the holiness of the holy according to our basic definition of a symbol. But participation is not identity; they are not themselves *the* Holy. The wholly transcendent transcends every symbol of the Holy. Religious symbols are taken from the infinity of material which the experienced reality gives us. Everything in time and space has become at some time in the history of religion a symbol for the Holy. And this is naturally so, because everything that is in the world we encounter rests on the ultimate ground of being. This is the key to the otherwise extremely confusing history of religion. Those of you who have looked into this seeming chaos of the history of religion in all periods of history from the earliest primitives to the latest developments in California will be extremely confused about the chaotic character of this development. But the key which makes order out of this chaos is comparatively simple. And the key is that everything in reality can impress itself as a symbol for a special relationship of the human mind to its own ultimate ground and meaning. So in order to open up the seemingly closed door to this chaos of religious symbols, one simply has to ask, "Which is the relationship to the ultimate which is symbolized in these symbols?" And then they cease to be meaningless; and they become, on the contrary, the most revealing creations of the human mind, the most genuine ones, the most powerful ones, those which control the human consciousness, and perhaps even more the unconsciousness, and have therefore this tremendous tenacity which is characteristic of all religious symbols in the history of religion.

Religion, as everything in life, stands under the law of ambiguity, "ambiguity" meaning that it is creative and destructive at the same time. Religion has its holiness and its unholiness, and the reason for this is obvious from what I have said about religious symbolism. Religious symbols point symbolically to that which transcends all of them. But since, as symbols, they participate in that to which they point, they always have the tendency (in the human mind, of course) to replace that to which they are supposed to point, and to become ultimate in themselves. And in the moment in which they do this, they become idols. All idolatry is nothing else than the absolutizing of symbols of the Holy, and making them identical with the Holy itself. In this way, for instance, holy persons can become god. Ritual acts can take on unconditional validity, although they are only expressions of a special situation. In all sacramental activities of religion, in all holy objects, holy books, holy doctrines, holy rites, you find this danger which I like to call demonization. They become demonic in the moment in which they become elevated to the unconditional and ultimate character of the Holy itself.

IV

Now I come to my fourth consideration — namely the levels of religious symbols. I distinguish two fundamental levels in all religious symbols: the transcendent level, the level which goes *beyond* the empirical reality we encounter, and the immanent level, the level which we find *within* the encounter with reality. Let us first look at the first level, the transcendent level. The basic symbol on the transcendent level would be God himself. But we cannot simply say that

God is a symbol. We must always say two things about him: we must say that there is a non-symbolic element in our image of God — namely that he is ultimate reality, being itself, ground of being, power of being; and the other, that he is the highest being in which everything that we have does exist in the most perfect way. If we say this we have in our mind the image of a highest being, a being with the characteristics of highest perfection. That means we have a symbol for that which is not symbolic in the idea of God — namely "Being Itself." It is important, and I think more than important, to distinguish these two elements in the idea of God. Thus all of these discussions going on about God being a person or not a person, God being similar to other beings or not similar, these discussions which have a great impact on the destruction of the religious experience through false interpretations of it, could be overcome if we would say, "Certainly the awareness of something unconditional is in itself what it is, is not symbolic." We can call it *"Being Itself,"* *esse qua esse, esse ipsum,* as the Scholastics did. But in our relationship to this ultimate we symbolize and must symbolize. We could not be in communication with God if he were only "ultimate being." But in our relationship to him we encounter him with the highest of what we ourselves are, *person.* And so in the symbolic form of speaking about him, we have both that which transcends infinitely our experience of ourselves as persons, and that which is so adequate to our being persons that we can say, "Thou" to God, and can pray to him. And these two elements must be preserved. If we preserve only the element of the unconditional, then no relationship to God is possible. If we preserve only the element of the ego-Thou relationship, as it is called today, we lose the element of the divine — namely, the unconditional which transcends subject and object and all other polarities. This is the first point on the transcendent level.

The second is the qualities, the attributes of God, whatever you say about him: that he is love, that he is mercy, that he is power, that he is omniscient, that he is omnipresent, that he is almighty and all this. These attributes of God are taken from experienced qualities we have ourselves. They cannot be applied to God in the literal sense. If this is done, it leads to an infinite amount of absurdities. This again is one of the reasons for the destruction of religion through wrong communicative interpretation of it. And again the symbolic character of these qualities must be maintained consistently. Otherwise, every speaking about the divine becomes absurd. A third level on the transcendent level is the acts of God. For instance, when we say, "He has created the world," "He has sent his son," "He will fulfill the world." In all these temporal, causal, and other expressions we speak symbolically of God. And I would like here to give an example in which the four main categories of our finitude are combined in *one* small sentence, *"God has sent his son."* Here we have in the word "has" temporality. But God is beyond *our* temporality, though not beyond every temporality. Here is space; "sending somebody" means moving him from one place to another place. This certainly is speaking symbolically, although spatiality is in God as an element in his creative ground. We say that he "has sent," that meant that he has caused something. In this way God is subject to the category of causality. And when we speak of him and his Son, we have two different substances and apply the category of substance to him. Now all this, if taken literally, is absurd. If it is taken symbolically, it is a profound expression, the ultimate Christian expression, of the relationship between God and man in the Christian experience. But to distinguish these two kinds of speech, the non-symbolic and the symbolic, in such a point is so important that if we are not able to make understandable to our contemporaries that we speak symbolically when we use such language, they will rightly turn away from us, as from people who live still in absurdities and superstitions.

Now consider the immanent level, the level of the appearances of the divine in time and space. Here we have first of all the incarnations of the divine, different beings in time and space, divine beings transmuted into animals or men or any kinds of other beings as they appear in time and space. This is often forgotten by those within Christianity who like to use in every second theological proposition the word, "incarnation." They forget that this is not an especially Christian characteristic, because incarnation is something which happens in paganism all the time. The divine beings always incarnate in different forms. That is very easy in paganism. This is not the real distinction between Christianity and other religions. Let me say something here, about the relationships of the transcendent to the immanent level just in connection to the incarnation idea. Historically, one must say that preceding both of them was the situation in which the transcendent and immanent were not distinguished. In the Indonesian doctrine of "*Mana*," the divine mystical power which permeates all reality, we have some divine presence which is both immanent in everything as a hidden power, and at the same time transcendent, something which can be grasped only through very difficult ritual activities known to the priest. Out of this identity of the immanent and the transcendent the gods of the great mythologies have developed in Greece and in the Semitic nations and in India. There we find incarnations as the immanent element of the divine. The more transcendent the gods become, the more incarnations of personal or sacramental character are needed in order to overcome the remoteness of the divine which develops with the strengthening of the transcendent element.

And from this follows the second element in the immanent religious symbolism — namely, the sacramental. The sacramental is nothing else than some reality becoming the bearer of the Holy in a special way and under special circumstances. In this sense, the Lord's Supper, or better the materials in the Lord's Supper, are symbolic. Now you will ask perhaps, "only symbolic?" That sounds as if there were something more than symbolic, namely "literal." But the literal is not more but less than symbolic. If we speak of those dimensions of reality which we cannot approach in any other way than by symbols, then symbols are not used in terms of "only" but in terms of that which is necessary, of that which we *must* apply. Sometimes, because of nothing more than the confusion of signs with symbols, the phrase "only a symbol" means "only a sign." And then the question is justified. "Only a sign?" "No." The sacrament is not only a sign. And in the famous discussion between Luther and Zwingli, in Marburg in 1529, it was just this point on which the discussion was held. Luther wanted to maintain the genuinely symbolic character of the elements, but Zwingli said that the sacramental materials, bread and wine, are "only symbolic." Thus Zwingli meant that they are only signs pointing to a story of the past. Even in that period there was semantic confusion. And let us not be misled by this. In the real sense of symbol, the sacramental materials are symbols. But if the symbol is used as *only* symbol (i.e., only signs), then of course the sacramental materials are more than this.

Then there is the third element on the immanent level. Many things, like special parts of the church building, like the candles, like the water at the entrance of the Roman Church, like the cross in all churches, especially Protestant churches, were originally only signs, but in use became symbols. I call them sign-symbols, signs which have become symbols.

V

And now I come to my last consideration — namely, the truth of religious symbols. Here I must distinguish a negative, a positive, and an absolute statement. First the negative statement. Symbols are independent of any empirical criticism. You cannot kill a symbol by criticism in terms of natural sciences or in terms of historical research. As I said, symbols can only die if the situation in which they have been created has passed. Symbols are not on a level on which empirical criticism can dismiss them. I will give you two examples, both connected with Mary, the mother of Jesus, as Holy Virgin. Here you have first of all a symbol which has died in Protestantism by the changed situation of the relation to God. The special, direct, immediate relationship to God, makes any mediating power impossible. Another reason which has made this symbol disappear is the negation of the ascetic element which is implied in the glorification of virginity. And as long as the Protestant religious situation lasts it cannot be reestablished. It has not died because Protestant scholars have said, "Now there is no empirical reason for saying all this about the Holy Virgin." There certainly is not, but this the Roman Church also knows. But the Roman Church sticks to it on the basis of its tremendous symbolic power which step by step brings her nearer to the Trinity itself, especially in the development of the last decade. If this should ever be completed as is now discussed in groups of the Roman Church, Mary would become co-Saviour with Jesus. Then, whether this is admitted or not, she is actually taken into the divinity itself. Another example is the story of the virginal birth of Jesus. This is from the point of view of historical research a most obviously legendary story, unknown to Paul or to John. It is a late creation, trying to make understandable the full possession of the divine Spirit of Jesus of Nazareth. But again its legendary character is not the reason why this symbol will die or has died in many groups of people, in even quite conservative groups within the Protestant churches. The reason is different. The reason is that it is theologically quasi-heretical. It takes away one of the fundamental doctrines of Chalcedon, viz., the classical Christian doctrine that the full humanity of Jesus must be maintained beside his full divinity. A human being who has no human father has no full humanity. This story, then, has to be criticized on inner-symbolic grounds, but not on historical grounds. This is the negative statement about the truth of religious symbols. Their truth is their adequacy to the religious situation in which they are created, and their inadequacy to another situation is their untruth. In the last sentence both the positive and the negative statements about symbols are contained. Only a few words about the absolute statement about the truth of religious symbols. I said that religion is ambiguous and that every religious symbol may become idolatrous, may be demonized, may elevate itself to ultimate validity although nothing is ultimate but the ultimate itself; no religious doctrine and no religious ritual may be. I believe that if Christianity claims to have a truth superior to any other truth in its symbolism, then it is the symbol of the cross in which this is expressed, the cross of the Christ. He who himself embodies the fullness of the divine's presence sacrifices himself in order not to become an idol, another god beside God, a god into whom the disciples wanted to make him. And therefore the decisive story is the story in which he accepts the title "Christ" when Peter offers it to him. He accepts it under the one condition that he has to go to Jerusalem to suffer and to die; that means to deny the idolatrous tendency even with respect to himself. This is at the same time the criterion of all other symbols, and it is the criterion to which every Christian church should subject itself. ❖

RELATION OF METAPHYSICS AND THEOLOGY

INTRODUCTION

The difficulty of the problem put before us is that every answer, no matter how general and abstract it tries to be, is the expression of a special metaphysical understanding of metaphysics and of a special theological understanding of theology. There is no court above them to decide about them. This refers immediately to the definition of the two concepts, the relation of which is under discussion, metaphysics and theology. In the context of this paper, only the result of much philosophical and theological arguing can go into the definition, not the arguments themselves.

I
DEFINITIONS

There are two problematic factors which must be considered in every definition of metaphysics, the first of which was effective for a long time, the other only recently. Metaphysics has suffered under the unjustified connotation that the "meta" in metaphysics points to a realm above the physical realm. This connotation was strongly supported by the Latin word "supranatural" which designated the realm of the divine above nature. Finally the term "experience" in its empiricistic application pushed metaphysics into the role of a "speculation" without an experiential basis. Against these distortions metaphysics should be defined as the analysis of those elements in the encountered reality which belong to its general structure and make experience universally possible. Metaphysics then is the rational enquiry into the structure of being, its polarities and categories as they appear in man's encounter with reality.

If this is accepted one may ask why one should not use the term "ontology" for this enterprise. It is the structure of being which is under inquiry, and this is what ontology is supposed to do. But the difficulty is that there are structures of less universality like nature, man, history, which also precede in logical dignity anything concrete in their respective spheres but which are not structures of being as such, and which, consequently, are not objects of ontology in the strict sense of the word. Therefore if the word "metaphysics" can be saved from its supranaturalistic connotations, it should be used. If, however, this is impossible, the term ontology must be enlarged so that it embraces all structures which constitute reality. Both ways are open.

The term "theology" needs equally careful consideration. It is burdened not only with semantic difficulties. Its literal meaning: *logos* of *theos*, the rational word about God, immediately leads to the question of where and when God has become manifest and in which situation his manifestation can be received. And here theology leaves the philosophical road. It asks the question of the concrete situation in which the manifestation of the divine has appeared. Theology deals with the concrete revelatory experience in which human beings have been grasped by an ultimate concern. Theology is existentially related to the concrete place at which the divine self-manifestation has been received. As theology it is bound to this place in time and space even if it claims universal validity. And that theology does. As the *logos* of *theos* it tries to show the universal validity of the concrete manifestation of the ultimate on which it is based. This is the reason why the early Christian theologians called Jesus as the Christ the *Logos*. *Logos* is the principle of the divine self-manifestation in nature and history. There is no *theo*-logy where there is no concrete, revelatory experience. And there is no theo-*logy* where there is not the universal claim for truth. This unity of the concrete-existential and the universal-essential gives theology its special position, its greatness and its dangers.

Theology is not religion, but it presupposes religion. Every religion expresses itself in symbols of its ultimate concern. These "symbols of faith" are the subject matter of theology. Theology, in spite of its name, is not "science of God," but it is the *logos*-determined interpretation of the symbols of God's self-manifestation in a concrete situation. These symbols are not arbitrary interpretations of the concrete revelatory experiences. But they appear within this experience itself. They are not created intentionally, but they are born in the same dimension in which the revelatory experience takes place. In and through its symbols the religious encounter with reality opens up the dimension of reality in which ultimacy appears. There is no other way of expressing our encounter with the holy than in symbols. Therefore, the "*logos* of *theos*," theology, is the *logos* of the symbols in which His manifestation expresses itself.

II

THE EXISTENTIAL GROUND OF METAPHYSICS

The definitive, or more exactly, circumscriptive, task performed so far emphasizes the divergent traits of metaphysics and theology. They are counterbalanced by convergent trends in both of them. Metaphysics (or ontology in the broader sense) is directed towards the observation and analysis of the categorical structure of being and its general spheres. It does not ask the question of its own existential roots. It does not look at itself and the ultimate concern underlying it. But the fact that metaphysics is directed towards being and its universal characteristics does not imply that it has no existential roots. It certainly has them, for the philosopher is a human being, and in every philosophical school human interests and passions are a driving force. No philosophy is without an ultimate concern in its background, whether this is acknowledged or denied. This makes the philosopher a theologian, always implicitly and sometimes explicitly. It is possible and even not difficult to trace the implicit theological elements in every philosophy, even that which restricts itself to logical analysis. The reasons given for this restriction betray an ultimate concern about man's relation to reality. The nature of this concern is sometimes openly expressed in the philosophy of religion of such a system. But it is manifest also in its logic and epistemology, in its philosophy of nature and its doctrine of man.

The effect of this existential element on metaphysics has not the character of interference. The experiential basis and the logical structure of a metaphysics are not affected. But the direction in which the question is asked and the dimension of reality which is opened up for experience are partly determined by the character of the ultimate concern in a philosopher. As a philosopher he looks at the structures and categories of being; but the way in which he looks, the potentialities and the limits of his vision, are existentially conditioned. This makes him a non-intentional theologian and produces from his side the common ground on which a conversation with the theologian is possible. It is partly for. this reason that a spiritual conversation between Plotinus and Origen, between the Stoics and Tertullian, between Cicero and Augustine, between Aristotle and Thomas, between Spinoza and Schleiermacher, between Hegel and

Kierkegaard, between Kant and Ritschl was possible. Intellectual history is full of these examples up to the present day. But in all these cases the common existential ground, whether in terms of agreement or in terms of conflict, is only one reason for the possibility of such conversation. The other reason follows from the nature of theology.

III
THE METAPHYSICAL FORM OF THEOLOGY

Theology is the *logos*-determined interpretation of symbols of ultimate concern. It is directed toward the ultimate concern, as it has appeared and expressed itself in a religious group. It is not world-directed as metaphysics, but existence-directed. It looks at the place where it stands, where the self-manifestation of the divine has occurred and is effective from one generation to the other. In traditional theology, it is dependent on revelation — if revelation is not taken in the distorted sense of an authoritative divine information. Revelation is the self-manifestation of ultimate reality in ecstatic experiences expressed in symbols. Theology does not create, but it interprets symbols. And these interpreted symbols may become creeds and doctrines and dogmas which often are also called symbols, but in the particular sense of signs through which the members of a community recognize each other. The way in which symbols produce doctrines is dependent on theology. The way doctrines become dogmas is dependent on decisions of the Church. Dogmas are parts of the canonic law; doctrines are creations of the theological *logos*, based on the symbols of revelatory experiences.

In this function the theologian uses metaphysics. Biblically oriented theologians in all periods of church history have contradicted this statement; but they never could prevail against the main trend of theological thought which used metaphysics for the interpretation of the Christian symbols. Not even the neo-Kantian theologians of the second half of the 19th century who rejected metaphysics for the sake of epistemology and value theory, were an exception. There was too much partly hidden, partly quite open metaphysics in their anti-metaphysics.

Metaphysics cannot be avoided in any theology. For in order to interpret religious symbols, theology must use concepts which are either taken directly from a metaphysical system or which have already entered the general language without normally reminding of their philosophical origin. Anti-metaphysical writings by theologians are full of such metaphysical terms, like nature and history, time and space, subject and object, mind and spirit, person and self, becoming and being. Ordinary language is justified in using them without further analysis. Theological language is not, as long as it claims to be theology. Usually anti-metaphysical theologians fall into the trap of assuming a particular metaphysics without being aware of it, as for instance today a kind of unreflective nominalism which makes them suspicious of the ontological use of the term "being."

The reason for the ever-repeated attack of the theologians on the use of metaphysics in theology is the awareness of the theological element in metaphysics itself. It arouses the fear that the substance of the divine self-manifestation and the genuine meaning of the symbols may be lost or distorted. Doubtless this is a danger; and the early church was aware of it when it used concepts created by Greek philosophers whose existential background is symbolized by Apollo and Dionysius. They countered the danger in three ways — as Thomas also did when he received Aristotle. They rejected concepts which express Greek existence more than metaphysical analysis, and cannot be taken into Christian existence, e.g., the eternity of the world or the circular character of time. They accepted others which have the same strongly existential character, but can be taken into Christian existence, e.g., the *logos* or the *pneuma*. Third, they tried to formalize the Greek concepts as much as possible, e.g., *physis* or *hypostasis*. This task is a permanent one in theology and refers to such terms as "history," "person," "self," our present discussions.

IV
METAPHYSICAL AND THEOLOGICAL ATTITUDES

The philosopher is directed toward being, its structures and categories, the theologian toward a self-manifestation of the divine and its symbolic expressions. This can lead to the question whether or not there is a radical contrast in the attitude of the two toward truth. The metaphysician, one can say, keeps himself in analytic detachment; the theologian is existentially involved. The former is determined in his attitude by methodological doubt, the other by what is usually called faith. The word "faith" in such context is then defined as believing in statements without evidence, including the unbelievable and improbable. It is indeed impossible to combine these two attitudes. They can be together in one and the same person only if the two spheres of truth have no relationship to each other at all. This, of course, would exclude a theological approach to the truths of faith. But this is not a picture of the real situation. Faith is not the belief in statements without evidence, but it is the state of being ultimately concerned, and the symbols expressing it have criteria of adequacy to what they are supposed to express and they have ontological implications which demand detached consideration. This removes the contrast of the metaphysical with the theological attitude. The involvement of the theologian has not the character of authoritarian subjection, but it has the character of a double risk, an existential one and a theoretical one. The first, the risk of faith, is a risk about the meaning of one's being. The second, the risk of argument, is a risk about the rational, analytic, and constructive element in theology. But this double risk is also the risk of the metaphysician. In his ultimate concern he takes the risk of faith as every human being. As a philosopher he takes the theoretical risk of error. Neither the theologian nor the philosopher has unconditional certainty about the contents of his faith or the results of his reasoning. In both of them doubt and the courage of affirmation are within each other. Therefore, the history of philosophical and theological thought is overwhelmingly a history of interdependence of theology and metaphysics and not of their lying side by side.

V

ESSENTIALIST AND EXISTENTIALIST METAPHYSICS AND THEIR THEOLOGICAL SIGNIFICANCE

The relation of theology and metaphysics has been deepened by the independent rise of existentialist philosophy. There are elements of Existentialism in most essentialist philosophers; but only in the first half of the 20th century has Existentialism appeared as a philosophical method as well as a universal style of cognitive and artistic self-interpretation of man. It is this side of Existentialism which makes it very important for the theological work of today. It would be a comprehensive description of present-day Protestant theology (including my own) if I went into the concrete problems of existentialist theology. But the following general statements may be made.

Existentialism helps theology to formulate the questions, and in doing so it exerts an indirect, formal influence on the answers. But it does not give the answers. Every answer concerning ultimate concern is given out of the experience of the self-manifestation of the ultimate. Theology, on the other hand, has opened up spheres of questions with which

Existentialism deals and is able to give it a focus and a definite direction, but it does not create the questions which are implicit in the human situation.

No matter how important Existentialism is for theology, it does not reduce the importance of essentialism for it. For Existentialism in purity cannot exist because it needs universals — essences — to make statements at all, even about existence. This is equally true of theology, which cannot exclude essentialist metaphysics. Only in confrontation with the essential structures of being can Existentialism speak. An existentialist theology as such is as impossible as a purely existentialist ontology. ❖

THE IDEA OF GOD AS AFFECTED BY
MODERN KNOWLEDGE

I

Our subject is indeed intriguing because it is similar to an equation with several unknown numbers. In this case, it is the meaning of most of the words in the title that represent the unknown quantity. There is the phrase "idea of God." What does this mean? It can stand for a symbol which is used in all religious language or it can mean a conceptualization of these symbols — the concept of God. The word "modern" can be meant to cover everything since the Renaissance, which is the modern period of history. But it can also mean contemporaneous. In Latin the word "knowledge" can mean either *scientia* or *sapientia* — science or wisdom. Both are ways of knowledge.

Thus I must make a few definitions about the meaning of these words before starting the lecture proper. Since the title indicates that the idea of God *is* affected by modern knowledge, it is obviously the *concept* of God that is meant and not the symbol, God; although a change in our concept of God may have an indirect influence on our use of the symbol of God in religious language. Since God is the concept of something which resists conceptualization, it becomes necessary to refer to both science and wisdom in interpreting the term *knowledge*. This means that we must at times transcend the scientific realm and look at the realm of the arts where usually more wisdom is deposited than in science and even philosophy. In using the word *modern* I shall simply decide it to mean contemporaneous, although we cannot speak about anything contemporaneous fully and profoundly without references to the whole modern period.

The lecture will take the form of two main parts, the first showing why the idea of God cannot be influenced directly by modern knowledge; the second part showing the ways in which it has been and can be influenced indirectly. Speaking about the fact that the idea of God *cannot* be influenced directly by modern knowledge brings to mind several foundations in America, similar to the one under whose auspices we are gathered here, which were inaugurated by people who experienced the height of their intellectual maturity at the end of the 19th or the beginning of the 20th century and who were deeply concerned about the situation of their time with respect to the problem of God. Their chief objective when they established foundations was to show that the attack on the idea of God does not have ultimate truth — that the denial of the existence of God can be overcome by philosophical reflection. So these foundations were thought at that time to be a wall of defense against a naturalistic philosophy of a special type — that which reduces everything to the simplest elements of nature as, for instance, the attempt to construct the world out of atomic particles, thus removing the independence of man's intellectual and spiritual life and removing the truth of the idea of God. But this situation is not real any longer in this year, nineteen-hundred fifty-seven.

When Karl Barth was asked to give the Gifford Lectures in Scotland which were founded in that period and which expected the lecturer to develop a natural theology in order to defend on philosophical grounds the idea of God, he started his lectureship with the statement, "I must confess that I don't believe there is such a thing as natural theology." This was the opposite of everything the founder of the

Gifford Lectures wanted him to say. Nevertheless he gave them.

I have stated that the basic presupposition of natural theology has ceased to be accepted by both those who attack the idea of God and those who defend it. Both groups are critical of *one* presupposition which was accepted in this period, namely that God is a being beside and above other beings whose existence can be spoken of in terms of affirmation or denial. One saw God on the level of any other reality, the existence of which can be argued for or against. This kind of discussion is no longer valid. The very presupposition that the idea of God points to such a highest being has become questionable, and even more on the side of the defenders of the idea of God than on the side of the attackers. Those who attack it still like to put God into the totality of existing beings because this makes it easier for them to deny the existence of God.

If God were what these critics and defenders declare him to be — a being alongside others, then it should be possible to find such a being in the context of reality either by direct sense impressions or at least by indirect conclusions from sense impressions as is done with all other objects which exist. But this method never succeeded. God never has been found; and those naturalists of the 18th or 19th century who boasted of this fact of not finding him were right. But they were looking in the wrong place!

The other possibility would be that if God cannot be reached by sense experiences, or conclusions derived from them, he might become manifest as a spiritual being, a self like other selves, by internal psychological experiences or by an extra-sensory person-to-person communication between an infinite and a finite person. But this is as questionable as all the so-called spiritualistic experiences. I just heard that one of my predecessors in these Garvin Lectures gave the whole doctrine of immortality on the basis of such experiences; however, I do not think we should build either the idea of eternal life (as I would say with the Bible instead of "immortality") or our idea of God on such shaky ground.

There is a third method, much higher than these, to which I already referred when I mentioned the Gifford Lectures, that of natural theology. This means a theology which does not refer to revelation, but which is based on the natural abilities of the human mind. This method had its greatest day when Thomas Aquinas developed his famous five arguments for the existence of God. Here, of course, God is not meant in terms of a being existing alongside other existing beings, either in terms of sense experience or psychological experiences. But the arguments do lead to what the word God means in all religions — that which is ultimate in being and in meaning, that which is the ground and foundation of being and not a being alongside others.

This kind of arguing is safe against science and wisdom, but it is not safe from philosophical criticism. It was criticized in the Middle Ages by a man who exceeded even Thomas Aquinas in critical power, namely, Duns Scotus. He refuted Thomas by saying that you can never reach on the basis of the finite the infinite. No argument for the so-called existence of God can ever reach God; in this Duns Scotus and much of the Protestant tradition agree. God can only be known through himself. He cannot be known by the work of the intellect which argues for him, and the uses of this human intellectual effort as a basis for man's relation to God. What is reached by your highest intellectual reasoning is only the *question* of God, but it is not God. God grasps you where and when he will, but he cannot be forced down from heaven, either by good moral behavior or by good intellectual reasoning. The arguments for the existence of God do not lead to him.

Now if God is not a being, if he is not within the context of finite things which are open to scientific research, then the idea of God cannot be influenced directly by science. This is most important because all the conflicts between religion and science are rooted in a confusion between the dimensions of being which are present in God and those which are present within the encountered world. For instance, we have the religious idea of God as "creator" and we have the description of the development of the physical world in billions of years. And even if today we find it plausible to say that the world started five billion years ago instead of five thousand, this is not an argument for the creation of the world by God five billion years ago, but rather an argument for one of the movements of reality, from contraction to expansion, and from expansion to contraction.

Or, another example, when we speak of "providence" as God's directing creativity and imagine a divine activity which again and again interferes with the processes of reality, then we are in for a fundamental conflict with the scientific description of processes which derives the state of things in the present moment causally from the state of things in the preceding moment. Or if we take the religious symbol of "miracle" and describe it — as some orthodox theologians do — as the destruction of the structure of reality for the sake of revealing the divine and then as the reestablishing of it by a special act of God, science rightly raises its protest. Or, if we think of the understanding of biblical literature as dictated through a spiritual recording machine into the souls of the disciples so that every word is itself a divine word, then historical research must raise its protest. In all these respects (and many others could be mentioned) it seems as if modern science has deeply influenced and even destroyed many tenets of the traditional idea of God.

But now let us look carefully at the situation. Are these conflicts caused by modern knowledge? No. Insistently and definitely no. They are produced by a confusion of dimensions — a metaphor which I like to apply when I speak about the relationship of the infinite and the finite, the divine and the human. They are not on the level of existing objects related to each other to be recognized in an equal way, to be defended or attacked in their characteristics and even in their existence itself, as is done with every other reality in time and space — and rightly so. But when this is done with God and his relation to reality, then it is profoundly wrong. It is a confusion of dimensions. But it may be something still deeper. It is probably an attempt to escape the always-present and disturbing reality of the divine in a world which is determined by industrial society with its knowledge and control of reality wherein there is no use for God. Therefore, if you first bring him down to the level of a thing within the world of things and then deny his existence, you do exactly what the intellectual leaders tried to do from the very beginning of industrial society in the early eighteenth century.

Why do I like the metaphor, dimension? Usually one speaks of levels or strata in the world with the inorganic realm comprising the lowest level, the living being a higher level, the psychological realm coming next, the spiritual or cultural level still higher, then the religious realm, and on the highest level the supranaturalist world: God and "divine things." But this is not a good way of speaking about our world and about God. There are no levels; there are dimensions. And dimensions are always within each other. They cut through each other in one point — this much we can take from the spatial metaphor. But if they cut through each other at every point, they cannot interfere with each other. They are united in one point, but are not in conflict with each other. And this is the great advantage of the metaphor of dimensions. If we speak of the dimensions of the inorganic, we see it always present in the dimension of the spiritual and vice versa: they do not interfere with each other. And if we speak of the ultimate dimension, the divine cannot interfere with or be interfered with by something in the other dimensions.

If this is the case, two consequences can be derived. The first is that we cannot apply to God the categories of our finite world. For instance, God cannot be understood as a cause who interferes with other causes as one beside others. God is not *a* cause as he is not *a* being. And if we apply to God the category of causality, which we *always* must apply, we must do it symbolically. God is not a cause, but the ground of the whole chain of causes and effects.

Let us consider another category, substance. God is not a separated substance, a being beside others. If he were, he would be subordinated to the whole of being and to the ground of being, but he himself *is* the ground of being. Therefore, if we use such words of him as, for instance, personality, we do it symbolically and not in the way in which we apply it to ourselves.

Or when we speak of our world, we speak in terms of space. Then we apply this category to God — he is in heaven and we are on earth. But as all classic theologians knew and often have expressed it, God is nearer to each of us and to each grain of sand than we and it are to ourselves, in spite of the fact that at the same time he transcends everything. Here all these spatial categories are, in their proper sense, destroyed. Or when we apply to our world the category of time and put God into it and speak of the everlasting time in which God lives, then we actually do not mean time — which is a form of finitude — but we mean eternity which transcends the disrupted moments of the temporal process.

This is the one consequence of the use of the concept of dimension. There is another consequence connected with this, namely the general character of our speaking of God. Religious language is symbolic language. Yet a symbol does not mean a sign which can be arbitrarily changed, but stands for the reality which it expresses, to which it points and which it represents. Therefore, we must say that religious language as symbolic language is not less true and not less adequate, but more true and more adequate than ordinary language. Literalism brings God down to that reality which can be approached scientifically and practically.

II

In the first part, I tried to show that the idea of God *cannot* be influenced directly by science. I will speak now of the ways in which the idea of God has been influenced indirectly by modern scientific development. It was when man started to deal with his world as one of calculable and manageable objects that the problem arose which we discuss tonight: How is this world which is so different from the mythical and pre-mythical world of early mankind related to the religious symbols? The answer is twofold. There are two dimensions and there are two languages: the dimension of the finite which uses the language of the day and of science, and the dimension of the infinite which uses the language of symbols. The necessity of making this distinction is the first influence of modern thought on the idea of God. Let me now carry this through to special points.

Take the Copernican-Newtonian image of the universe and compare it with the Greek, medieval, and biblical image of the universe. In the biblical and the medieval, we have a tri-partite structure consisting of a world above, a world below, and between them the earth. God belongs to one, the demonic sphere to the other, and man is the battlefield between them. Powers come down and go up, and man's ultimate destiny is determined in the spatial symbols of heaven and hell. This imagery was destroyed when the earth lost its central place in the cosmos and became only one of many other stars. The world became an infinite universe. The idea of other worlds which had other beings who are related to God also became a possibility, although not yet a reality. Man experienced this reduction of his central position in this universe as a tremendous shock and the anxiety it produced is recognizable as an undercurrent in the lives and thought of many men in the eighteenth and nineteenth century. Even today, looking at the sky produces anxiety because of the realization that the earth is only a particle in the universe and no more. Theology must cope with this situation much more than it has in the past.

History is another sphere of scholarly research which had a great indirect effect on religious ideas. When some theological groups tried to build Christian faith on historical research, they did just what cannot be done. Their effort confused dimensions and language, resulting in what we today recognize as basically a failure. But the *indirect* influence of the historical understanding of the symbols applied to God and the Christ in the Old and New Testament, the removal of superstitious elements in interpretation and text, the distinction between historical, legendary and mythical elements in biblical literature all had a great liberating influence on Protestant Christianity — which is the only religion able to allow and even encourage historical research into its own sacred sources.

A third problem of an indirect influence of science on religion is that of depth psychology. Depth psychology is more than a scientific movement. It has transformed the whole intellectual climate of our century. The rediscovery of levels of human being which had been shut off by rationalism and Enlightenment had a decided indirect influence on religion. It undercut the intellectualistic and moralistic interpretation of Christianity and made possible a reevaluation of the classical Christian doctrine of man. One can see again the ambiguity of man's existence, the demonic darkness as well as the light of reason in him. This rediscovery of the unconscious in man made it further possible to understand a symbol like "divine grace" — grace as a reality in the presence of God accepting us in spite of our separation from him. This is an indirect help that science gives towards a reinterpretation of the idea of God.

Finally, I come to that realm which more than anything else has indirectly influenced Christian thought today, namely, the philosophy which is usually called existentialist (which should not be identified with the philosophy of Sartre in Paris). Existentialism is a reaction of man to his becoming an object in the analysis and management within the industrial society since the eighteenth century. In fact, the first one who expressed this in full clarity and in most important concepts was Pascal. As a mathematician, he himself was a supporter of the development of science, but as a human being, he protested against the loss which threatens every human being — the loss of himself in industrial society. From this follows a description of the human predicament which anticipates much of the wisdom found in the twentieth century's art, literature, drama, poetry. As the style of this century, Existentialism reveals man's predicament: his having to die, his being estranged, his being threatened with the loss of meaning, his becoming an object among objects.

This I think is the greatest thing which modern thought has contributed to the idea of God. We can understand that the idea of God is the answer to the question implied in man's very existence, in his predicament, in his finitude and estrangement. God is not an object of argument in which his existence or non-existence is discussed. Neither is God a concept given to us by religious authorities, but he is the liberating answer to the question of our having to die, of our being in guilt, of our being threatened with losing the meaning of life. In this correlation the idea of God has received a new meaning for our time. Modern thought has helped to open up the meaning of "God" in a new way. To do this is better than to engage in debate on the existence or non-existence of God.

Although I did go into the discussion of the idea of God in the form in which it was seen around the turn of the century, I hope that I have been able to show something about the relationship of the idea of God and modern thought as we must see it in the present situation of both religion and the sciences.❖

27410371R00186

Made in the USA
Middletown, DE
17 December 2015